Language and Society in Japan

Language and Society in Japan deals with issues important to an understanding of language in Japan today, among them multilingualism, language and nationalism, technology and language, discriminatory language, and literacy and reading habits. It is organized around the theme of language and identity, in particular the role of language in constructing national, international and personal identities. Contrary to popular stereotypes, Japanese is far from the only language used in Japan, and the Japanese language itself does not function in a vacuum, but comes with its own cultural implications for native speakers. Language has played an important role in Japan's cultural and foreign policies, and language issues have been and continue to be intimately connected both with certain globalizing technological advances and with internal minority group experiences. Nanette Gottlieb is a leading authority in this field. Her book builds on and develops her previous work on different aspects of the sociology of language in Japan. It will be essential reading for students, scholars and all those wanting to understand the role played by language in Japanese society.

NANETTE GOTTLIEB is Reader in Japanese at the University of Queensland. Her previous publications include *Word Processing Technology in Japan* (2000) and *Japanese Cybercultures* (2003).

Contemporary Japanese Society

Editor:
Yoshio Sugimoto, La Trobe University

Advisory Editors:
Harumi Befu, *Stanford University*
Roger Goodman, *Oxford University*
Michio Muramatsu, *Kyoto University*
Wolfgang Seifert, *Universität Heidelberg*
Chizuko Ueno, *University of Tokyo*

Contemporary Japanese Society provides a comprehensive portrayal of modern Japan through the analysis of key aspects of Japanese society and culture, ranging from work and gender politics to science and technology. The series offers a balanced yet interpretive approach. Books are designed for a wide range of readers including undergraduate beginners in Japanese studies, to scholars and professionals.

D. P. Martinez (ed.) *The Worlds of Japanese Popular Culture*
0 521 63128 9 hardback   0 521 63729 5 paperback

Kaori Okano and Motonori Tsuchiya *Education in Contemporary Japan: Inequality and Diversity*
0 521 62252 2 hardback   0 521 62686 2 paperback

Morris Low, Shigeru Nakayama and Hitoshi Yoshioka *Science, Technology and Society in Contemporary Japan*
0 521 65282 0 hardback   0 521 65425 4 paperback

Roger Goodman (ed.) *Family and Social Policy in Japan: Anthropological Approaches*
0 521 81571 1 hardback   0 521 01635 5 paperback

Yoshio Sugimoto *An Introduction to Japanese Society* (2nd edn.)
0 521 82193 2 hardback   0 521 52925 5 paperback

Vera Mackie *Feminism in Modern Japan: Citizenship, Embodiment and Sexuality*
0 521 82018 9 hardback   0 521 52719 8 paperback

Ross Mouer and Hirosuke Kawanishi *A Sociology of Work in Japan*
0 521 65120 4 hardback   0 521 65845 4 paperback

Language and Society in Japan

Nanette Gottlieb

The University of Queensland

CAMBRIDGE
UNIVERSITY PRESS

CAMBRIDGE UNIVERSITY PRESS
Cambridge, New York, Melbourne, Madrid, Cape Town, Singapore, São Paulo, Delhi

Cambridge University Press
The Edinburgh Building, Cambridge, CB2 8RU, UK

www.cambridge.org
Information on this title: www.cambridge.org/9780521825771

© Cambridge University Press 2005

This publication is in copyright. Subject to statutory exception
and to the provisions of relevant collective licensing agreements,
no reproduction of any part may take place without
the written permission of Cambridge University Press.

First published 2005
Third printing 2009

Printed in the United Kingdom at the University Press, Cambridge

A catalogue record for this book is available from the British Library

ISBN 978-0-521-82577-1 hardback
ISBN 978-0-521-53284-6 paperback

Cambridge University Press has no responsibility for the persistence or accuracy
of URLs for external or third-party internet websites referred to in this publication,
and does not guarantee that any content on such websites is, or will remain,
accurate or appropriate. Information regarding prices, travel timetables and other
factual information given in this work are correct at the time of first printing but
Cambridge University Press does not guarantee the accuracy of such
information thereafter.

Contents

Figures

Preface

This book is a study of the major cultural, social and political aspects of language in Japan. It focuses on the interaction between the language and the people it serves from an overarching social rather than specifically linguistic perspective, with the intent of contributing to the study of the sociology of language in Japan. The term "language in Japan" may seem on the surface to be unproblematic; when we look more closely, however, we find dimensions not apparent at first glance. The Japanese language itself, for instance, is not a monolithic, unchanging entity as the term implies, although some of the ideological arguments both prewar and postwar have been devoted to making it seem that way. Like any other language, it exhibits dialectal variations, differences in usage based on gender and social register, subcultural jargons and foreign influences. No language functions in a vacuum; it comes with its own freight of wider cultural implications for its native speakers. One of the objectives of this book is to tease out those implications and examine how they manifest themselves in practice in relation to Japanese itself (Chapters One, Three and Four). The other is to show the diverse range of languages other than Japanese spoken in Japan today and their sociocultural contexts (Chapter Two).

The organizing theme of the book is the interconnection between language and identity. I will identify and discuss some of the issues which past and present debates have foregrounded as important to an understanding of the role of language in constructing national, international and personal identities over the modern period (defined as beginning with the Meiji Period in 1868) right up to the present day. Language has played an important role in Japan's cultural and foreign policies, and language issues have been and continue to be intimately connected both with globalizing technological advances and with internal minority group experiences. We shall see how the institutions of the schools and the media played a part in disseminating the desired standard form of the language. We shall also see how the print and visual media put brakes on the use of language which incited protest from marginalized sections of the community (Chapter Six). Chapter Five will provide a picture of literacy in practice: what the writing system is, how people learn to read and write, what problems they may encounter, and what they do with the knowledge once they have it.

Language issues today extend to the Internet, whether accessed by computer or, more likely, by mobile phone. We shall see how the technology that made possible the electronic use of written Japanese has resulted in certain changes in writing practices and self-identification, not least in the development of a new dimension of written Japanese in the emoticons favored by chatroom users and in the subversive use of script by bright young things. The anonymity of the Internet has resulted in the phenomenon of online hate speech of the kind no longer permitted in the print and visual media: if word processing constituted the acceptable face of technology, as I argue in Chapter Seven, then this aspect of Internet use constitutes the dark side, allowing free use of the kind of language that has largely disappeared from other media.

I make no claim to have covered all areas of language use in today's Japan, and doubtless some readers will wish I had focused a little more on this and a little less on that. What I have done is provide an analysis of significant aspects of the diversity of Japan's linguistic landscape in both its spoken and written aspects and an understanding of how that landscape has changed (and in some cases been manipulated) over the last 140 years. The link between ideology and language policy (Chapters Three and Four) gives a good indication of how philosophies relating to the Japanese language have been made to serve the purposes of the state, while policies relating to Ainu and English represent in the one case an attempt to erase the depredations of a century of assimilation and in the other to acknowledge the realities of the world situation in which Japan is a participant. Below it all, object of the policies, lies the highly literate population of readers and writers which underpins any analysis of language in Japan. I commend their story to you and wait with interest to see what the future brings in terms of ongoing developments in linguistic identities.

An editorial note or two: where no page number is given in a reference, this indicates that the document was read online. Japanese names are given in the usual Japanese order, i.e. surname first.

Acknowledgments

Thanks are due to a great many people who have helped me at different times with the research conducted for this book, in particular to Dr. Akemi Dobson, whose excellence as a research assistant is unsurpassed. Thanks to her tireless searching and categorizing of data, I was able to complete the book in a much shorter time than would otherwise have been possible, and I am very grateful to her. I would also like to thank the staff of the Nissan Institute of Japanese Studies at St. Antony's College, Oxford, who extended me their hospitality as a Senior Associate Member during Michaelmas Term in 2002, and the Australian Research Council, which has funded research for several of the projects from which this material is drawn. I am deeply indebted to the two anonymous readers who read and commented upon the drafts of both the original proposal and Chapter Four. Their suggestions and comments contributed to a very useful reshaping of the original research design and I thank them for their time and consideration.

Sections of this text are based on my earlier work, supplemented by new research specifically undertaken for this purpose. The discussion draws on my books *Language and the Modern State: The Reform of Written Japanese* (1991), *Kanji Politics: Language Policy and Japanese Script* (1995), *Word-processing Technology in Japan: Kanji and the Keyboard* (2000), *Language Planning and Language Policy: East Asian Perspectives* (2001, edited with P. Chen) and *Japanese Cybercultures* (2003, edited with M. McLelland). It also refers to articles published in the *Asian Studies Review* and *Disability & Society*.

1 The Japanese language

Let me begin by asking a question: how do we define the term, "the Japanese language"? Odds are that those both unfamiliar and fairly familiar with Japan alike will answer at once, "the language that is spoken by people in Japan." And of course, they would be quite right, up to a point.

Pressed for a similar definition of the English language, the answer would require more thought, since English is patently not just the language spoken in England by the English but, like French and Spanish, is spoken in a variety of local forms throughout a great number of countries of the world, legacies of former empires and the commercial and cultural webs spun between countries around the world. Arabic, too, is the official language of over twenty countries and Chinese in one form or another is spoken widely throughout East and South East Asia and in the countries of the Chinese diaspora.

In the case of Japanese, while geography likewise plays a part in definition, the geography is limited to that of the Japanese archipelago. Japan once had an empire too, and Japanese was spoken in its colonies, as we shall see, and to some extent remains so: in the former colony of Taiwan, for example, elderly people who were children during the days of the Japanese empire were brought up to speak Japanese as their first language and speak it still. Yet for most people the definition given above is the first which springs to mind. It is perfectly true, of course, that Japanese is the language spoken in Japan by the Japanese people, but such a definition is much too simplistic. It prefigures Japanese as a monolithic entity, assuming (though not making explicit) that every Japanese person speaks the same kind of Japanese, that nobody outside Japan speaks the Japanese language and that every person living in Japan views the language in the same way. As we shall see, however, there is much more to language in Japan and to the Japanese language.

We might usefully begin by considering what we mean when we speak of a Japanese person. Through analysis of relevant statistics, Sugimoto (2003:1) arrived at the conclusion that a "typical" Japanese would be "a female, non-unionized and non-permanent employee in a small business without university education," where typical equates to most representative of trends in today's Japan. This analysis puts paid to the stereotype of the educated male "salaryman" (white-collar worker) working for a large company that most people might envisage when faced with the term "typical Japanese." But how do we define a person as Japanese in the first place? No simplistic answer based on any purported reality of homogeneity of ethnicity, language or sociocultural experience is possible. Rather, our answer must take into account the day-to-day actuality of diversity in Japan. Sugimoto (2003: 185–188), discussing this issue, notes that "some 4 percent of the Japanese population can be classified as members of minority groups," with that proportion rising to around 10 percent in the area around Osaka. He analyses the characteristics of examples of fourteen specific groups within Japan in relation to seven characteristics by which "Japaneseness" may be assessed,[1] questioning the validity of some and demonstrating that different views of what constitutes "the/a Japanese" may be held depending on how those dimensions are interpreted and applied.

Fukuoka (2000: xxix–xxxiv) conducts a similar analysis based on permutations of ethnicity (broken down into blood lineage and culture) and nationality. He arrives at a list of eight theoretical clines:

- "pure Japanese" (Japanese lineage, socialized to Japanese culture, hold Japanese nationality)
- "first-generation Japanese migrants" to other countries (Japanese lineage, socialized to Japanese culture, but hold foreign nationality)
- "Japanese raised abroad" (Japanese lineage, Japanese nationality, socialized to foreign culture), e.g. *kikokushijo* (returnee children)
- "naturalized Japanese" (foreign lineage, socialized to Japanese culture, Japanese nationality), e.g. *zainichi kankokujin/chūgokujin* (resident Koreans/Chinese) who have taken out citizenship
- "third-generation Japanese emigrants and war orphans abroad" (Japanese lineage, socialized to foreign culture, foreign nationality), e.g. the offspring of migrant Japanese who return to Japan to work
- "*zainichi* Koreans with Japanese upbringing," i.e. those resident Koreans who have not taken Japanese citizenship (foreign lineage, foreign nationality, socialized to Japanese culture)
- "the Ainu" (Japanese nationality, different ethnic lineage, socialized to a different culture). Very few would fit this category, given the century of forced assimilation
- "pure non-Japanese" (foreign lineage, socialized to a different culture, foreign nationality), i.e. *gaijin* (foreigner)

For Sugimoto's female worker to be "typical," we would have to go by the numbers and put her squarely into the first category above. Each of the other categories, however, represents a sizable chunk of people who either live in Japan or lay claim to one degree or another of "Japanese-ness." Many of them speak Japanese as their native language; others speak it as a second or foreign language; and some speak other languages as well. Even those who represent the majority of the population speak and write Japanese differently, depending on age, gender and education.

Language is a key aspect of identity formation, both personal and national, and a person's view of "the Japanese language" will vary depending on the nature of that person's interaction with it. To a Japanese person living in Japan the Japanese language will be the native language, spoken from childhood and used daily; exactly what "the Japanese language" means in this context, however, is open to discussion and needs to be viewed in the context of local variation and national policy on language standards. To people outside Japan, Japanese may be a heritage language, the language of their forebears, spoken by emigrant mothers and fathers and passed down to children born in Japanese communities outside Japan. To still others, it is a foreign language which offers the learner the chance to take on a multiplicity of identities, the language of a superpower eagerly studied to improve employment prospects, the means of communicating at grassroots and business level in a rapidly globalizing world.

To a person from one of the countries from which workers flock to Japan to take up menial jobs and send money home, for example, Japanese is the passport to learning to survive in their new country. To those involved with business and smart enough to realize the advantages of language proficiency, Japanese can be viewed as one of the keys to improving their company's prospects in Japan. To exchange students studying at Japanese universities, Japanese is the language through which they make grassroots connections which may stand them in good stead for the rest of their lives. To many in East and South East Asia, Japanese is the language both of an economic superpower and of a former enemy; in the case of Korea, a former colony, the former apparently takes precedence over the latter, South Korea having the largest number of overseas learners of Japanese in the world (Japan Foundation Nihongo Kokusai Sentaa 2000). The list has as many variations as there are individuals involved with the language. In other words, as with any other language, the term "the Japanese language" refers not to something monolithic, unique and unchanging but rather to a multifaceted and constantly developing entity which can have different meanings for different users.

Far from functioning in some kind of linguistic and social vacuum, a language carries its own freight of wider cultural implications for its native speakers and for those who choose to learn to speak it. To understand what this has meant in the case of Japanese, we need to examine the major philosophy which has influenced people in the first of those categories: the Nihonjinron view of Japanese language and culture.

The Nihonjinron view of the Japanese language

The ethnocentrist Nihonjinron[2] literature, the dominant trope for Japanese society in schoolbooks and scholarly literature on Japanese society for most of the postwar period, has portrayed the language as static and as somehow uniquely different in important functions from all other languages. Within the Nihonjinron framework, Japan is portrayed as linguistically homogeneous (i.e. Japanese is the only language spoken there), and the Japanese language itself as a uniquely difficult and impenetrable barrier even for the Japanese themselves, let alone others. In this view, race, language and culture are tied together and cannot be separated.

A 1982 book by American scholar Roy Andrew Miller, *Japan's Modern Myth*, took issue during a period at which Nihonjinron literature was particularly flourishing with what he described as the mass of theories and misconceptions that the Japanese had built up around their own language:

The myth itself essentially consists of the constant repetition of a relatively small number of claims relating to the Japanese language. All these claims share one concept in common - something that we may call the 'allegation of uniqueness'. All these claims have in common the allegation that the Japanese language is somehow unique among all the languages of the world . . . From this essential claim of absolute uniqueness, for example, it is only a short step to simultaneous claims to the effect that the Japanese language is exceptionally difficult in comparison with all other languages; or that the Japanese language possesses a kind of spirit or soul that sets it apart from all other languages, which do not possess such a spiritual entity; or that the Japanese language is somehow purer, and has been less involved in the course of its history with that normal process of language change and language mixture that has been the common fate of all other known human languages; or that the Japanese language is endowed with a distinctive character of special inner nature that makes it possible for Japanese society to use it for a variety of supralinguistic or nonverbal communication not enjoyed by any other society – a variety of communication not possible in societies that can only employ other, ordinary languages. (10–11)

Miller demonstrates (while at the same time debunking) the manner in which this myth constructs an indissoluble link between the country's language and race, culture and even morality, and functions to keep the linguistic barrier between Japan and the outside world unbreached. "It is the myth that argues that there is a need for foreigners to learn the

Japanese language but also simultaneously claims that the Japanese language is so uniquely difficult that it is all but impossible for anyone to learn it, whether Japanese or foreigner." (20) Dale (1985:60–61) likewise takes issue with the manner in which, in the Nihonjinron tradition, perfectly ordinary Japanese words have been loaded with ideologically constructed "nuances" which can be understood only by Japanese, so that attempts by foreigners to translate are doomed to failure. He speaks of this practice as "an academic metadiscourse, implicated with intertextual reverberations of uniqueness, that raises a semantic bamboo curtain between Japan and the outside world."

Outside academic circles, the view of the Japanese language as a barrier both in Japan and in the world at large remained robust throughout the twentieth century, even well after the Japan Foundation[3] began its efforts to promote the study of Japan overseas in the 1970s. To draw just a few statements at random from the wealth of popular literature on Japan over this period: "his language is extremely difficult; it is a formidable barrier to complete interchange of thought with the foreigner . . . this language barrier, believe me, accounts for nine-tenths of the Asiatic mystery" (Clarke 1918: 3–4); "the Japanese language looms as a never-never land which few dare to explore. It simply is not a tourist's dish. Moreover, anybody who has acquired by some gruesome brain manipulation the faculty to speak Japanese realizes how futile were his efforts. His difficulty in communicating with the Japanese has merely grown in depth" (Rudofsky 1974: 156–157); "language difficulties are one of the major sources of misunderstanding between the Japanese and other peoples" (Wilkinson 1991:244).

And yet: millions of non-Japanese can testify to the fact that they are able to speak, read and write Japanese, a reality which confounds the Nihonjinron claims of race and language being one and indivisible and of the Japanese language being uniquely difficult and impenetrable for foreigners. Spoken Japanese is actually no more difficult than French and much easier than German. Learning to read and write takes longer, of course, owing to the nature of the script, but many people manage it not just successfully but outstandingly well (Dhugal Lindsay, for example, the young Australian marine scientist living in Japan who recently became the first foreigner to win a prestigious Japanese-language haiku prize, or Swiss-born author David Zoppetti, who won Japan's Subaru Literature Award for a novel written in Japanese). The Nihonjinron myth of linguistic homogeneity in Japan, too, has been challenged by recent studies, notably Maher and Macdonald (1995), Maher and Yashiro (1995) and Ryang (1997), all of whom deal with language diversity in Japan, as we shall see in Chapter Two.

What, then, is "the real story" about language in Japan? This chapter will discuss the varying ways in which the term "the Japanese language" can be interpreted. We will begin by looking at who speaks Japanese in the world today and why, and will then turn to a discussion of some of the major characteristics of Japanese and the manner in which some of them are changing.

Who speaks Japanese in the world today?

Japanese today is spoken by most of the 126.5 million people in Japan. The main areas where it is spoken outside Japan, following earlier periods of limited Japanese diaspora, are the west coast of North America, Hawaii and South America, although many people of Japanese descent living in those areas no longer speak their heritage language. In other countries, Japanese is learnt as a foreign language and during the Japanese economic boom of the 1980s became one of the top languages of choice for students with their eyes on a career involving working in a Japan-related business, either in Japan or in their home country.

Weber (1997, cited in Turner 2003) lists the number of secondary speakers of Japanese (defined as those who use the language regularly or primarily even though it is not their native language) as eight million. This figure, going by his definition, seems unlikely to include the two million students of the language worldwide identified by a 1998 Japan Foundation survey published in 2000. The number of overseas learners has greatly increased since the 1970s, actually doubling between 1988 and 1993, as a result of the activities of the Japan Foundation and of governments such as state and federal governments of Australia since the 1980s, all of which have devoted policies and funding to increasing the number of people learning Japanese. Much of this increase, however, including the late 1980s *tsunami* of learners, was predicated on Japan's status as an economic superpower, which meant that the primary motivation for studying Japanese was job-related rather than intrinsic curiosity in a majority of cases.

The Director of the Japan Foundation's Urawa Language Institute, Katō Hidetoshi, suggests that the total number of learners of Japanese worldwide is likely to be around five million, given that the most recent survey figure of two million referred only to those studying at the time of the 1998 survey and did not take into account those who had figured in earlier surveys. Once those studying informally or learning to speak on an experiential basis are also added in, perhaps a total of ten million people are now able to speak Japanese as a foreign language (Katō 2000: 3).

What kind of Japanese do they speak?

The standard form of Japanese, designated as such by the National Language Research Council in 1916 and spoken and understood throughout the country, is called *hyōjungo* and is based on the speech of the Tokyo dialect, in particular the dialect of the Yamanote area of the city. Standard Japanese is used in writing and in formal speaking situations. In casual interaction, however, people usually speak a variant called *kyōtsūgo* (common Japanese). This is close to Standard Japanese in all its main features but not as formal; it includes contractions, for example, and people living in regional areas might include expressions from their local dialect (Neustupný 1987: 158–160). Regional dialects, which were accentuated by the political segmentation of Japan during the feudal period, do remain, and some of them are quite markedly different from those of other areas. However, the overarching use of the standard language throughout Japan overcomes any communication difficulties this might cause. The Japanese taught to overseas learners is uniformly standard Japanese; those few books meant for non-Japanese which have been published on dialects are for personal interest rather than formal study.

Standard Japanese

Today, a visitor to Japan who can speak the language takes it for granted that they will be understood anywhere in the country, but this was not always the case. To understand just how important the development of the standard language was to what we now think of as modern Japan, we must consider the language situation in pre-modern Japan, i.e. until the Meiji Restoration in 1868. During the period during which Japan was unified under the Tokugawa Shogunate (1603–1867), Japan was divided into upwards of 250 autonomous domains called *han*,[4] each ruled by its own feudal lord, or *daimyō*. The military rulers in Edo (today's Tokyo) kept a very tight control on the feudal lords of each region in order to prevent challenges to their authority. Except for a very few categories of people, such as the *daimyō* themselves on their mandatory periods of travel to Edo, religious pilgrims and wandering entertainers, travel outside one's own domain was forbidden. The linguistic consequence of this was that local dialects flourished, unaffected by more than occasional contact with passers-through from other places who spoke a different dialect.

Until the middle of the Tokugawa Period, the lingua franca of these times, at least among those in a position to travel and therefore to need a lingua franca, was the dialect of Kyoto, which was then the capital. This was widely perceived as the "best" form of spoken Japanese because of the upper-class status of its speakers; although power had begun to shift to the east some time before, with the earlier Kamakura Shogunate, Kyoto remained both the city where the emperor lived and the centre of culture. Around the middle of the eighteenth century, the language of Edo, seat of power of the Tokugawa military rulers, became a second contender for lingua franca. Over the preceding 150 years, Edo had begun to develop its own distinct culture and its language then began to exert an influence on other parts of Japan (see Twine 1991: 210–213).

In 1868, however, with the overthrow of the Tokugawas and the restoration of the Emperor Meiji to power, things began to change rapidly. In order to create a unified modern state, the better to fight off the perceived threat from colonizing western powers after Japan was reopened in 1854, statesmen and intellectuals began to put into place during the last three decades of the nineteenth century the required infrastructure: a modern press, an education system, a postal system, an army, transport and communications systems such as railways and telegraphs, and much, much more. By about the middle of the 1880s it became clear that a standard form of both spoken and written Japanese was needed, not only to play an important unifying role in enabling communication between citizens from one end of the archipelago to the other but also to form the basis for the future development of a modern written style based on the contemporary spoken language. The modern novels which began to appear in the 1880s used the dialect of Tokyo as the basis for realistic portrayals of modern life; thus, their adoption of educated Tokyo speech strengthened the claims of that particular dialect as the matrix for the standard language by modeling it in the novel.

The active co-operation of the intellectual elite of a speech community is required for the standardization of its language (Garvin 1974: 71). From the mid-1890s, men such as Ueda Kazutoshi (1867–1937) adopted a centralist approach to the issue of standardization, forming interest groups and lobbying for a government-supported approach. When eventually the National Language Research Council, Japan's first language policy board, was formed in 1902 as the result of their efforts, one of its tasks was to conduct a survey of the dialects in order to settle upon one as the standard. There was already by this time substantial support for the choice of the Tokyo dialect: the Ministry of Education had stipulated in 1901 that the Japanese taught in schools would be that of middle- and upper-class Tokyo residents and subsequent textbooks had therefore begun to disseminate this throughout Japan. It was only a matter of time before the standard was formally defined in 1916 as the Japanese spoken by the educated people of Tokyo, specifying the speech of the Yamanote district.

While school textbooks disseminated the written form of the standard, the most influential organization in spreading the spoken form was
Nippon Hōsō Kyōkai (NHK, Japan Broadcasting Corporation) through
radio and, later, television. NHK is a public broadcasting organization
but not a state organ; it places considerable importance on its role as a
modeler of correct language, issuing pronunciation dictionaries and other
language-related publications and from time to time conducting surveys
on aspects of language. The advent of national broadcasting in the 1920s
presented a fortuitous opportunity to model the recently adopted standard in spoken form for listeners throughout Japan. Today, the heavy television viewing habits of the Japanese ensure that exposure to the standard
is constant (Carroll 1997: 10–11).

Dialects

The presence of a standard language, of course, is little more than a communicative convenience and does not mean that no layers of linguistic
diversity exist in addition: quite the opposite, the fact that there is a need
for a standard acknowledges that they do. Regional dialects continue to
flourish, and dialectology is a strong field of research in Japan. An interesting Perceptual Dialect Atlas which offers insight into how Japanese
people living in different areas perceive both the use of the standard language and the characteristics of various dialects is maintained online by
linguist Daniel Long of Tokyo Metropolitan University.[5] Respondents
native to eight different areas of Japan were asked to indicate in which
areas they thought that standard Japanese was spoken. The results from
respondents from the Kanto area around Tokyo show that they believe
standard Japanese to be spoken only in the central part of Japan, from
a core in Tokyo reaching across to the west coast and diminishing as it
goes. Hokkaido (but not the other major islands of Shikoku and Kyushu)
is included as a standard-speaking area in their perceptions, though at a
fairly low rate. This research also elicited perceptions of which areas use
the most pleasant and the least pleasant speech, and which areas are seen
to use a specific dialect. Again looking at the responses from the Kanto
group of respondents, the results are highest for the area in and around
Tokyo, tapering off to less than 20 percent in the rest of the country,
while a higher proportion of Kansai respondents nominated the Kansai
area (in western Japan, around Osaka) and its surrounds, across to the
west coast.

Leaving aside the Ryukyuan dialects in Okinawa Prefecture, the major
categorization of dialects is into eastern Japan, western Japan and Kyushu,
although Kyushu may be subsumed into western Japan (Shibatani

1990: 196). Dialects vary in terms of lexical items (including, of course, the names of items specific to that particular region, such as particular local foods and drinks): one example is the use of *bikki* instead of the standard *kaeru* for "frog" in Miyagi dialect and *ango* for the same thing in Chiba Prefecture's Chikura dialect. Verbal inflections will usually differ as well: in Osaka dialect, for example, *mahen* is used instead of *masen* in the negative inflection, while in Nagoya *janyaa* replaces *de wa arimasen* for "is not" and in Fukuoka *n* is used instead of *nai* for negative verbs, e.g. *taben* for "don't eat," which in standard Japanese would be *tabenai*. Particles vary too: in Miyagi dialect, *–ccha* is added for emphasis (*yo* in standard Japanese) while in Nagoya dialect an elongated *yō* fulfils the same purpose.

    Dialects underwent a period of repression during the first half of the twentieth century during which the newly designated standard language was being disseminated through the newspapers and the national broadcaster. Children who were heard to speak dialects at school were often punished and ridiculed as a means of discouraging local usage (although of course those same students returned home in the afternoon to families who spoke the local dialect). As time passed, and more and more children became educated in the standard, they themselves became parents who were able to speak that standard, so that with time the degree of fracture between standard and dialect blurred, though never disappearing. Ministry of Education guidelines for teaching *kokugo*[6] still clearly stated in 1947 and 1951 that dialect expressions were to be avoided in favor of "correct forms," i.e. the standard language. Pressure was particularly applied in rural areas, where people were likely to go elsewhere to look for employment and could find their chances diminished if they did not speak the standard (Carroll 2001: 183–184).

    As we see in Chapter Five, the current national curriculum guidelines for *kokugo*, issued in 1998, provide for students in the latter years of elementary school to be able to distinguish between dialect and standard; this is presumably applied in terms of the local dialect in the area in which the school is located. Students at middle school are expected to develop an understanding of the different roles of the standard and the dialects in sociolinguistic terms. This represents a complete change from the previous prohibition of dialects, although "despite the more positive comments on dialects in curriculum guidelines, the emphasis is largely on tolerance, rather than any active promotion of dialects" (Carroll 2001: 186). Policy statements from the National Language Council in the 1990s urged a new respect for local dialects, probably in response to the policy of regionalism which informed government directions from the late 1980s. The 1995 report, for example, while it restated the centrality of *kyōtsūgo* for purposes of communication throughout Japan, stressed that dialects should be valued as an important element in the overall picture of a rich and beautiful national language, showcasing the vibrancy of the people and cultures of local areas (Kokugo Shingikai 1995:432). While this might seem like a nod in the direction of cultural and linguistic diversity, we need to remember that cultural diversity here is firmly located within the boundaries of the Japanese language itself. As we shall see in Chapter Two, minority languages in Japan face a very different situation.

Influences from other languages

No language exists in a vacuum. All are influenced to varying degrees by others with which they have contact. We need only think about the number of widely-accepted Americanisms or words and expressions from non-English languages current in Australia today to see this in action. Any native speaker of English (or for that matter, French, German, Spanish and a host of other languages), even without detailed knowledge of or contact with Japan, will know what *sushi* means, or, thanks to Tom Cruise's recent blockbuster film, *samurai*. The two major linguistic influences in the case of Japanese have been Chinese and English (see Loveday 1996). Around 60% of today's Japanese vocabulary, or at least of that part of it found in dictionaries, is made up of loanwords from other languages. Around 6% of these are from western languages, but the vast majority come from Chinese (Backhouse 1993: 74, 76). *Kango*, Sino-Japanese words, reflect the long history of language and cultural contact between China and Japan since the fifth century (see Twine 1991). Most Japanese hardly think of these as loanwords, however, as over the centuries they have become absorbed so thoroughly into Japanese as to seem not at all foreign. Even those words which had to be specifically created in the Meiji Period (1868–1912) using Chinese characters (*shinkango*, or new Sino-Japanese words) in order to express new concepts such as *kenri* (rights) or describe new objects (*denwa*, telephone) have long been accepted as natural Japanese. The focus of discussion on loanwords rests with the other category, *gairaigo* (foreign loanwords), which come from western languages, predominantly English.

While Backhouse gives the number of *gairaigo* in the Japanese lexicon as around 6%, Honna (1995:45) puts it higher, at around 10% of the lexicon of a standard dictionary. We could be forgiven for thinking that it was much higher even than that, since magazines, advertisements, department store counters and restaurant and fast-food outlets all push loanwords at anyone walking down a street in Tokyo. "Present day Japanese is literally inundated with an inordinate number of loanwords borrowed chiefly from English in various forms" (Suzuki 1991:99). The spread of computers in particular brought with it a flood of new terms from English, e.g. *mausu* (mouse), *fuairu* (file) and *kurikku* (click). Compulsory English study at school may also have been a contributing factor in the preponderance of English loanwords.

In just the same way as the Australian press carries occasional opinion pieces about the influx of Americanisms into Australian English, so Japanese papers now and then publish letters from readers bemoaning the popularity of *gairaigo* in Japanese, particularly among young people. The matter has been examined at official levels as well: the National Language Council warned against the practice of using foreign words where Japanese equivalents exist, particularly in public government documents where readers unfamiliar with the loanwords might be confused (Kokugo Shingikai 1995:437). The Ministry of Health and Welfare attempted to address this issue by replacing loanwords with Japanese equivalents in medical care programs for elderly people, who were least likely to understand the loanwords; it ran into difficulties with finding appropriate Japanese equivalents, however, and had to put the initiative on hold (Honna 1995:46).

In 1995, the Agency for Cultural Affairs, located within the Ministry of Education,[7] carried out a survey which indicated that most respondents did not view the overuse of loanwords with any particular alarm, which perhaps accorded with the increasing internationalization of Japanese society since the 1980s. The survey nevertheless found evidence of a few who feared that using a loanword rather than its Japanese equivalent could lead to a loss of respect for the national language and a consequent breakdown in its traditions. Intergenerational communication could suffer as a result, since the most enthusiastic users of loanwords were younger people. Subsequently, the National Language Council acknowledged in a position paper that while the use of loanwords was to a certain extent unavoidable, given the progress of internationalization and the development of new technologies, a cautious approach was appropriate in general communication where misunderstandings might disrupt communication (Kokugo Shingikai 1995: 449–450).

A more assertive approach has been taken by Prime Minister Koizumi. In 2002, a panel was formed at the National Institute for Japanese Language at his request to provide some suggestions on stemming the flow. Following extensive surveys, this panel has to date produced three lists of *gairaigo* found not to be widely understood, with suggestions for Japanese equivalents to use instead. *Anarisuto* (analyst), for example, should be replaced with *bunsekika, konsensasu* (consensus) with *gōi*, and *shinkutanku* (thinktank) with *seisaku kenkyū kikan*.[8] Japan is not the only nation to have adopted this stance; most notable among others are France and Russia. The State Duma in Russia approved a draft bill in 2003 defending the Russian language from foreign contamination and prescribing penalties for the use of foreign-derived words where adequate Russian equivalents exist. However, since the drafters of the bill were unable to refrain from using the words they sought to root out, this led to lively comment in the press. The Upper House has now deferred discussion of the proposals indefinitely and President Putin, unlike Koizumi, is not pushing the issue at all.

The trend to overuse, however, seems certain to continue among younger users concerned with image and its role in personal identity. Very often, a loanword is used when a perfectly functional Japanese word already exists, for a variety of reasons ranging from euphemism to status-marking in the belief that using the foreign loanword will give a sophisticated image, for example, *biggu-na* instead of *ōkii* for "big." The link between foreign-ness (or rather, knowledge of things foreign) and construction of a cosmopolitan personal identity has been well documented across cultures, and Japan is no exception. Sprinkling conversation or text with *gairaigo* can be considered to mark the user as someone "in the know," sophisticated and cosmopolitan, much as phrases from French (and Latin before that) used to appear in English conversation in certain circles for the same purposes: to exhibit education and underline the user's supposed sophistication. In Japan, in addition to these more weighty reasons, loanwords are often used just for the sheer fun of it, in language play.

Men, women and other subcultural variations

One well known area of variation in Japanese is the manner in which speech conventions differ between the genders. Not only do certain specific conventions confirm the gender identity of the speaker, they can also be used to flout assigned gender identity. Sometimes this is done deliberately as when gay Japanese men use markers of women's speech:

Gay men who wish to perform a feminine role (in Japanese, *onēsan*, or 'big sister') can do so simply by switching to a female-coded speech pattern. The film-critics and panel stars, Osugi and Piiko, do not cross-dress at all, but use hyper-feminine *onēsan kotoba* (literally 'big-sister speech') which marks them as transgendered. (McLelland 2000: 47)

At other times, it is unwitting (as in the case of foreign men who pick up some Japanese from bar hostesses and think they are speaking correct

Japanese without realizing that the female characteristics of the speech are inappropriate for a man).

The major differences occur in verb forms used, personal pronouns, sentence final particles and use of honorifics. Men will use the short, impersonal form of the verb and its imperative in speech in informal situations, e.g. *iku yo* for "I'm going" and *ike* for "go!", where a woman would use *ikimasu* or *iku wa* and *itte (kudasai)*. The personal pronoun *ore* is used only by men, with women referring to themselves as *watashi* or *atashi*. Certain sentence final particles, e.g. *wa* with a rising intonation, are reserved for women, others, e.g. *zo*, for men. In general, women have traditionally used more honorific language than men (see Ide 1982 and 1991), and many Japanese women (but certainly not all) pitch their voices higher (see Loveday 1981). Shibamoto (1985) found that women often reverse the normal word order, putting the subject after the predicate, and drop particles more often than men.

In recent years, however, the gap seems to be narrowing. Okamoto (1994, cited in Adachi 2002), for example, reports on the phenomenon of unmarried female university students' use of an abrupt speech style which incorporates sentence-final particles usually reserved for men. Since around 1990, schoolgirls have been using the pronoun *boku*, once the preserve of men (particularly young men and schoolboys), to mean "I." This was originally confined to the period of schooling, in which girls felt able to compete with boys on equal terms, and tapered off after the girls left school (Reynolds 1991: 140–141), but more recently it has remained in use among young women after they leave school. There have also been changes in the relative degree of honorifics use in informal contexts. Whereas a 1952 report on polite speech by the National Language Council had criticized the overuse of honorifics and euphemisms by women, a similar investigation conducted in the early 1990s found almost no difference between the language use of men and women in this respect (Kokugo Shingikai 1995:432–433). Differences still remain, of course, but the lines are less clear-cut than they once were.

As with any language, subcultures (defined by Sugimoto 2003:5 as "a set of value expectations and life-styles shared by a section of a given population") among speakers of Japanese use variants of language as a kind of group identity code intended to set themselves apart and, in some cases, exclude outsiders. Examples of this in English are the language of computer nerds and of police and the military. In Japan, subculture variants often include an excessive use of foreign terms: *ko-garu-go* (high school girl-talk, gal-talk), for example, is liberally sprinkled with English terms, many from American pop culture, which in some cases have been adapted to fit Japanese grammar. *Hageru* in this idiom, for example, is a verb meaning to buy a Häagen-Dazs ice-cream, formed by adding the *–ru* verb ending to the first part of the trade name.

Kokugo and *Nihongo*

One interesting feature about Japanese is that it goes by two different names. A native speaker will refer to it as *kokugo* (lit: language of our country, our language) rather than *nihongo* (lit: language of Japan). Classes in language in Japanese schools for Japanese students are *kokugo* classes and the textbooks are *kokugo* textbooks; classes where Japanese is taught as a foreign language are *nihongo* classes and most textbooks have *nihongo* in the title. Most, if not all, of the twentieth-century debate about language reform used the term *kokugo kairyō*, not *nihongo kairyō*. The term *nihongo* is reserved for the Japanese which is taught as a foreign language to non-Japanese. In the case of English, this distinction is observed by adding a few more words to the name of the language: native-speaker students go to English classes at school, whereas non-native speakers study English as a Second Language (ESL) or English as a Foreign Language (EFL). In Japanese, however, the actual native-speaker word for the language is different, although the language itself is of course the same, clearly designating the insider-outsider tenets of the Nihonjinron stance on language. In the push by the Japan Foundation to promote the study of Japanese around the world since the 1970s in line with Japan's growth as an economic superpower, it is always *nihongo* which is to be spread, never *kokugo*, although *kokugo* was what was taught in schools in the two pre-war colonies of Taiwan and Korea. Linguist Kindaichi Haruhiko speaks of this use of *koku* to indicate Japan in words such as *kokushi* (Japanese history) as "one indication of our feeling that distinctions should be made between Japanese and foreign things. The writing of foreign words in stiff katakana to distinguish them from other words as if they were objects of our enmity is an expression of that same feeling" (1978: 154). In the matter of "ownership" of the language, the use of *kokugo* indicates that it remains firmly in Japanese hands.

Many in Japan, however, aspire to see Japanese become an international or world language. Several things would be necessary for this to occur, not least among them the development in Japan of a different mindset in relation to global use of language rather than local. With any international language, the issue of "ownership" is usually of keen interest to those whose first language it is not. In the case of English, for example, Suzuki has argued that as English is an international language the English can no longer lay claim to sole ownership and that Japanese English ought to be accepted as a legitimate variant (Suzuki 1987: 113–118).

Katō recently made a similar point in relation to Japanese. Musing on the number of learners identified by the Japan Foundation's 1998 survey, mentioned above, and other evidence of international interest in Japanese,[9] he pointed out that Japanese had progressed from being the preserve fifty years ago of a small and select group of scholars to the point where it was now offered as a language elective in schools in many countries, even in primary schools in Australia and New Zealand and elsewhere. Given that the role and position of Japanese in the world had changed such that it was no longer a minority language spoken only by those born and raised in Japan, he suggested, a re-evaluation of earlier attitudes and beliefs was in order.

First among the steps he proposed for "liberating" Japanese to play a role as an international language was one well known to those familiar with the World Englishes debate: namely, that native speakers of the language should stop demanding perfection from non-native speakers. In much the same way that Phillipson (2002:7) draws a distinction between English as a globalizing language and global English, which exists only as an abstraction, Katō argues that native speakers of Japanese must concentrate not on the mistakes made by non-native speakers but rather on the communication event taking place. If Japanese becomes a world language like English, communication – and not perfect grammar – will be the most important thing; not even native speakers themselves adhere to a consistent, ideal standard of perfection in their use of Japanese.[10] In Katō's view, the final responsibility for successful communication rests not with the non-native speaker but with the native speaker, who can easily infer what was meant from the context, regardless of grammatical inaccuracies. Given that local Englishes are replete with differences from the UK or US versions and yet are accepted, the Japanese propensity to focus on small mistakes makes it difficult to view Japanese as a world language, with all that this entails in terms of local appropriations (Katō 2000: 10–17).

This is a valid point, and one which has not until now been made with any degree of conviction about Japanese. Until the almost coy inside-outside mindset encapsulated by the *kokugo/nihongo* terminology divide becomes less entrenched, Japanese has little hope of becoming a world language, which by its very nature would be open to and used by many. Quite recently, however, a small departure from this practice occurred when the Society of Japanese Linguistics voted in early 2003 to change its Japanese name in 2004 from Kokugo Gakkai to Nihongo Gakkai. In a 2002 survey, also, seventy-four universities were found to have changed the name of the department concerned with Japanese language to Nihongo Gakka, while only twenty-nine retained the name

Kokugo Gakka. There is thus evidence of some change at tertiary levels of education; the same change, however, is unlikely to occur in elementary and high schools (Okada 2003).

We have examined in this chapter some of the issues relating to the seemingly unproblematic phrase "the Japanese language" as it relates to the national language of Japan. In the following chapter we will look in detail at the variety of other languages spoken in Japan.

2 Language diversity in Japan

As we saw in Chapter One, Japanese is not the only language spoken in Japan, although it is of course, as the national language, the main one. It has never faced the struggle for dominance against the language of a colonizing power we find in other parts of Asia and elsewhere; there has been no other contender for the status of national language. That does not mean, however, that Japan's linguistic profile lacks complexity. Regional dialects, the minority languages in use among various ethnic groups and the powerful influence of English mean that the linguistic landscape is far from one-dimensional. This chapter will examine the ways in which minority and other languages have played an important role in the construction of Japanese identity, either by defining an "other" against which the "self" (or "the nation") can be delineated, as in the case of the Ainu and the Okinawans, or by enabling an expanded notion of the self as citizen of the world.

Ainu

The Ainu language was reputed to be in danger of dying out until a 1997 law mandated its protection and promotion. The Ainu people themselves, who today number around 25,000[1] and live mainly in the northern island of Hokkaido, experienced considerable oppression at the hands of the Japanese over the last four centuries, during which time the use of their language had been at one time mandatory and then later proscribed. For two hundred years before the Meiji Period, the Matsumae clan and the Japanese in charge of the trading posts drafted Ainu men as fishermen in places far away from their home villages. It was important, during this period, that Ainu people were perceived as non-Japanese, as the barbarian periphery of Japan, and they were therefore forbidden to speak or write Japanese, to adopt Japanese dress and practices or to learn agricultural skills. Mogami Tokunai, a Tokugawa official of this period, suggested that Matsumae policy "sought to dramatize the cultural and ethnic distinctiveness which divided the two people, in turn using this distinctiveness to demarcate boundaries in the north" (Walker 1999:124). To couch this in more practical terms, the ban was intended "to minimise the danger of Ainu's destabilising the status quo; a situation that would have been inconvenient for the government intent on confining the natives to the island and which would have occurred if the Ainu had been able to freely communicate with the outside world and brought new information to and from their territory" (Taira 1996).

After the Meiji Period, however, Japan, in the interests of nation build-ing, needed to define its northern borders in relation to nearby Russia. It thus became crucial to assert that the Ainu were in fact Japanese in order to maintain a claim on Hokkaido as Japanese territory. Ainu people were therefore given Japanese citizenship and subjected to a policy of assimi-lation which forbade them to use their own language or to practice many of their customs. Ainu children were to be educated only in the Japanese language. Difference, in other words, was subjugated to the needs of the state, as "with this, the status of the Ainu was transformed from that of an oppressed racial group into a minority in a modern nation state" (Baba 1980: 63). Ueda Kazutoshi, as we shall see in a later chapter, was one who argued fervently in 1894 that language was a tool for creating a cohesive nation. Tellingly, he expressed gratitude that Japan, not being a multi-ethnic state like some of the European nations he had experienced in his recent years of study abroad, had no need to proscribe the use of other languages within its borders (Ueda 1894: 1–11). The existence of the Ainu language had apparently escaped his attention; nor, indeed, would recognition of its presence have suited the nationalist project of conflating language with national spirit.

The Ainu language is what is known as a language isolate, i.e. "a lan-guage which has no known structural or historical relationship to any other language" (Crystal 1987: 326). In other words, it is not a member of any known language family. The Japanese language also fits this category: although it has been considered to be a member of the Altaic language group (see Miller 1971), theories have been advanced for genetic relation-ships with other languages in relative geographic proximity (see Shibatani 1990: 94 for a detailed list). Within Ainu itself, there are regional vari-ations, as detailed in linguist Hattori Shiro's 1964 dictionary of Ainu dialects.

As a result of the assimilation policy described above, the Ainu lan-guage dropped out of daily use in many areas but was preserved through oral transmission of songs and stories, there being no written form of the language. DeChicchis (1995: 110) identifies four main types of present-day Ainu speakers: "archival Ainu speakers, old Ainu-Japanese bilinguals, token Ainu speakers, and second language learners of Ainu." Recordings of the speech of those in the first category, most of whom are no longer living, earn them this designation; the second is self-explanatory, referring to older members of the community who grew up speaking both Ainu and Japanese. The "token Ainu speaker" group requires more explanation: this term describes those who normally speak Japanese but retain a few stock words and expressions of Ainu which they occasionally sprinkle into their conversation. Lastly, there are those who study Ainu as a second language either for heritage reasons or from personal interest: these are the people who populate the Ainu language classes held at various universities, community education and other venues.

DeChicchis (1995: 112–115) also provides us with a useful overview of bibliographies and publications on Ainu language, concentrating on the four main subcategories of glossaries, archival texts, linguistic studies and books for the popular market, as well as a discussion of the audio and video recordings available. At Tokyo University, which has a long connection with the Ainu language,[2] the Department of Dynamic Linguistics[3] hosts the International Clearing House for Endangered Languages (ICHEL), which also lists an extensive bibliography of work done on the Ainu language, nearly all of which dates from 1990.[4] ICHEL's own publication series includes a book written in English on the Ainu language (Tamura 2000, translated from a Japanese original which appeared in the 1988 *Sanseido Encyclopedia of Linguistics*). The Endangered Languages of the Pacific Rim Project at Kyoto University likewise provides bibliographies of publications on Ainu both in western languages and in Japanese.[5]

In terms of non-Japanese scholars, John Batchelor, who had come to Japan as a Christian missionary in the nineteenth century and is credited with being the first westerner to learn the Ainu language, published many works on Ainu, including an Ainu-Japanese-English dictionary in 1938. The best-known western scholar of the Ainu language today is Danish scholar Kirsten Refsing, whose works include a study of the Shizunai dialect (Refsing 1986) and a massive ten-volume edition of early European writings on Ainu language (Refsing 1996).[6]

Maher (2002: 172) recapitulates the marked propensity of Japanese linguists during the twentieth century to insist that the Ainu language was all but gone: "The death of Ainu was announced in the early part of the twentieth century. Remarks on the de facto disappearance of the Ainu language have been standard from the earliest ethnographies of Ishida (1910), Goto (1934) and Kubodera (1939)," to give but a few of the studies he cites. And yet, he reminds us:

Although Ainu is not a language of everyday communication, it is dubious to equate ethno-linguistic vitality of a language only with psycho-linguistic capacity (i.e., possession of spoken fluency). It is a language of archival and literary study, recitation, speech contests and song – from traditional to jazz – with a radio program, newsletters and Ainu festivals that feature the language and scores of small language classes throughout Hokkaido. Of course, within all this diverse use of Ainu, there is code-mixing with Japanese among some speakers. (Sawai 1998)

Following a remark by then Prime Minister Nakasone in 1986 to the effect that Japan was a mono-ethnic nation, Ainu activism began to reassert itself, newly invigorated by contact with other ethnic minorities around the world during this decade. Three members of the Ainu Association of Hokkaido (AAH) in 1987 attended a meeting of the International Labor Organization (ILO) which discussed the revision of ILO Convention No. 107, removing from it the reference to assimilation of indigenous peoples into mainstream dominant cultures. Making a clear connection between identity politics and language, the subsequently released AAH statement stressed over and over the fact that the Ainu people had their own language; that fact was viewed as an important political tool in their struggle to gain recognition as an indigenous minority in Japan in the late 1980s. The document reads, for example: "in the field of education, the law trampled down the dignity of our people's own language"; "this people's own language, culture, life-customs, and so on are still retained."

The overarching legal document pertaining to Ainu people during all but a few years of the twentieth century was the *Hokkaido Former Aborigines Protection Act*, which stipulated a policy of total assimilation, including mandatory education in the Japanese language. The goal of Ainu activism from the 1980s on was to replace this discriminatory law – even the term "former aborigines" had offensive connotations – with one which would recognize the status of the Ainu people as separate and valued for their difference. A court case brought by two Ainu men (one of whom was the high-profile Kayano Shigeru, the first Ainu man to be elected to the Diet) over the construction of the Nibutani Dam on ancestral lands saw a ruling by the Sapporo District Court in 1997 that the Ainu fitted the international definition of an indigenous people. Subsequently, the Ainu Cultural Promotion Act (CPA), commonly referred to as the Ainu New Law, came into being on 1 July 1997, replacing the disputed Protection Act.

As we shall see in more detail in Chapter Four, which discusses the policy approach to languages, the Foundation for Research and Promotion of Ainu Culture established later that year took as one wing of its activities the promotion of Ainu language, focusing its attention on ethnicity rather than on more substantive issues related to indigenous status. The Foundation's four main activities are: promotion of research on the Ainu; the revival of the Ainu language; the revival of Ainu culture, and the dissemination of and education about Ainu traditions. In terms of Ainu language teaching, the first Ainu language schools in Japan actually predated the New Law by a decade or so: the Nibutani Ainu Language School was opened in 1983 by Kayano Shigeru and another opened in Asahikawa in 1987 (Hanazaki 1996: 125). After government-sponsored promotion of language classes began in 1997, the number of classes and radio broadcasts increased. The website of the Foundation for the Research and Promotion of Ainu Culture[7] offers rudimentary details of that organization's teacher training programs and of Ainu radio broadcasts. Several websites currently exist where those interested in learning Ainu can begin to do so: http://ramat.ram.ne.jp/ainu/, for example, offers audio files of common Ainu phrases and numbers and also features a map of areas where Ainu is spoken.

Ainu activists are not happy with the CPA, Siddle (2002: 413) reports, since Ainu culture remains defined in terms of difference with no recognition of the hybridity that is as much a feature of present-day Ainu culture as it is of other cultures, and no mention of the Ainu struggle against colonial oppression and discrimination. "Official Ainu culture is thus limited to language and the creative or artistic production of objects or performances in clearly defined contexts largely divorced from everyday life." Even the promotion of Ainu language ignores present-day realities, choosing to equate language with identity without recognizing that most Ainu pour their creative energies into dance and handicrafts rather than Ainu-language cultural production and that in fact most of the Ainu language classes in Hokkaido are attended by Japanese. The cultural promotion activities do not contribute to Ainu economic stability (Siddle 2002: 414). Ainu representatives told a meeting of the UN's Permanent Forum on Indigenous Issues in 2002 that the Law had "mostly benefited Japanese scholars, while the Ainu culture was being 'Japanized', a cultural invasion that could be seen as a new form of colonization" (United Nations 2002).

Despite the increased emphasis on teaching Ainu, then, the reception of the New Law by those it most concerns has not been rapturous, because it seems to stereotype them into yet another cultural ghetto based on cultural traditions without recognizing the clearly visible lingering effects of the earlier assimilation policy in the way today's Ainu live their lives and in their present-day interests. And yet Maher (2002: 174–175), using the Ainu New Law as his example, wisely cautions against discounting interim solutions which may seem fragmentary and imperfect:

Interim, piecemeal solutions can provide momentum, time and space to think more about the multilingual situation in Japan, as the Ainu saying opines: *Naa somo kuokere* (the work is always unfinished) . . . However, in the absence of a broad acceptance or understanding of a multilingualism framework, it is possible to move forward by making use of many types of institutions, events and people, some of which may appear, mistakenly, hostile. Thus, paradoxically, the Nakasone speech, *inter alia*, continues to serve as an important ideological axis for cultural theorists, and provide activists with a touchstone for continued social action.

The cultural promotion activities may not be what Ainu activists had hoped for. Nevertheless, the fact that they exist is an improvement over the former situation and in time they may provide a useful launch pad for future activities while raising awareness of the Ainu language itself in the meantime.

Okinawan

The Okinawan languages (also referred to as the Ryukyuan languages) include those languages spoken across the group of islands stretching from Amami-Ōshima near Kyūshū in the north to Yonaguni-jima near Taiwan in the south. Okinawan is thought to have separated off from Japanese before the eighth century CE and to have developed along its own trajectory thereafter. It is not a dialect of Japanese as is often mistakenly believed, although it does tend to be called the Okinawan dialect for political reasons (rather than linguistic) (Matsumori 1995: 20),[8] presumably for the same nation-building purposes which informed the treatment of Ainu. It is an independent language, not intelligible to speakers of standard Japanese, but with historical connections and consonances. Today, speakers of Okinawan also speak standard Japanese, although the reverse is not necessarily true: the younger generation may be heading towards a monolingual command of Japanese only, as young people shift away from areas in which older bilinguals live and as standard Japanese dominates the structures of everyday life (Matsumori 1995: 40).

Okinawans are the largest ethnic minority group in Japan today (as opposed to the largest recognized minority group, the Burakumin, who are themselves Japanese and therefore not an ethnic minority). It is difficult to know how to arrive at a figure for this population: the 2002 population for Okinawa Prefecture is given as a total of 1,339,000, of whom "Japanese" are separated out at 1,332,000, or 96.6% of the population (Statistics Bureau 2002). Presumably the remaining 3.4% refers to non-Japanese such as the Americans living on United States bases. Of the Japanese section of the population, however, no distinction is made between those with Okinawan lineage and those without. Taira (1997: 142), presumably conflating residence in Okinawa with Okinawan descent, which of course will to a large extent be true, gives the population of the Okinawan minority group as 1.3 million in their home islands with another 300,000 living in other parts of Japan and an equivalent number living overseas in places like Hawaii.

Like the Ainu, the Okinawans were caught up in Japan's haste to build a unified modern nation during the Meiji Period. Just as a policy of forced assimilation was applied to the Ainu in order to solidify the perceived porosity of Japan's northern border in Hokkaido, so the indigenous population of the Ryukyus[9] was likewise treated in the south. The Ryukyus had been invaded by the Satsuma clan, native to Kyushu, in 1609, bringing to an end the sole domination of the Ryukyu kingdom rulers, at least in the Amami Islands. In 1879, however, the islands were annexed by the Meiji government and turned into the new prefecture of Okinawa. As a result, the indigenous inhabitants of the former kingdom were absorbed willy-nilly into and disguised by the myth of a mono-ethnic Japan which was to prevail for more than a century after that, just as had happened with the Ainu, in a kind of instant transformation of ethnicity to serve the ends of the state.

As happened with the Ainu, however, political absorption, while convenient at the level of nationalist rhetoric, did not equate to cultural acceptance in everyday life. Nor did it entail allowing education to occur in the native language, in this case Okinawan. In 1916, as we saw in Chapter One, the dialect of the Yamanote district in Tokyo was officially named the standard variant of Japanese, henceforth to be used throughout the Japanese archipelago as the official form of Japanese. The Education Ministry then embarked on a program of spreading the standard through textbooks and schools throughout Japan. During this period, children who were found to be speaking their own regional dialects at school were often subjected to punishment and/or ridicule. It was important for the needs of the classroom that everybody be able to use the common language, and therefore infractions were not permitted. In Okinawa, punishment took the form of being made to wear the *hōgen fuda* (dialect placard):

Because they had their own language, culture and history, the people of Okinawa had to endure excessive measures as the Japanese government worked to make them "Japanese." For example in public schools, the use of the Okinawan language was forbidden. A student who spoke even a word of the Okinawan language in class was forced to wear a dialect placard (*hōgen fuda*) around his or her neck, enduring humiliation until another student made the same mistake and was in turn, forced to assume the role of class dunce. Okinawa prefecture governor Ota Masahide once stated that process of making Okinawans "Japanese" resulted in human alienation. (Aikyo 1998: 6)

Okinawans themselves would seem to have been complicit in the practice. Matsumori (1995: 32) reports that Okinawans were quick to adopt the rhetoric of standardization in the early part of the twentieth century and later. Students at a Naha[10] school in 1916 themselves agreed to countenance the use of the dialect placard. "Wearing the wooden placard was considered a disgrace and resulted in a lowered grade. And, according to the rules, the only way a student could get rid of it was to catch another student using Ryukyuan to whom it could be passed on" (Rabson 1996). Interestingly enough, during the period of United States occupation after the war when use of Okinawan dialect was encouraged by US funding of a radio station to broadcast in it, dialect placards reappeared in the schools at Okinawan instigation to discourage children from speaking their dialect, as most Okinawans supported a return to Japan and knew that they would need to be able to speak standard Japanese when that day came (Rabson 1996). The practice seems to have persisted until the 1960s (Carroll 2001: 64); indeed, older scholars I spoke to in the early 1990s in the course of research for a book on language policy recalled personal memories of the system.

In contrast to the marked prewar discrimination against Okinawans, the 1990s saw an "Okinawa boom," led to a large extent by popular music. Through the popularity of bands such as Rinkenband, Kina and later The Boom, which combined elements of traditional Okinawan music with modern rock and other traditions, the sense of Okinawa as a rich, exciting local culture endowed it with, in Maher's terms (2002: 176), "cultural cool." His perceptive analysis of the likely impact of this factor on the revitalization of both Okinawan and Ainu languages is worth citing in full here:

Contrasting Ainu with Korean social "cool" Ainu fares less well in this respect. Quite simply, it lacks prestige, cultural and linguistic capital (Bourdieu 1991). This contrasts with Okinawan and, more complicatedly, post-modern Korean, which have been categorized as cultural values by the middle class. Ainu's image is ethnic, indigenous and rural (*daishizen no naka* – "in the virgin wild") rather than urban. Immutable ethnicization is how Ainu is presented and promoted – now "officially" the Ainu Promotion Act – and is another reason for some negative reaction. We are now well into the ethnic boom and Ainu fares well among persons with stereotypic sympathies (e.g., environmentalists, "the left"), and those who might drop in at the one ethnic Ainu restaurant in metropolitan Tokyo. It is difficult to see growth in appeal outside the cultural cliché. Again, we contrast this with the popularity of funky Okinawa as both physical territory and cultural idea. **Cultural cool fosters interest in language. Perhaps language revitalization might emerge as a by-product of a cultural cool that overleaps older motivations such as ethnic duty and the maintenance of ethnic orthodoxy.** (p. 176, my emphasis added)

Certainly the cultural coolness of Okinawa is confirmed on many fronts (e.g., Henshall 1999: 75; Taira 1997: 142). If this does indeed lead to language revitalization, then the Ainu language promotion being undertaken by the Foundation for Research and Promotion of Ainu Culture may pay fewer dividends than would attention to the non-traditional cultural activities undertaken by today's Ainu, such as rock bands and art festivals. Promotion of such activities, which include the non-traditional Ainu Art Project and the popular jazz-influenced band Moshiri, part of the World Music boom (Siddle 2002: 416), would better suit the aspirations of Ainu activists dissatisfied with the current promotional activities and could over time lead to Ainu losing the cultural-cliché image described by Maher and becoming invested with a greater "cultural cool," which in turn could raise the stock of the Ainu language in the public's perception.

Meanwhile, as is the case with Ainu, the Internet has a role to play in offering "tastes" of language. Websites offer interested visitors audio-files of common Okinawan phrases and more,[11] or non-audio-supported introductions to the language. One such website headlines its text with the unequivocal statement that "Japanese IS NOT the native language of Okinawa,"[12] in case anyone should be under the mistaken impression that it was. At the top end of Japan, then, we see technology being used to reassert the status of an indigenous language as an indigenous language; at the bottom end, to assert linguistic independence from Japan altogether, perhaps as a precursor to the long-debated independence of Okinawa itself.

Korean

Japan's resident-alien ethnic Korean population (known as *zainichi kankokujin*, or *zainichi* for short), as of 2002 numbered 625,422, accounting for one third of the total foreign population (Ministry of Justice 2003) and making them Japan's largest minority group after the Burakumin and the Okinawans. These figures do not include those Koreans who have taken Japanese citizenship, and are therefore not an accurate guide to the number of people who actually speak and write Korean in Japan: some of those included among the 625,422 are third- and fourth-generation residents who have no knowledge of their heritage language and speak only Japanese, while some of those who have taken citizenship (and are therefore not included here) do speak Korean. The Korean population, itself a diverse group encompassing young job-seeking newcomers from South Korea and permanent residents of Japan, North- or South-Korean affiliation, and those who have taken citizenship and those who have not (Okano and Tsuchiya, 1999: 111–112), is clustered in large urban centers such as Tokyo, Osaka and other cities, where Koreatowns function both as a focus of shared community aims and as a visible manifestation of the vibrancy of this section of Japan's population (see Maher 1995a for details, and Sabin 2002 for a description of Kawasaki's Koreatown).

Longstanding historical factors have meant that Koreans in Japan have been subject to discrimination on a par with that experienced by the Burakumin (see Chapter Six, and see Weiner 1997: 83–84 for details), although in recent years the Korean community, like the Okinawans, have seen "cultural cool" confer a kind of social cachet on being Korean through rock bands, soccer players and other manifestations of popular culture:

Does multiculturalism in post-modern Japan reside in the celebration of mere "difference" or in some other kind of lifestyle hybridity and cultural mixing? . . . Korean cool is much in evidence in Japan. Being a minority is, after all, being someone. Korean cool is linked to weekend trips to Korea, Korean *Este* (body conditioning salon), rock music, Japanese culture in Korean, film, *kimchi* and Korean language classes in university (attended also by *zainichi* Korean students). Korean-Japanese writers have won major literary prizes and the "cool" world of recently established J-League soccer teams features many Korean soccer players. (Maher 2002: 176)

Maher, as we saw earlier, suggests that a growth in awareness of the groups to which this concept of cultural cool attaches may in turn lead to an acceptance of the concept that Japan is in fact multilingual, despite the strong and persisting popular belief that it is monolingual. Certainly the more people become accustomed to hearing Korean spoken or sung in certain contexts, the more they will come to realize that Korean is being spoken *in Japan* by people who live there, rather than by visitors. The fact that only around 20% of young *zainichi* Koreans are estimated to be able to speak Korean (Fukuoka 2000: 27), however, may mean that this realization could be a long time coming through any more generalized exposure to the language outside of Koreatowns.

Korean is maintained as a community language through the activities of resident groups such as *Mindan* (Korean Residents Union, pro-South Korea) and *Sōren* (General Association of Korean Residents in Japan, pro-North Korea, also known as *Chongryun*). Both these organizations run their own school systems which teach curricula both in Korean and Japanese, *Sōren* having a much larger number of schools than *Mindan* and also a four-year university in Tokyo (see Ryang 1997 for details). Korea University was until very recently particularly important for chil-dren educated at these schools since the Japanese government would not allow them to apply to enter national universities because they had not gone through the standard Japanese education system.[13] This created the anomalous situation whereby a student from Korea could apply for entrance to a prestigious national university and be accepted as an international student, but a Korean-background student who had grown up in Japan, spoke Japanese as his/her first language and had been educated in Japan, albeit at a non-government school, could not (Tanaka 1991: 164–166, cited in Sugimoto 2003). From April 2004, however, this rule has been changed; graduates of all foreign schools in Japan will be permitted to sit for university entrance examinations, including the 1,000 or so students who graduate from Korean schools each year. The original decision, announced in March 2003, that only graduates of foreign schools affiliated with Europe or America could do so was expanded to include them after complaints that the original plan was racist. Kyoto University had already announced in 2002 that it would accept graduates of foreign schools in Japan (Mainichi Shimbun 5 August 2003).

In addition to ethnic community schools, Korean is also taught through community education classes. NHK, the national broadcaster, has offered weekly Korean language classes since the 1980s, prompted by the advance of Japanese companies into Asian markets (NHK 1999). In 2000 a report commissioned by then Prime Minister Obuchi on Japan's goals in the twenty-first century recommended that Japan pay greater attention to developing *rinkō* (neighborly relations) with Korea and China:

To achieve this, we should increase the amount of school time devoted to the study of Korean and Chinese history and the history of these countries' relations with Japan, particularly in modern times, and dramatically expand our programs of Korean and Chinese language instruction. In addition, we should develop a sense of neighborliness by providing multilingual information displays at major locations throughout Japan that include Korean and Chinese alongside English. (Prime Minister's Commission 2000)

Korean-language signs are much in evidence at Narita airport and other places in Tokyo in recent years, perhaps as a result of this report. The Narita International Airport website offers a Korean-language version; Kansai International Airport (Osaka's airport) offers both Korean and Chinese versions, as does the JR (East Japan Railway Company) site. A report on the teaching of Korean in Japanese schools listed details of 246 schools which in September 2003 were either offering classes in Korean or planned to introduce them by 2005, up from 165 in a 1997–1998 survey of 5,493 schools (The Japan Forum 2003). The Korean language classes are variously called Hangul, Kankokugo, Chōsengo or (since 1990) KankokuChōsengo. A message on the Network for Korean-Language Education in High Schools bulletin board in 2003 made the point that Korean should not be subsumed under the rhetoric of "diversifying foreign language education," as the education reforms of 1987 had suggested,[14] and viewed as coming in second-best to the dominance of English and Chinese, but should be viewed rather as a community language to promote the concept of multilingualism in Japan (Oguri 2003). This network, established in 1999, maintains an active website at http://www.iie.ac.kr/~jakehs/index.html to promote the teaching of Korean in Japanese schools.

International events which have contributed over recent years to a rising awareness of Korean culture in Japan include the 1988 Seoul Olympics, a gourmet boom in Japan which has prompted interest in Korean cuisine, and an ethnic boom where Asia is seen as cool. Local events include an increase in the media visibility of Korean singers, journalists, newsreaders and writers (Maher 1995a: 99). The soccer World Cup final held jointly in Korea and Japan in 2002 also contributed to an increase in interest in things Korean; in an Internet survey conducted immediately after the final had finished, more than half of respondents felt it had led to an improvement in Japan-South Korean relations (Japan Times Online 2002). *Zainichi* authors (writing, of course, in Japanese) have won prestigious literary awards for their fiction dealing with the Korean experience in Japan. Korean films have been big hits (see Sōzō 2001). Popular culture is the driving engine behind these events. Whether that leads in time to an increased uptake of Korean language study in Japan in recognition that Korean is not solely a foreign language, but is actually one of the languages of Japan, remains to be seen; it may signal no more than an increased acceptance of Korean ethnicity, but on Japanese terms.

Chinese

Japan's Chinese community in 2002 numbered 424,282 (Ministry of Justice 2003), most of whom live in large cities in the Tokyo-Yokohama conurbation, the Kansai region of western Japan and parts of Southern Kyushu (Maher 1995b: 126). Early immigrants settled in Yokohama, Nagasaki and Kobe; the Chinatown in Yokohama is the world's oldest and largest (Chang 1998).

Vasishth (1997) questions but then ends by affirming the "model minority" view of Chinese diaspora groups[15] in relation to this group in Japan, deconstructing the history of oppression and marginalization that the stereotype conceals (see also Nagano 1994). The assumption behind the "model minority" image is that such a minority is doing so well in terms of affluence and education that its members no longer experience discrimination. It is true that today the Chinese community is in general more affluent than, say, the Korean or Okinawan minorities, but this follows a long history of discrimination and persecution reliant upon anti-Chinese attitudes which continue today, such as those displayed in the comments made in 2000 and discussed in Chapter Six by Tokyo's Governor Ishihara, imputing a purported rise in crime to Chinese, Koreans and illegal immigrants. The Tokyo Overseas Chinese Federation on that occasion held a special meeting to protest strongly against the governor's remarks (*People's Daily* 2000).

Many of the Chinese community now live outside the Chinatown areas to which Chinese were originally confined in the early Meiji Period and work in the professions, or own restaurants or food-industry businesses. In 1975, Vasishth (1997: 134) reports, patterns of residence reflected province of origin, with Chinese living in Kanagawa being mainly Cantonese, in Osaka from Jiangsu and in Kyoto and Nagasaki from Fujian. Schools teaching in Japanese and Chinese, which like the Korean schools were until recently not accredited by the government for university entrance exams, educate the children of the postwar wave of Chinese immigrants from Taiwan, although many children attend mainstream Japanese schools. The Chinese and Korean languages were added comparatively recently (1997 and 2002) to the list of foreign languages students could choose from in the national university entrance examination, joining English, French and German (Izumi *et al.* 2003). Chinese-language newspapers and web-based news sites such as RakuRaku China provide other outlets for use of Chinese in Japan. Whereas Cantonese was spoken by the majority of the prewar immigrants, the majority of the postwar influx speak Mandarin (Maher 1995b: 127).

Outside the Chinese community schools, Chinese (Mandarin), like Korean, is taught in a number of other schools: in a 1998 report by The Japan Forum, 353 schools across Japan, many of them private schools, either taught Chinese or intended to introduce it by 2001, compared to 165 with Korean (52 schools offered both). This reflected a big increase for both languages since 1987, thought to be the result of the release in that year of the final report of the Ad-Hoc Council on Education which recommended *inter alia* that the range of elective subjects in the high school curriculum be expanded. In 1991 a group of Schools for Collaborative Research on the Diversification of Foreign Language Education began research on foreign languages other than English; two reports ensued in 1993, the first of which suggested that the languages of neighboring Asian countries be introduced into the curriculum of middle and high schools (The Japan Forum 1998). A survey conducted by the Yomiuri Shimbun in January 2004 found that 67% of respondents thought universities needed to place greater emphasis on giving students the foreign languages they would need to play a role in the international community: after English, Chinese and Korean were nominated as strong contenders (ELT News 2004).

English and other European languages

We shall see in Chapter Four the policies which have been adopted at government level with regard to the teaching of English. The present chapter will concentrate on the history and current state of the teaching of English and other European languages in Japanese schools.

English was brought into middle schools as an elective subject in 1947, where it was seen as a "window to the world." The aim of the curriculum was to teach students to "think in English," not to think in Japanese and translate it into English, i.e. to treat English as a living language rather than as an object of study. Ironically, in view of the direction the curriculum later took, listening and speaking were listed as primary skills, reading and writing as secondary skills. The method of instruction was premised, in theory at least, on an audiolingual approach (Ministry of Education 1947). Four years later, the preface to the 1951 Course of Study for English made it clear that no guidelines would be issued by the Ministry for the teaching of foreign languages other than English, as the study of such languages, compared to that of English, was minuscule in scale. Teachers of other languages were exhorted to refer to the Course of Study for English (Ministry of Education 1951).

A student completing the nine years of compulsory education today would therefore have studied English for three years; those who complete a further three years (the majority of students) would have studied for six years. While English was not a compulsory subject (except at certain schools), it was taken by most students because of the foreign language requirement for many university degrees and the consequent emphasis in high school and university entrance exams on English (Kitao *et al.* 1994). The central university examination system tests students applying to national and public universities through multiple-choice questions in the six areas of mathematics, science, history, language arts, humanities and foreign languages; some private universities may require only three or four of these areas (Moriyoshi and Trelfa, n.d.). After the new Course of Study was introduced in 2002 following the introduction of the five-day school week, foreign language education became a required subject at middle and high school (MEXT 2003a).

Despite the emphasis on listening and speaking in the 1947 Course of Study, Japanese proficiency in spoken English has been historically poor, given that extensive classroom practice time based on written multi-choice tests is required for the university entrance examinations, resulting in a focus on reading and writing. One view of this is that since spoken English levels were so poor, the most noticeable end result of the six years of compulsory English education has been the creation of a high proportion of loanwords from English in the Japanese lexicon (Honna 1995: 57–59). It is certainly true that Japan has historically scored very low among Asian nations' mean scores in the Test of English as a Foreign Language (TOEFL)[16] score rankings, and this has prompted various knee-jerk reactions. In 1998, as we see in Chapter Four, Japan's score ranked 180th among the 189 countries in the United Nations (Inoguchi 1999: 1). The test and score data summary for 2001–2002 showed Japan as twenty-ninth out of thirty nations on the computer-based test and fourteenth out of fifteen on the paper-based test (TOEFL 2003). In July 2003, the Ministry of Education, Culture, Sports, Science and Technology (MEXT) issued a press release unveiling a strategic plan for improving the English abilities of Japanese citizens which linked progress in this area with Japan's ability to participate on the world stage:

With the progress of globalization in the economy and in society, it is essential that our children acquire communication skills in English, which has become a common international language, in order for living in the 21st century. This has become an extremely important issue both in terms of the future of our children and the further development of Japan as a nation. At present, though, the English-speaking abilities of a large percentage of the population are inadequate, and this imposes restrictions on exchanges with foreigners and creates occasions when the ideas and opinions of Japanese people are not appropriately evaluated (MEXT 2002).

This was followed up in March 2003 by an action plan setting specific proficiency targets for junior and senior high school graduates; universities were exhorted to set their own targets such that graduates could use English in their work. Specific steps detailed the strategies to be used to achieve these targets, including upgrading of teacher proficiency and of pedagogical methods and also improving motivation for learning English through study abroad and other means (MEXT 2003a).

The JET (Japan Exchange and Teaching) program[17] introduced in 1987 was intended in part to promote a shift towards a more communicative focus in language teaching in junior and senior high school language classrooms in order to foster internationalization. Assistant Language Teachers (ALTs) are placed in English, French and German classrooms to assist Japanese teachers and provide students with native-speaker contact. An evaluation of the program's effectiveness carried out in 2001 reported high degrees of satisfaction from primary, junior and senior high schools taking part. Primary schools spoke of perceived increases in student interest in foreign languages and cultures, ease in mixing with foreigners and willingness to try communicating in English; high schools reported an increase in the number of students attempting the Step Test in Practical English Proficiency (Eiken), officially accredited by the Ministry of Education in 2000 (MEXT 2001a). The major emphasis of the program, it is clear, is on English. The program continues its annual intake of ALTs from around the world: the 2003–2004 intake, for example, included 2,582 ALTs from the USA, 1,165 from the United Kingdom, 368 from Australia, 340 from New Zealand, 942 from Canada and 103 from Ireland, all major English-speaking countries. Much smaller intakes were accepted from France (9), Germany (3), China (12), Korea (4) and a long list of other countries (JET Programme 2003).

Whether languages other than English are taught depends on the school. Japan has no overarching national language policy which determines which community languages should be taught (hardly surprising in view of the monolingual belief still largely prevailing) or which languages should be strategically introduced with a view to Japan's regional and international linkages. English is by default the catch-all solution to engagement with the rest of the world. This is reflected by the gradually increasing but still very small enrolments in foreign languages other than English at high schools: in 1998 3.5 and 0.9 students in every 1,000 studied Chinese, dropping to 2.1, 1.1, 0.5 and 0.2 for French, German, Spanish and Russian respectively (The Japan Forum 1998). A total of twenty-two languages were taught in 551 schools that year (about 60% of them government schools) to about 40,000 students. Chinese was the most widely taught, in 372 schools, followed by French in 206, Korean in 131, German in 109 and Spanish in 76 (MEXT 1999, cited in The Japan Forum 1999). These figures accord reasonably well with the 1993 Keidanren (Confederation of Japanese Industry) survey reported by Maher (1995a: 93): when asked which languages they thought would be important for Japan in the future, businessmen and "salarymen" responded that they would be English (50%), Chinese (25%), French (5.7%), German (5.4%, Spanish (5%), Korean 4.7% and others too small to mention. Classification of responses by age showed that those over forty chose European languages, those under forty Asian languages (in addition to English).

Interestingly, an examination of the Ministry of Education's Course of Study guidelines[18] over the years turns up changes in approach. In 1947, the name of the subject in the Course of Study, which covered both middle and high schools, was "English" and not "Foreign Languages." Four years later, the name had changed to *Gaikokugoka: Eigo-hen* (Foreign Language curriculum, English section), with other languages to follow the English curriculum guidelines. After this, the guidelines no longer treated middle and high school curricula together. Looking first at the progress of the guidelines for middle school, which falls still within the period of compulsory education: in the 1958 revisions, that format had changed. The overall objectives of learning a foreign language were stated first, followed by year-level goals for English, German and French in separate sections. The same format recurred in the next revision in 1969, with a sociocultural dimension of understanding through language of the way foreigners lived and thought now added to the previously linguistic objectives. This format remained mostly unchanged through the revisions of 1967. In 1989 the year-level objectives were stated in terms of the four separate skills of listening, speaking, reading and writing, whereas previously listening and speaking had been treated together. Students' affective motivations were also to progress with the year levels, from "interest" in the first year of middle school to a positive desire to use the language in the third. By 1998, the middle school guideline revisions, referring now to *Gaikokugo*, reflected the changes which had been occurring since the education reforms of the previous decade. "Foreign language" was now a compulsory subject and English was to be selected. Other languages could be offered as electives. The objectives now referred specifically to communication, with listening and speaking singled out as essential to communicative competence. The course of study was laid out not in terms of objectives by grade level as formerly, when the focus had been on linguistic structures, but in terms of functions (greeting, shopping, traveling and so on) to be mastered.

The preface to the *Gaikokugoka* (Foreign Languages) section of the revised high school Course of Study guidelines in 1956 pointed out that it would now be possible to take a second foreign language elective in schools which had many students wishing to do so. The guidelines listed the objectives for English, French and German when taught as the first foreign language, and again when taught as the second foreign language. These differed in that the former sought to extend students' abilities in the four macroskills, whereas the latter sought the same but to inculcate those skills with regard to a "simple" modern language. Four years later, "foreign language" was listed as a compulsory subject; this changed in 1970. By 1978, "foreign languages" included five English-related subjects, distinguished by emphasis on different skills; this increased to seven in 1989, three of which were subjects in oral communication. The objectives include inculcation of a willingness to communicate. In 1999 the English subjects were restructured and one was made compulsory. As in the 1989 revisions, emphasis was placed on a student-centered approach to teaching. The 1991 report of the Central Deliberative Committee on Education (Chūō Kyōiku Shingikai) recommended that the number of young people from other countries who teach languages in Japanese schools through the JET program be increased in order to improve the standard of foreign language teaching and that the Course of Study guidelines be revised to promote a greater emphasis on communication (MEXT 1991).

Clearly the Course of Study guidelines over the years have reflected a move towards a communicative function-based approach to language teaching, pushing for greater student participation and less "chalk and talk" by the teacher. Whether these guidelines have been followed to their maximum extent, though, is debatable. JET program participants tell of top academic schools with high aspirations for tertiary study among their student body where the focus remains firmly on the fill-in-the-blank preparation for the entrance examinations and both teachers and students resist distraction, while other less academically focused schools welcome the more communicative approach in their classrooms (McConnell 2000).

In the private sector, language teaching is big business at private language academies, and occasionally the newspapers contain stories of such schools which have disappeared with their customers' fees. The Japan Association for the Promotion of Foreign Language Education, an association of private language schools, attempts to regulate this industry by stipulating a code of practice; member schools advertise their affiliation with this body to assure clients of their credibility. The languages on offer through these schools, apart from English, include Chinese, French, German, Italian, Korean, Latin, classical Greek and Spanish, with several of the larger schools, such as DILA (http://www.dila.co.jp/) offering a much wider range. We can get a good idea of the range and frequency of the languages taught at private academies from the ALC website (www.alc.co.jp).

A growing number of Japanese universities have begun teaching both undergraduate and postgraduate programs in English in a bid to attract higher numbers of international students who might otherwise have been deterred by the difficulty of studying Japanese to the level required for entrance to university programs. Short-term exchange programs were also set up in 1995 following a recommendation from a Ministry of Education conference on the progress of the plan to achieve the government's target of having 100,000 foreign students studying in Japan. At least seventeen universities have had such short-term exchange programs, in which courses are taught in English, approved since then. Some private universities, such as the International Christian University in Tokyo, also teach in English.

Internationalization and foreign language learning

The learning of foreign languages, predominantly English, has been a major thrust of the government's push for greater internationalization of Japanese society since the 1980s, as we have seen in the exemplar of the JET program. Policy document after policy document, discussion paper after discussion paper has focused on the need for Japanese to learn to speak English better and more widely. Little more than lip service seems to have been paid to the idea of learning other languages, apart from the paper referred to above which called for wider teaching of Chinese and Korean, "neighbor languages." In response to a question in a 1995 survey carried out by the NHK Broadcasting Culture Research Institute as to what (if any) language/s respondents could speak other than the one they used at home, 89% said none and 9% nominated English. To another question in the same survey, 76% of respondents ticked "agree" or "somewhat agree" to the proposition that foreign languages should be taught more thoroughly in schools in Japan (NHK Broadcasting Culture Research Institute 1995).

And yet, as we have seen, languages other than English are *not* taught very widely in schools, although growth in Korean and Chinese is evident over the last few years. The dominance of English reflects a trend which began in Japan in the early Meiji Period. Up until that time the foreign language most studied was Dutch, given that the Dutch were the only Europeans allowed to maintain a toehold in Japan, on a little island called Deshima in Nagasaki Harbor, during the more than two hundred years for which Japan closed itself off to the world as a reaction to fears of European colonial ambitions during the late sixteenth and early seventeenth centuries. A school of studies known as *rangaku* (Dutch studies) flourished during this period. When the period of isolation came to an end, however, it soon became evident that Dutch was not a major international language and that English was the one most needed for contact with the west, particularly the United States and Britain. Japan's international relations with western powers since then have focused to a large extent on English-speaking countries, although German and French were important in the early modern period when Japan modeled its army on the Prussians and its legal codes on the Napoleonic codes.

The lack of a national strategic plan for the role of both community and foreign languages in Japan's present and future activities is one factor contributing to the low rates of language study in schools, with of course the exception of English. Another is the old Japanese belief that Japanese people cannot learn other languages, a formerly surprisingly well entrenched conviction despite all evidence to the contrary in the form of

students who return from study abroad virtually bilingual, depending on
the amount of time spent in the other country. Returnees (*kikokushijo*),
as the children of parents who have been posted abroad for business and
other reasons are known, often come into Japanese schools knowing less
of their own language than of the language they acquired overseas; a huge
literature exists which details the problems these children face and the
strategies that have been taken to deal with them (see, for example, Pang
2000; Goodman 1990).

The origins of this belief, Miller (1982: 222–253) contends, lie in the
layers of illogical argument with which what he terms Japan's modern
myth – the belief in the extraordinary uniqueness of the Japanese language which manifests itself in different ways relating language to society, race and culture – has coated Japanese views of language learning.
While it is certainly true that all languages involve a certain level of difficulty for adults in learning them, "the construction that the myth places
upon this kernel of truth, the universal experience of difficulty that we all
have in learning a foreign language, is that the Japanese experience this
difficulty to a greater extent than anyone else *because they are Japanese*"
(my emphasis added). Miller, while at the same time pouring scorn on
this belief in terms of its universality, isolated some local factors which
may cause Japanese difficulty in speaking foreign languages. One is the
sound structure of Japanese itself, with its relatively small number of syl-
lables and their fixed consonant-vowel structure, which makes it difficult
for Japanese tongues to deal with runs of vowels or consonants in foreign words. Another is the marked preference for hiring only Japanese
nationals in permanent positions in Japanese universities and schools to
teach foreign languages rather than native speakers of those languages,
and the skewing of language teaching away from communicative proficiency towards answering written examination questions. "What is actually implied by 'using English' in a Japanese sociolinguistic context is
'using English to pass the university or other admissions examinations'"
(254).

That was more than twenty years ago. Since then, the reforms to
Japanese education in the mid-1980s have included a marked swing to
embracing the concept of communicative language teaching, backed up
with large injections of government funding, through the JET program
after 1987. English conversation was introduced into Japanese elementary
schools as an internationalization-oriented elective in Period of Integrated
Study activities from 1997, and in 2002 was taken up by approximately
50% of public elementary schools (MEXT 2003a). The Action Plan to
Cultivate "Japanese with English Abilities" aims to build on this by having at least one third of such classes led in student-centered activities

by native English speakers or junior high school English teachers and to support the undertaking with research and materials development. Ten thousand high school students are to study abroad each year. Between 2003 and 2005, as part of the plan to increase the English-speaking abilities of Japanese, 100 high schools are to be designated as Super English Language High Schools (SELHis) which will teach part of their curriculum in English. From 2006, the central university entrance examination will include a listening test in addition to a written test. Japan's government, then, is serious about developing the English abilities of its citizens. It will be interesting to evaluate in ten years' time what effect these strategies have had. In the meantime, however, it would seem that belief in the ability of individual Japanese to learn other languages is growing, helped along by the changes in teaching methodology (which may increase once the domination of the written-only central admissions test is broken), by grassroots practical experience through young people studying abroad or meeting foreign students studying in Japan, and by Internet-related activities which require English.

In this chapter we have seen something of the diversity of language used in Japan, from Japanese as the mainstream language to minority languages such as Ainu, Okinawan, Korean and Chinese, and to foreign language study trends and attitudes. In terms of the experience of minority language users, Maher encapsulates their difficulties "not merely as a 'minority problem' but more as an overarching problem of hegemonic practice" (2002: 176), and we have seen that without exception these groups have gone through experiences of discrimination and marginalization that have without doubt affected their ability or desire to speak their own languages to a certain extent. In the case of foreign language study, it is English which has proved the hegemonic power which has eclipsed the study of other foreign languages in a short-sighted approach to foreign language policy, although we are seeing encouraging signs with the growth in the number of schools offering Korean and Chinese. In the private sector, of course, other languages are available on demand for those willing to pay; the public sector, however, has a long way to go to achieve a reasonable spread of language provision.

3　Language and national identity: evolving views

In this chapter, we will examine earlier overt ideological connections between language and identity and engage in more speculative theorizing about what the more recent variations might be. During Japan's modern period the language (often confused with the writing system) has functioned as a marker of shifting cultural identity. Contrasting views on how the language should develop sparked heated and often bitter debate during the twentieth century as the evolving demands of history placed a new importance on the role of language in modernization and in Japan's interface with the world. I will discuss the major views put forward on the role of Japan's language in the construction of a particular cultural identity relative to the circumstances of the time, up to and including the present.

Personal and national identity in a modernizing Japan

To go back to the very beginning of Japan's modern period in 1868, the language practices then in use would have clearly identified someone in terms of class and location. As we saw in Chapter One, the pre-modern division of Japan into multiple closed-off domains meant a highly segmented society and a complicated network of regional dialects. Dialectal variations could be extreme: the dialects of Kagoshima in the south and Sendai in the north-east, for example, were mutually unintelligible (Hattori 1960: 733). None of the dialects, even that of Kyoto or Edo, was officially designated as the standard language; that would not happen until 1916, although in practice these functioned as lingua franca for those able to travel. Within each domain, of course, the local dialect *was* that region's standard, used for the normal purposes of communication between residents who were unlikely, given the restrictions on travel, to have occasion to communicate with speakers of other dialects from different regions. Any Japanese, therefore, would be identifiable in terms of region by the dialect they spoke.

In terms of written Japanese, identity in terms of social class was strongly marked by the system of writing then in use. Not only orthography but stylistic genres as well indicated whether the user was a member of the educated elite. During the pre-modern period, "educated" meant the upper classes, aristocrats and *samurai*, who were the only ones for whom education was officially provided in the form of domain schools at which students were drilled in the Chinese classics and the writing of innumerable characters. Those who were not members of the upper classes were not necessarily illiterate; far from it, self-education among townspeople and villagers flourished in the *terakoya* (temple schools), lending libraries did a roaring trade (see Kornicki 1998) and Japan had a higher rate of literacy during the late pre-modern period than Europe. The growing influence of the merchant class in the eighteenth and nineteenth centuries saw rapid growth in the number of private schools for the lower classes in both rural and urban areas, giving basic instruction in the three Rs along with moral and occupational training. Some commoners acquired only the bare essentials of literacy; others developed an advanced ability to read and write, though usually only in certain areas.[1]

An upper-class educated man (and I use the word advisedly, rather than "person") in the pre-modern period could be expected to have a familiarity with the Chinese classics, to be able to read and write *kambun* (Sino-Japanese) and *sōrōbun* (its epistolary equivalent) and in general to be familiar with the Japanese classics and their literary conventions as well. Writing (or at least the then prevailing idea of the written language of public life between educated men) was far from being an easy approximation of speech on paper; the several varieties of formal written Japanese adhered to classical traditions which resembled the spoken language only slightly. These varieties, or styles, are today collectively known as *bungotai* (literary styles based on classical forms), to differentiate them from *kōgotai*, the modern written colloquial style which is based on – though not entirely identical to – today's spoken Japanese. Today's *kōgotai* did not exist at the beginning of the modern period. It developed over time during the Meiji and subsequent periods, in response to the social changes during Japan's modernization which meant that a democratic written language was needed to replace the existing conventions which carried strong overtones of the power structure and values of the feudal period.

To understand the nature of written Japanese at the time and how it related to identity, we need to look briefly at the four major written conventions then in use: *kambun* (Sino-Japanese), *sōrōbun* (epistolary style), *wabun* (classical Japanese) and *wakankonkōbun* (a style combining elements of both Chinese and Japanese). Each of them, although necessarily having incorporated newer lexical items over the centuries, relied heavily on the use of archaic literary conventions and idioms: *kambun* and *sōrōbun* on classical Chinese and *wabun* on classical Japanese. *Wakankonkōbun*, while it combined both these traditions, did so with a heavy admixture of contemporary elements which made it less arcane (for details, examples and history of the development of each of these four styles, see Twine 1991a).

Sino-Japanese was the form of writing used in official documents, criticism and exposition, history and critical essays, early Meiji translations of western literature and in general in upper class education. The term *kambun* (literally "Chinese writing," denoting the Chinese language as used in Japan), actually encompasses several different types of Chinese or Chinese-influenced writing in Japan, including *jun kambun* (pure Chinese, or a Japanese attempt at writing Chinese as a foreign language using Chinese word order[2]) and *kambun kundoku* (Chinese read as Japanese with the help of diacritics and glosses to indicate word order and pronunciation, or written out in full as Japanese with a combination of Chinese characters and Japanese phonetic katakana).

We may wonder why Chinese should have played such an influential role in written Japanese, until we realize that in the sixth century, Japan, having no writing system of its own, adopted the Chinese writing system along with Buddhism during a period of extensive cultural borrowing. Chinese was originally written as a foreign language in Japan. Over time, however, systems such as the phonetic kana scripts were derived from the Chinese characters to indicate both those features of Japanese grammar not present in Chinese and the Japanese pronunciation of the words which the characters represented. It might have seemed only natural that the role of Chinese would diminish once the Japanese had developed writing systems of their own, but this did not happen. The use of Chinese or one of its derivatives signified erudition and prestige. As such, men chose to continue writing in that vein, and kana writing based on classical Japanese speech was left to women. *Kambun*, valued for its conciseness and formal erudite tone, enjoyed a prestige higher than that accorded to other forms of writing right up until and into the Meiji Period, bolstered along the way by the Tokugawa Shogunate's revival of Confucian studies.

Sōrōbun used the verb *sōrō* as its copula. Men used this as their epistolary style in both public and private correspondence. Unlike *kambun*, which remained the province of the upper class, *sōrōbun* – descended from a modified form of classical Chinese developed in the Middle Ages in Japan – was used by commoners as well in correspondence, records and public notices. Commoner education included classes in *sōrōbun*, despite the fact that its marked Chinese influence made it quite difficult to master.

Originally written in Chinese characters alone, by the beginning of the Meiji Period it had evolved into a mixture of characters and katakana.

Wabun, on the other hand, was not Chinese-derived but rather descended from the court literature of the Heian Period (794–1192). Once kana scripts had been developed by the ninth century, it became possible for the literate few to write down Japanese in a manner approximating the way it was spoken. As we have seen, however, the prestige script of Chinese remained the one used by men, and kana were known as *onnade*, women's writing. Court ladies used kana to write the great early classics of Japanese literature, among them *The Tale of Genji*, which is known as the world's first novel. The soft elegance inherited from Japanese poetry lent to *wabun* a preference for graceful circumlocution and euphemism, with long meandering sentences very different from the brevity of *kambun*, lexicon drawn predominantly from native Japanese words and a marked preference for the use of such rhetorical devices as pivot words.[3] Honorifics, rare in *kambun*, were abundant in *wabun*. In the early Meiji Period, *wabun* was used by women in correspondence, men in correspondence to women or near relatives, court ladies in the diaries which had been traditionally kept since the days of *The Tale of Genji*, essays by neo-classical scholars and some translations.

The fourth major literary style, *wakankonkōbun*, was essentially *kambun kundoku* made softer by a mixture of classical Japanese; it also incorporated colloquialisms from the eleventh century on. This became the major general-purpose literary style outside those areas in which *kambun*, *sōrōbun* and *wabun* were mandated. Its uses were many and varied: Buddhist sermons, plays, fairytales, ballad-dramas, certain genres of Tokugawa Period fiction, the dialogue passages in popular novels, prose poems and essays. Its grammar was still that of a past age and its nucleus was Chinese, but the familiarity imparted by the use of Japanese expressions made it popular with the many literate townsmen of the Tokugawa Period.

Going back to our theme of identity, then, both the variant of spoken language a person used and their degree of literacy and knowledge of the above literary conventions would have functioned to identify what part of Japan that person came from and whether the degree of education they possessed stamped them as upper or lower class. That was about to change, however, as the Meiji Period wore on, bringing a swift and all-encompassing transition from old to new. In quick succession came a national postal system (1871), a national education system (1872) and a modern communications network featuring, rail, telegraph and telephone networks. After 1870, the publication of newspapers and journals mushroomed. The lifting of the earlier restrictions on travel and choice of occupation led to a new freedom of social interaction and mobility. At national, community and personal levels, life changed on a scale not previously experienced.

The changes in language over this period reflected what was happening in society at large. A written language predicated on classical conventions and on notions of class made redundant by the sudden abolition of the previous four-tier class system[4] now inevitably came under scrutiny in terms of whether it helped or hindered the modernization process. What was needed was a new written style based on modern speech which everyone could read and write and which was based on a standard language taught and used throughout the country. The orthography needed to be overhauled: kana spellings based on the speech of the classical era[5] still in use needed to be replaced with a streamlined system of kana spelling reflecting modern speech, and a limit needed to be placed on the number of Chinese characters to be used and to be taught in schools for daily use. Advocates of language reform argued that these changes would simplify the education system by reducing the time needed to learn to read and write, would facilitate full literacy and would result in a language able to be more or less uniformly spoken and written throughout Japan.

Although this may seem like good common sense from our present historical perspective, it was not an uncontested position. In fact, with the possible exception of the standard language, these reforms were bitterly fought. Colloquial Japanese had long been considered too vulgar and wordy to be used in writing, except where the dialogue of popular fiction demanded it. To suggest that a modern written style be based on contemporary speech was viewed as an affront to centuries of belief that *kambun* and *wabun* and their derivatives were the only forms of writing possible for educated people of refined sensibilities. To suggest that the existing orthography be rationalized was tantamount to rejecting centuries of literary and cultural tradition. Language, in short, was a sacred cultural icon which embodied all that was good and true in the worldview of those keen to retain the status quo. Because those who reacted in this way were to a large extent those in power, it was a long time before any serious consideration was given to the issue of language reform, although both script and style reform were debated from time to time in newspapers and journals during the latter part of the nineteenth century.

The major engine which drove the development of a modern written style during this period was the newly emerging modern Japanese novel. Because authors such as Futabatei Shimei (1864–1909), the writers of the later Naturalist school and the great anti-Naturalist writers dealt with the alienation and psychological trauma experienced by their characters in the new Japan, it became imperative to develop a new way of writing flexible and contemporary enough to properly express personal issues of identity and change. Futabatei's *Ukigumo* (The Drifting Cloud, 1887–1889) is generally regarded as Japan's first major modern novel, both because Futabatei, under the influence of Russian literary theory, used new techniques of psychological realism in depicting the main character's inner turmoil and because in order to do so he pioneered the use of the Tokyo dialect in his text, on the grounds that the character's thoughts could only be realistically conveyed in the language used in his everyday life. Later authors such as Yamada Bimyō (1868–1910), Shimazaki Tōson (1872–1943) and others, through successive waves of literary endeavor, developed and polished the style further, until in the works of the Shirakaba group of authors in the years around 1920 the modern colloquial style reached perfection as a literary medium which from then on held unchallenged sway in the novel. Outside literary circles, and spurred on by their revelation that it *was* in fact possible to create a polished written style based on speech, progress in simplifying the language used in textbooks had been made by 1910; newspapers veered away from the traditional styles in the 1920s; and finally, the 1940s saw colloquial style being used in official documents and government decrees.

We can see from this string of developments that the relatively static relationship between language and identity that pertained in 1868 began to shift and change during the ensuing decades as former social structures were broken down and new ways of doing things emerged. Language became important to the identity of the new "modern" Japanese in several ways, marking him/her as a citizen of an emerging modern nation state where one language acted as a unifying force understood (in theory, at least) by all citizens and where the kind of written language that a citizen should be exposed to in the press and use in his/her daily life was coming increasingly under scrutiny. At the macro level, concepts of personal identity in relation to language remained fluid during this period, under tension from opposing views of how language should function and what it should represent. Just as the structures of the past were changing, so too, though at a much slower rate, were mindsets about speech and writing.

Personal identity was soon to be linked with national identity through the medium of language. In the 1890s, following Japan's victory over China in the Sino-Japanese war (1894–1895), nationalistic sentiment led to a new interest in language issues. Prominent among those engaged in the debate at this time was Ueda Kazutoshi, whom we first met in Chapter One. Ueda had just returned to Japan from his studies of western linguistics in Germany. He was very much influenced by the western view of writing as secondary to speech and therefore a perfectible resource rather than a sacred icon which must not be tampered with. As linguistics lecturer at Tokyo Imperial University and later head of the Education Ministry's Special Education Bureau, he threw his energies into lobbying the government to establish a body to research and oversee the implementation of a standardized form of written Japanese based on the contemporary spoken language, as we saw in Chapter One. What motivated him more than anything else was the connection he saw between national identity and the treatment of language. The Japanese language, he asserted, could be greatly improved by the adoption of a standard form of the language and of the colloquial style in writing. Ueda did not view this as tampering with tradition or destroying a respected cultural icon; far from it, to refine the national language – which he described as the spiritual blood binding Japan's people together – was to treat it with respect. Japanese, as the identifying mark of the state and of its people, must be respected and protected, not through allowing it to stagnate but through modification appropriate to the circumstances (Ueda 1894). A standard language and a modern written style were, in his view, interdependent; both were essential to the future development of language in modern Japan.

We have seen some of the ways in which language related to shifting and fluid views of identity in mainland Japan during this period of sudden change. Identity issues for the Ainu and Okinawan populations were of course much greater. Dragooned into service as "Japanese" for the purposes of establishing the geographical borders of the nation state, they were assimilated to the point of being unable to receive education in their own languages. For these sections of Japanese society, identity as a Japanese citizen equated to erasure of personal identity through the most intimate identity marker of all: their own language.

Language issues in the Meiji Period, then, functioned as a symbol of modernized Japan: as a marker of personal identity and later also of identity as a national subject. Not everyone viewed either of these in the same way, however; most of those in power or positions of influence rejected the idea of manipulated language change. The calls for script reform that began to surface in the 1870s and 1880s[6] were opposed just as vehemently as the development of a modern written style. Chinese characters had formed the basis of written Japanese since the sixth century. Over the intervening centuries, they had become not just a form of writing, which could be altered as circumstances might demand, but a value-laden cultural institution, yardstick of erudition and marker of power and prestige. Those who espoused such values in regard to the writing system were therefore very strongly opposed to any attempt to rationalize it. As we shall see in the following section, language (and to a large extent this meant characters) came to function as an icon of ultranationalism under a militarist government.

Language and ultranationalist identity

We have seen that during the Meiji Period those who held that language represented some sort of ineffable connection to Japan's heritage and encapsulated the indescribable but unique essence of the Japanese spirit managed to suppress ideas that language might be changed, although as time went on novelists and people like Ueda and his followers took the argument out of their hands. Nevertheless, such people continued to hold powerful positions in government, and it was government through which any codified change would have to be approved. As we shall see in Chapter Four, proposals on script reform put to the government by the language policy bodies established in the early twentieth century were routinely knocked back.

The debate about language reform as an attack on national values centered on script to a much larger extent than might have been expected. In one sense, of course, given the complexity of the orthography at that time, a concentration on script was entirely natural, but in another it was ironic, given that characters had after all originated in China and not Japan. There is a widespread tendency in Japan to this day to conflate language with script (see, for example, Brown 1985 and Unger 1987: 98–104). Discussions of the difficulty of Japanese invariably center on the writing system. The same attitude informed the earlier arguments of those who were against change: to change the script in some way would be to change the language itself. The ultranationalism that developed and became increasingly powerful in the early part of the twentieth century therefore played a reactionary role in terms of language. The link between the status quo in language and a particular kind of identity in this view could not be disentangled without irreparable harm to both. In the years following the Manchurian Incident in 1931, when Japan occupied Manchuria and the power and influence of the military grew, extreme right-wing militarists came to dominate the political and intellectual climate in Japan. Two particular concepts were key to their views on language.

The first of these, *kokutai* (national polity), denoted "the development of a distinct pattern of national unity around the emperor" (Mitchell 1976:20). This term and its connotations came to be surrounded with an almost mystical aura of nationalism, to the extent that a 1937 Education Ministry-issued book *Kokutai no Hongi* (The Fundamentals of Kokutai) was banned in schools during the subsequent Allied Occupation of Japan (1945–1952). Forming one of the basic constructs within *kokutai* was *kotodama*, "the spirit of the Japanese language," a term used to imply an inseparable connection existing between the unique Japanese language and the essence of the Japanese spirit. Chinese characters in particular, sanctified by centuries of use in Japan, were particularly venerated. It was only possible to express Japanese thought through the existing script, in which so much tradition resided; not unnaturally, therefore, any attempt to tamper with that existing script system equated to a treasonous violation of *kokutai* itself. Where nationalism had provided a positive stimulus for efforts by Ueda and others to reshape language in the wake of the first Sino-Japanese war, ultranationalism now acted as a deterrent to language reform by emphasizing that any such reform would be an attack on the national identity of Japan's citizens.

During this period, therefore, a Japanese person was being reminded constantly through the school system and through the press of the link between language and heritage, the ineffable essence of being Japanese. Using the Japanese language stamped them not simply as being Japanese in ordinary terms but as being an important cog in the *kokutai* system, part of a mystical whole set apart from other peoples and linked back through the ages to the wellsprings of national tradition in a nexus which more than anything else was considered to shape identity at this time. Identity here was conceptualized not as something fluid and multifaceted but as something static and unchanging, solid but at the same time vulnerable to attack. Such attacks were firmly repulsed, both by government which repulsed proposals for script reforms, and in some cases by the police: in June 1939, for example, some Waseda University students who supported replacing characters with the western alphabet were accused of anti-nationalist sympathies and arrested by the secret police (Kitta 1989:53). Clearly, only one form of identity was permissible at this time.

Language and the citizen of empire

Concurrently with the developments described above, the Japanese language began to play an important role in the two colonies of Taiwan (1895–1945) and Korea (1910–1945). This added a new dimension to the linguistic and other identity of Japanese citizens, that of citizen of a colonial power whose language was used outside its own borders. The policy adopted in Taiwan was one of assimilation, in which the teaching of the Japanese language had first priority, with the threefold aim of providing a standard language for communication between the disparate groups who lived on the island, raising the cultural level of the Taiwanese, and assimilating them by teaching them the Japanese way of doing things (Tsurumi 1967:133). Japan's experience in Taiwan later provided the model for its language policy in Korea, where Japanese was again used as the medium of education, in order to assimilate the Korean people spiritually and culturally as subjects of the Emperor.

By the end of 1942, Japan had three kinds of territory under its control: the two colonies and the mandate of Micronesia, which Japan had held since 1922; areas such as Manchuria and North China under the nominal control of a puppet government; and occupied areas under military control in South East Asia, known as the Nanpō (southern region). With the Japanese Greater East Asia Co-Prosperity Sphere thus established, the Japanese language was to be disseminated in order to afford the peoples of East Asia an understanding of and respect for the "Japanese spirit" so that they would become loyal subjects of the Emperor. Japanese was to be seen not as a foreign language but as the common language of the Co-Prosperity Sphere, one wing of the historic creation of a new order which by its nature as a lingua franca facilitating communication and business would bring together the diverse peoples of this vast region (Etō 1943: 66–68). Japanese and not Chinese was the natural choice for this role not only because of the political and cultural force of Japan but also because of the intrinsic superiority of the language itself (Shinohara 1944: 24). The influence of *kotodama* now extended far outside Japan's borders.

Many felt that Japanese at this time was poised to become a world language like English and French on the international scene. One writer remarked, for example, that Pearl Harbor had launched Japanese on the road to becoming an international language; just as English had become a world language after England's defeat of Spain, Japanese would soon rise to equal stature after Japan defeated the United States (Tsurumi 1942: 3–5). The close connection between strategies to disseminate Japanese and the construction of the new world order became a favorite theme. Responsibility for the teaching of Japanese in the two colonies lay with the governments-general there. In the territories occupied after the Pacific War broke out in 1941, the military – specifically the Propaganda Corps of the General Staff Office – were put in charge of spreading the language. Teachers were trained, textbooks were written, methodologies were debated and the field of teaching Japanese as a foreign language was given a boost through publication of the findings of related research activities. The main focus of the textbooks, given that the aim was to assimilate subjects of the Emperor, was on presenting a picture of life in Japan rather than on incorporating material relevant to local areas. In the colonies, Japanese was *kokugo*, the national language. Its status in Manchuria was that of one of the national languages; in puppet-government areas of

China, it was a foreign language; and in South East Asia and Micronesia it was taught as a compulsory school subject. The dichotomy between *kokugo* (Japanese for Japanese) and *nihongo* (Japanese for foreigners) discussed in Chapter One can be seen here reflected in the titles of textbooks, e.g. *Nihongo Tokuhon* (A Japanese Reader) produced for use in China.

When the war ended, the teaching of Japanese outside Japan, or at least that sponsored by Japan itself, came to a halt; indeed, a backlash occurred in the previously occupied territories, although evidence of colonial cultural policies lingered in Korea and Taiwan for quite some time. The kind of identity conferred on users of Japanese during the preceding years had been twofold: dutiful subject of the Emperor and consumer of Japanese culture on the one hand, and dutiful subject of the Emperor and colonial/imperial master on the other. What was to happen next, however, would sweep away the ultranationalistic views of language and identity with a vengeance as the end of the war ushered in both a new era in politics and a new view of the citizens of Japan and their linguistic rights.

Language and the sovereign citizen

Immediately after World War Two, language became an expression of Japan's new identity as a democratic society freed from the rule of ultra-nationalism and imperialism which had led it into conflict. The ultimate symbol of this was of course the new Constitution, today's "Peace Constitution," enacted in 1946 during the Allied Occupation of Japan. Chief among the changes in this constitution from the earlier 1889 Meiji Constitution was the fact that sovereignty now rested with the people of Japan and not with the Emperor, as Article 1 made clear from the outset: "The Emperor shall be the symbol of the State and the unity of the people, deriving his position from the will of the people with whom resides sovereign power."

The following passage, though dealing with an Okinawan context, sums up the sense of alienation from the construct of *kotodama* that the aftermath of the war inspired in relation to identity:

If we look at Okinawa through the constitutional patriotism definition of Jurgen Habermas, after the terrible experiences of the Rape of Nanking and the Battle of Okinawa (in particular the mass suicides of non-combatants), it is clear that Japanese citizens cannot be expected to look for a sense of identity in the "unbroken imperial line" or "the beautiful Japanese language" which are in the end nothing more than ideas developed by the government. The identity of the Japanese people can only be found in the model of a Japanese citizen defined in the postwar Japanese constitution. (Aikyo 1998:7)

In language terms, this shift in focus was symbolized by the fact that the new Constitution, the nation's premier legal document, was not only written in modern Japanese but also in today's combination of kanji and hiragana rather than the older kanji and katakana of official documents (see Twine 1991b). One of those responsible for this change was Yamamoto Yūzō (1887–1974), a novelist and dramatist keenly interested in language issues who argued that a strong connection existed between democracy and language. An editorial in the major newspaper Asahi Shimbun on 20 November 1945 sought to impress upon the drafters of the new constitution the importance of seizing this opportunity to produce a document written not in *kambun* but in a style that everyone could understand: it was essential that, in a Japan where democracy was becoming a reality with the enfranchisement of women and the lowering of the voting age, the document which was the source of the nation's laws be open and accessible to everyone. A subsequent period of argument was followed by a capitulation by the Minister of State, which led some to speculate that he may have felt that to use colloquial style in the Constitution, while a radical departure from tradition, would at least make it seem like an original Japanese document rather than the translation of an English original. The Constitution was then written in modern Japanese.

The postwar Japanese citizen, then, was newly empowered not only by the change in status to locus of sovereignty but also by the change in written language which enabled them, once educated, to read the laws of the land without undue difficulty. The connection between language and identity on a national-to-individual level had never been stronger. A second area in which this connection was underlined, indeed headlined, during the Occupation was the long-delayed script reforms. Released from the decades of right-wing dominance which had seen prewar proposals repressed (see Gottlieb 1995 and Seeley 1991), the revitalized National Language Council, which had gone into eclipse after 1942, was given government approval to proceed. The connection between language and democracy was a constant theme: how were the people in whom sovereignty now resided to participate effectively in public life if the period of compulsory education did not fully equip them with the level of literacy required to read political debate in the newspapers? Clearly it was time to do something about the writing system, to reshape it from its existing state into something more streamlined and up to date. In script reform terms, the democracy argument meant that because complex Chinese characters were a relic of the old ruling class they should be changed – numbers limited, shapes and numbers of possible readings simplified – such that everyone could handle them with ease. The slogan *kokugo wa kokumin zentai no mono* (our language belongs to *all* the people) was often heard during this period. The script reforms that will be described in Chapter Four followed in short order.

What sort of Japanese person did the new script policies imply? One who was – assuming that person to be not a member of a minority group – empowered to take part in public debate by virtue of being able to read without excessive difficulty, who could spend more time on education in other subjects by virtue of the scaled-down time needed to learn to read and who was no longer constrained by the dead hand of a writing system and written language which reflected feudal power structures and values. In short, the changes in the written language reflected the change in Japan itself, from imperialist state to democracy, no matter how contested the nature of that democracy may have been both then and now.

Those who held the old views on language and script had not of course gone away simply because they no longer held power. They bided their time until they were able to maneuver a partial political reversal of some of the reforms. While the psychological background to the postwar script reforms had been a desire to break with the past, this in time gave way to a sense that, although the reforms had indeed brought about a form of political disjunction, they had also led to a less than desirable cultural disjunction with prewar literary culture which needed to be addressed. We will see in Chapter Four how that came about.

Citizen of the world?

Once Japan had recovered from the disaster of the war and the years of desolation which followed, the economy began to grow strongly. By the mid-1970s, language was beginning to be regarded as a symbol of economic power and to become the subject of cultural policy promotion. The Japan Foundation was set up within the Foreign Ministry in 1972 with the brief of promoting Japanese culture overseas, and as we shall see in Chapter Four, a large part of its activities were devoted to fostering the study of Japanese language overseas in the belief that "the main pillar of international cultural exchange (is) the teaching of language" (Japan Foundation Nihongo Kokusai Sentaa 2000). The number of overseas learners of Japanese worldwide more than doubled between 1988 and 1993, and by 1999 the figure had reached approximately two million. To Japan-bashers during this period, these activities equated to a kind of cultural imperialism; to those who sought to benefit in terms of employment from Japan's economic miracle, they offered a way of increasing the prospect of employment with a Japanese company.

A hypothetical mainstream Japanese person during this period, therefore, could at a stretch be described in terms of affective linguistic identity as seeking cultural recognition for his/her language concomitant with Japan's economic power. Other economic empires had seen their languages spread far outside the borders of the metropolitan power; why not Japanese also? At the same time, however, as we saw in Chapter One, this period of greater prosperity afforded the leisure for introspection missing in the frantic postwar years and saw the flourishing of Nihonjinron literature which came into conflict with the search for external recognition by its insistence that the Japanese language was uniquely difficult and that only the Japanese (and sometimes not even they) could fully understand it. Language in this view functioned as a linguistic barrier, with language, race and culture inseparably linked.

This period, then, saw something of an identity split: on the one hand Japanese could consider themselves increasingly cosmopolitan in the sense that their language was now being promoted more and more strongly overseas, with willing uptake from those who saw in it the way to future prosperity or whose interest in Japanese culture, spurred by developments in fashion and popular culture, prompted them to learn the language in order to immerse themselves in the study of Japan. Government was keen to foster recognition of the language on the international scene, and it was during this period that the idea was first mooted that Japanese should become one of the official languages of the United Nations, in recognition of Japan's huge economic contribution to that body. On the other hand, against this stood the Nihonjinron view, widely held among Japanese people themselves, that they were isolated speakers of a uniquely difficult language, that they had no facility for learning foreign languages and that no foreigner could properly learn to speak Japanese. What, then, to do?

One novel but relatively short-lived proposal was put forward by Nomoto Kikuo of the National Language Research Institute[7] in Tokyo in the late 1980s. It came at a time in the 1980s when the power of Japan's economy was at its height, before the bubble burst and led to the recession of the 1990s, and when inside Japan itself the government emphasis on *kokusaika* (internationalization) was also strong. Within this framework, articles and books began to appear outlining reasons why Japan's language should attain a position of greater international prominence. Nomoto suggested that a kind of *kan'yaku nihongo* (Simplified Japanese), not as complex as the real thing, should be developed. The plan was that in order to foster the spread of Japanese on the international scene and to provide those seeking to use the language for business purposes with an easier version than the real thing, only a restricted range of adjectival inflections and verb forms would be taught, together with a basic vocabulary of 1,000 words.

The Simplified Japanese project married the two opposing views described above: that Japanese should become an international language but that it was too difficult for non-Japanese to learn properly. The deceptively logical solution to this impasse was to develop a dumbed-down version, with the stated aim of facilitating communication by pruning the linguistic complexity of "real Japanese" to a more manageable set of rules which could more easily be assimilated by non-Japanese learners: a kind of "us" and "them," which Nagata (1991) has described as linguistic apartheid. The project fudged the issue, however, of whether speakers of an artificially created simplified variant of a language – what really amounted to a pidgin – had any real chance of acceptance on equal terms by native speakers of that language, particularly in business, or whether their credibility would be perpetually marred by the perceived deficiencies of their Japanese. Nevertheless, the Agency for Cultural Affairs within the Education Ministry considered it worth funding for several years from 1988 and teaching materials were developed. The project was widely criticized both within and outside Japan and did not achieve any substantive result.

The twenty-first century

And finally, what of today? What kind of identity might today's Japanese person attain through the medium of his/her language? The last dozen or so years have probably not seen any really significant degree of change, i.e. Japanese remains important to economic and trade concerns but has made no real progress on the international scene in terms of influence. Despite its recent recession, Japan is still one of the world's major economies but, by comparison with languages such as English, French, Chinese and Arabic, remains under-recognized culturally in terms of its language (though not of other popular cultural forms such as anime, fashion, martial arts, kabuki and computer games). Strong western perceptions that Japanese is "too hard" remain. Nevertheless, as we saw in Chapter One, the number of students worldwide has grown. The economic significance of the language has clearly not diminished, as any visitor to tourist resorts frequented by groups from Japan will testify on seeing the multiple signs in shops. A recent Australian film, "Japanese Story," showed Australian mining executives meeting an important Japanese visitor with prepared Japanese speeches and handling intercultural communication issues such as the correct Japanese way of handling business cards with aplomb. In business, knowledge of Japanese remains an advantage.

We might think that the Internet would have played a role in spreading Japanese, but Japanese is rarely used on the Internet outside Japan.

The language remains, even in relation to this truly borderless technology, a local player, with the exception, of course, of those who access Japanese-language pages for research and teaching in Japanese Studies all around the world. Although Japanese rapidly established a web presence for itself in 1998 after a relatively slow start with Internet use (as we shall see in Chapter Seven), rising to become the second most widely used language on the Internet after English, it has now been overtaken by Chinese (Global Internet Statistics by Language 2003). In online terms as well as other terms, it is nowhere near an international language.

All of this should, in theory, leave our hypothetical Japanese citizen in something of a state of confusion in regard to language and identity, particularly given the suggestion – not well received – in 2000 that English might at some future stage become an official second language. I doubt very much, however, that this is the case. We have seen already that Japanese are comfortable with language diversity within the national language itself, if not yet in the sense of accepting the concept of multilingualism within Japan. Attitudes towards foreign language learning, moving away from the old belief that the Japanese somehow are just not good at learning other languages, are bound to change, and indeed have no doubt begun to change already, given the government's proactive stance on English education and communicative teaching and the number of Japanese students who study overseas. The building blocks are in place for a substantial shift of mindset here. It remains only to remove the existing impediments, such as the format of the university language entrance examinations which discourage communicative competence, and we will see a surge of language awareness and capability unlike any seen before. I do not think this is too optimistic a forecast. The world has changed, Japan has changed with it, and twentieth-century structures and ideas on language and identity are no longer as inflexible as once they were. Recognition of other languages used in Japan will come too, probably driven not by the popular culture successes of those who use the minority languages as much as by the fact of the increasing numbers of children speaking other languages in the public school system (MEXT 2001b). We might say, then, that views of language and identity are currently in a transitional stage; rather than Japanese as an international language becoming the next step, the recognition of Japan as a multilingual country is likely to be the road traveled, bringing us full-circle away from the Nihonjinron philosophy of language and identity.

4   Language and identity: the policy approach

In Chapter Three, we looked at the broad themes inherent in the ideology of language and identity. The present chapter will discuss how those themes played out in actual policy approaches to language management. Few things reveal more about a society's attitude to the role of language in national identity than the types of language policy it develops. To arrive at any real understanding of language in today's Japan, we need to know what the official views of language at government level have been, because language policy decisions reflect and attempt to come to terms with the linguistic implications of major social developments. Language policies originate in recommendations made by high-level government bodies set up expressly to deal with perceived language-related problems and to guide future development. As such, they illuminate – and sometimes confront head-on – the cherished beliefs of users of the language(s) in question. Debates over language policy frequently escalate (or perhaps descend) into full-blown furors, sometimes among members of the committees only, sometimes – as in the case, for example, of India in the 1950s – in the wider social arena. As we shall see in this chapter, twentieth-century language policy in Japan was no exception.

People sometimes assume that language policies in Japan deal only with the Japanese language itself, but this is not the case. The term "language policy" refers to the specific strategies formulated and implemented by language planners to achieve certain objectives: to restrict the number of characters in general use, for example, or to make it easier to teach foreign languages, in particular English. These usually take the form of laws, regulations or guidelines laid down by authoritative agencies and intended to direct, change, or preserve the acquisition, structure, or functional allocation of language codes. What, then, is the "language planning" on which this is based? Simply defined, it is "the organized pursuit of solutions to language problems, typically at the national level" (Fishman 1974:70). Others define it as "the activity of manipulating language as a social resource in order to reach objectives set out by planning agencies which, in general, are an area's governmental, educational, economic and linguistic authorities" (Eastman 1983:29), or, in a more restricted sense, as "deliberate efforts to influence the behaviors of others with respect to the acquisition, structure, or functional allocation of their language code" (Cooper 1989:45).

Language planning and language policy formulation occur in several areas in Japan today. The focal points of these activities reflect the country's historical and cultural background, the make-up of its population and its position in the international community. This chapter will examine three particular issues: language policy relating to the Japanese language within Japan; to other languages within Japan (Ainu and English); and to the teaching of Japanese as a foreign language, both inside and outside Japan. The discussion will bring together threads already picked up in earlier chapters and consider them from a policy angle.

Japanese as the national language

We might usefully begin by considering how language policy relating to Japanese as the national language has developed. Japan today has a century of hard-won experience with language policy formulation behind it. It faces an equally challenging set of contemporary and future issues as technological advances such as computerization impact on language. The history of these developments very clearly illustrates the major issues relating to language and identity in Japan in terms of its national language. As we saw in Chapter Three and will continue to explore in this chapter, they illuminate what social perceptions of the connection between language and identity have been in terms of Japanese identity as citizens in a modernizing nation, as subjects of the Emperor during wartime expansion, as members of a society climbing back from postwar chaos to affluence, and finally as members of the information society.

Language policy formulation began in Japan in 1902, when the government set up a small committee called the National Language Research Council (Kokugo Chōsa Iinkai) within the Ministry of Education. It did this in response to a growing groundswell of public opinion in favor of changing certain aspects of the language and in particular of the writing system, which were believed to be detrimental to the progress of modern Japan (see Twine 1991a). Those who raised initially sporadic but increasingly vehement voices in support of reforms of various kinds included educators, journalists, civil rights activists and novelists, most of whom were motivated by pragmatic concerns related to their own fields. Some saw characters as the enemy of progress because it took so much time to master them: time which could be better spent, they thought, on acquiring other learning more urgently needed for national development.

Script reform therefore became a goal, either through limiting the number of characters, abolishing them completely in favor of kana, or adopting the western alphabet, depending on the views of the advocate. Others believed that the development of a written style based on modern spoken Japanese rather than the archaic literary conventions discussed in Chapter Three was imperative to achieving their ends, be those education, writing realistic contemporary fiction or political education of the masses. Still others argued that Japan needed an official standard language which would override the multiplicity of dialects and unite the nation under one linguistic banner; this would foster a sense of national unity and identity as Japan entered the world stage again after two hundred and fifty years of self-imposed isolation.

Those who advocated language reform during the period from around the time of the Meiji Restoration in 1867 to the turn of the century were for the most part isolated intellectuals whose views found no favor with the majority. The small private script reform groups which formed in the 1880s proved insufficiently focused to push their then unpopular cause effectively. Despite the newly instituted national education system, scholarship and erudition (though not literacy per se) remained largely the preserve of the upper classes and were demonstrated by mastery of the old literary styles and of a very large number of characters. Many of the character forms were much more complex than today's simpler versions; kana spelling was based on classical speech centuries out of date. A thorough grounding in the Chinese classics was considered an essential part of the education of many of the men who now held power. To suggest that the literary conventions and the script which had formed the backbone of high culture for centuries should be in any way changed or simplified was thus tantamount in many people's eyes to heresy. Those advocating such a path were for the most part either ridiculed or ignored.

After the Sino-Japanese war of 1894–1895, however, an upsurge of national pride and confidence saw a renewed push for language to cast off the Chinese influence and return to its Japanese roots. This coincided with the return from Europe of the first western-trained linguist, Ueda Kazutoshi (also known as Mannen), who founded the linguistics department of Tokyo Imperial University and there trained many of the men who were to become influential in the twentieth-century script reform movement.

In 1898 Ueda and others established the Linguistics Society (Gengo Gakkai) to push these views. Its members, together with those of the Genbun'itchi Club (formed in 1900 by the Imperial Society for Education to promote the spread of a written colloquial style outside literature), petitioned both Houses of the Diet to establish a government agency to work toward achieving their aims. An initial committee was formed as a result, but Ueda and his supporters had something more high-powered in mind and kept up a campaign of pressure on the Education Minister and other politicians to establish a national body. The citizens of modern Japan needed a language which could be understood from one end of the archipelago to the other, regardless of local dialectal differences, and a modern written style based on that standard language and not on classical Chinese or Japanese. Only thus could a modern linguistic identity available to all Japanese be formed. Eventually, in 1902, the government agreed.

The National Language Research Council set itself four tasks: to investigate adopting a phonetic script, either kana or rōmaji; to encourage the widespread use of colloquial style; to examine the phonemic system of Japanese; and to settle upon a standard language from among the dialects. Over its eleven years of activity, it carried out many of Japan's first large-scale language surveys, documenting and classifying information which would in time provide the basis for policy decisions by later bodies. It did not succeed in formulating any lasting policies, in part because of the still strongly-entrenched, generalized political opposition to language reform of any kind. It did, however, succeed in its aim of delineating a standard form of Japanese in its normative grammars, *A Grammar of the Spoken Language* (Kōgohō 1916) and a supplementary volume in 1917, published four years after the Council itself had disappeared in an administrative reshuffle. In these books, the standard language was clearly defined as that currently spoken by educated people in the Yamanote district of Tokyo.

What was the overall impact of the Council's work and to what extent did political and social currents support or hinder this? It achieved its aim of defining the standard language because the government could see that a standard language was important to education, which was in turn important to national progress (for a discussion of the role and influence of language standardization, see Joseph 1987). It was also successful in promoting the advancement of the modern written colloquial, though this had already attained a momentum of its own in society as a whole. The Council was not at all successful with script reforms, however, because of that entrenched belief about script held by powerful men in the Diet: namely, that the written language was a sacred treasure which must on no account be tampered with lest the cultural heritage of the nation be lost. Ironically, of course, as we know, Japan's script was entirely derived from the Chinese, both through the initial adoption of the characters themselves and the later derivation of the phonetic scripts from the characters.

This struggle over script between the western-trained linguists who regarded script as secondary to language itself and those who treasured language traditions as an icon of national spirit was to characterize language planning and policy formulation during the entire first half of the twentieth century. Government input was revitalized in 1921 with the formation of the Interim National Language Research Council (Rinji Kokugo Chōsa Iinkai) and its replacement in 1934 with the National Language Council (Kokugo Shingikai), which remained in charge of language policy issues until 2000.[1] Both these bodies tried in vain to induce the Diet to accept proposals limiting the number of characters in use (an enduring concern to newspaper owners interested in increasing their circulation and educators wanting to cut the amount of time spent on teaching characters in schools). The Interim Council's members included scholars (Ueda among them), educators, journalists and writers committed to language reform, each for their own compelling set of reasons. Its brief was to find solutions to those aspects of language which caused difficulties in daily life and education; its members chose, therefore, to concentrate on investigating character limits, revising kana spellings and rationalizing written conventions such as the multiple pronunciations a character could have. Among its proposals were a list of 1,962 characters for general use (1923), a change to kana spelling based on modern Tokyo pronunciation (1924), modification of Sino-Japanese words to replace some of the more difficult characters with simpler ones (1926–1929) and simplification of character shapes in general (1926). For full details of events in the following discussion, see Gottlieb 1995 and Seeley 1991.

The government accepted neither of the major proposals on characters and kana. The former was warmly welcomed by twenty influential newspapers, however, who announced that they would adopt this approach from 1 September 1923. This plan, however, was thwarted by the great Tokyo earthquake which occurred on that day, leaving many of the newspapers unable to publish at all. The proposal to alter kana usage met with concerted opposition from ultranationalist classicists and others who believed, as we saw in Chapter Three, that script should not be changed artificially but should evolve naturally over time. Historical kana spelling, therefore, being like characters the product of long tradition, was viewed as a repository of the cherished cultural and spiritual values of the nation. Reaction to the proposal was so virulent that the Education Minister eventually had to announce in the Diet that he would not implement it. Seven years later, in 1931, a revised version of the proposal looked likely to succeed when the Education Ministry decided that – despite ultranationalist opposition – it would implement this policy in state textbooks once it had been passed by the Educational Administration Committee. Before that could happen, however, the Cabinet changed and with it the Minister; the Prime Minister then shelved the proposal on the grounds that it could disturb public opinion at a time when unity was important.

Attempts to democratize the written language by making it more accessible through reforms of this sort were thus viewed with deep suspicion by the conservative establishment. As long as the military, which upheld rigid views on the sanctity of tradition, held power, script reform was a lost cause. When the successor National Language Council tried a similar proposal to limit characters in 1942, Japan had already been at war for a long time, and attempts to change the sacred script, by then the repository of *kotodama*, were viewed as akin to treason. We saw in Chapter Three that *kotodama* (the spirit of the Japanese language) was a term used to encapsulate the belief that the national language (by which was usually meant the time-hallowed characters and historical kana usage), bound up as it was with the essence of the national spirit, was sacrosanct, never to be altered. Advocates of script reform were subject to right-wing vilification campaigns; foreign loanwords were dropped in favor of Sino-Japanese equivalents; and in general, tradition, rather than convenience, ruled. The officially sanctioned linguistic identity of the "good" Japanese of this period, at least as far as writing was concerned, depended on knowledge of the old forms of both kana and characters.

While this was happening in Japan itself, the Japanese government was pushing ahead with policies aimed at spreading the Japanese language abroad in the conquered territories, as part of a scheme to foster in the various peoples of the Greater East Asia Co-prosperity Sphere an understanding of "the Japanese spirit" and respect for the Emperor. The East Asia war was seen as a war of ideas in which language was both the advance guard and the rearguard (Nishio 1943); Japanese was to be the lingua franca of the Sphere. Many people at this time, judging from the literature of the period, felt that the words "language policy" referred only to the spread of the Japanese language overseas, not to the management of language issues at home, so that the next few years saw heated debate as to how the teaching of Japanese in the conquered territories should be handled (see Gottlieb 1994a and 1995).

The end of the war in 1945 brought an end to these activities. In Japan itself, a new intellectual current propitious to change emerged. With the fall from power of the ultranationalists came a golden chance for those who wished to initiate reform of the writing system. These men adopted "democracy," then a popular catch cry, as their slogan and argued cogently that existing script conventions were anti-democratic in that they made it needlessly difficult for all sections of the populace to participate in the written debate on public life in postwar Japan. Given the changes then sweeping occupied Japan, it was not difficult to find support for these views as people distanced themselves either voluntarily or with a nudge from elsewhere from the views which had underpinned the militarists. Some[2] mounted a renewed push for the abolition of characters through romanization or other means (see Gottlieb 1995 and Unger 1996), but the majority of members of the reconvened Council in 1945 favored the middle-of-the-road approach of limiting the number of characters for general use, modifying the shape of the more complicated ones, bringing kana spelling into line with modern pronunciation, and in general implementing related changes aimed at reducing complexity. This resulted in a slew of policy documents over the ensuing decade or so, of which the most important were the List of Characters for Interim Use (*Tōyō Kanji Hyō*, 1946), a list of 1,850 characters of which 881 were later designated to be taught during the nine years of compulsory education, and the policy on Modern Kana Usage (*Gendai Kanazukai*, 1946), which aligned kana spelling and modern pronunciation in all but a few specialized instances.[3] Other significant policies specified the number of different pronunciations a character could have in different contexts and how much of a word customarily written in a kanji-kana mix should be taken up by the character and how much by the appended *okurigana*.[4]

So far, so good, in the eyes of those who had now finally made some progress toward their goals. The policies were officially promulgated through Cabinet and became binding on all government ministries (though not on the private sector). As the Education Ministry was part of the government, this naturally meant that they were disseminated through school textbooks and that the postwar generation of school children grew up under their influence. Just because right-wing views had fallen from grace, however, did not mean that they had disappeared altogether. Conservative Council members such as Fujimura Tsukuru (1875–1953) were appalled by the changes, deploring the erosion of prewar literacy standards and worrying that people would no longer be able to read the literature of the past without substantial help in the form of annotations, dictionaries and other supports. To them, the reforms were the thin end of a wedge intended eventually to lead to the total abolition of characters (a fear not entirely unjustified, as some vocal members of the Council did in fact support this aim). The perceived "compulsory," government-mandated nature of the policies also caused concern, although in fact the changes were binding only on government offices and not on private citizens.

Spurred on by these worries, they began before long to plan a counter-offensive, devising a clever plan to draw public attention to what was happening in the Council. Many of them were also members of a private pressure group, the Council for Language Matters (Kokugo Mondai Kyōgikai, set up in 1958), which skillfully used the media to air concerns over the direction in which the Council's policies seemed headed. At the same time, sympathetic politicians in the Diet made speeches raising the specter of a communist-motivated national "dumbing-down" (a significant claim during that Cold War period). In 1961, disaffected Council members succeeded in focusing media attention on what they perceived as the stacking of successive Councils' memberships with script reform supporters by staging a well-publicized walkout from a general meeting. The subsequent coverage, which included a mock trial of the Council on television, did in fact put the issue in the public eye for long enough to persuade the Education Minister to change the method of selecting incoming members. In 1965, as a result of these upheavals and the later establishment of a subcommittee on language within the Liberal Democratic Party (see Gottlieb 1994b), the Council was asked to re-evaluate the postwar script reforms in the light of the concerns which had been raised.

The next twenty-five years, from 1966 to 1991, saw the postwar policies systematically evaluated and, in some cases, revised. The 1948 list limiting the number of different pronunciations a character could have in different contexts was expanded by 357 in 1973; also in that year, the expanded role accorded to *okurigana* in 1959 was reduced somewhat in a revised policy, restoring to a certain extent an emphasis on the role of kanji rather than kana in inflected words. The major change, however, and the one which took the longest to achieve due to its contentious nature, was the revision of the list of characters. At issue were the word *seigen* (limit) in the preface of the 1946 list and the number of characters, felt to be too restrictive. After eight years of deliberation and extensive consultation, the list was revised to today's List of Characters for General Use (*Jōyō Kanji Hyō*, issued in 1981). The main changes were an increase from 1,851 to 1,945 characters and the substitution of "guide" for "limit" in the accompanying documentation. Other policies, specifically the change to modern kana spelling and the simplification of complex character shapes, remained unchanged; they had by that time become so embedded through the education system that any attempt to revert to the prewar systems would have been counterproductive. The cycle of re-evaluation ended in 1991, with the final document being a revised policy on how to write foreign loanwords.

What had this re-evaluation actually achieved? It had succeeded to some extent in stopping the continuing erosion of prewar script conventions; no further reformist policies could be implemented during that period, and those already in existence were reviewed and in some cases revised. The extent of the revision, however, was perhaps not as great as its instigators might have wished. There had been no return to the prewar situation of virtually untrammeled orthographic freedom at a formal level; the postwar intervention of official policies continued to exist (albeit in slightly watered-down form), so that the much-contested involvement of government in the domain of writing remained. Nevertheless, the more radical members of the Council, those who had sought the eventual abolition of characters, were now muzzled, and indeed, sidelined for good. Supporters of the alphabet or kana as the national script lost whatever degree of influence they had had; today they continue their advocacy from within small private interest groups which have no representatives on the Council.

All this had taken place within an overall national context of a review of policies enacted during the Allied Occupation of Japan. Some Occupation policies, such as administrative decentralization of education and the police force, were revoked. The major script reform policies had also been enacted during the Occupation; this meant that their detractors had been keen to point out that they, too, had been foisted upon the unwilling Japanese by their conquerors. In fact this was not a tenable position, as the evidence shows. Isolated Allied staff members did indeed voice opinions as to the desirability of romanization and the 1946 report of the United States Education Mission to Japan gently suggested this as a possible avenue to be explored for the future. The clearly expressed belief of General MacArthur's office, however, was that the nature of the Japanese script was a matter for the Japanese themselves to decide and that was how things had developed, along the middle path of rationalization of the existing orthography rather than its wholesale abandonment.

The early 1990s, then, found the National Language Council having completed a major task. Its direction changed after that to a renewed concern with the spoken language. At first glance the new direction might seem to be no more than a natural consequence of the end of the script-related re-evaluation, but in fact other contributing factors had come into play during the 1980s. For one thing, an increased political focus on regionalism led to a reconsideration of the status of dialects, as we saw in Chapter One. For another, both the post-1970s emphasis on internationalization and the take-up of new technologies, in particular information technology, contributed to an increasing tendency to use (mainly) English loanwords instead of Japanese equivalents where they exist. This in turn contributed to an often-expressed view that the language is in a state of decline. The apparently decreasing ability of young people to use honorifics properly also features large within complaints of this sort, which appear regularly in newspapers in Japan. Japan is not alone in this concern with what are perceived as deteriorating language standards, of course. Language change often attracts such charges, particularly from older people (Crystal 1987:4), and we can find similar refrains in other countries where changes wrought by technology and increasingly fluid boundaries between languages appear to an older generation brought up with fewer choices to be eroding standards.

The Council took up both these issues in the mid-1990s. It concluded in 1995 that the use of loanwords was to a certain extent unavoidable, given the nature of the modern world, and that this was particularly true in specialist arenas, such as information technology. In non-specialist areas, however, as we saw in Chapter Three, it counseled caution; the use of words not universally understood could impede communication, particularly with older people (Kokugo Shingikai 1995: 449–450). With regard to honorifics, its reports advised in 1995 and again in 1997 that it was no longer so much the correct forms of honorifics that were important as knowing when their use was appropriate to achieve smooth communication (Kokugo Shingikai 1995: 432–433 and 1997). This represented a clear move away from the more prescriptive attitudes of the past toward a more holistic view of language and communication and also formed the refrain of the Council's final report on the subject (Kokugo Shingikai 2000) before its disappearance in an administrative reorganization in 2001.

The renewed interest in the spoken language did not mean, of course, that the Council no longer concerned itself with the writing system. One of the biggest changes of the 1980s, and one with the potential for enormous ramifications for how Japanese is written this century, was the invention of character-capable technology. This enabled both a rapid swing to the use of word processors and later computers and, by extension, the eventual construction of a substantial Japanese-language presence on the Internet in the second half of the 1990s. One of the pillars of the postwar script reforms was that characters would in the main continue to be written by hand, a Japanese typewriter being too time-consuming and cumbersome. The new technology, of course, changed that. Some have since suggested that the current policy on characters ought to be changed so that fewer are taught for reproduction and more for recognition, as word processing software contains many thousands more characters than the 1,945 characters for general use. Council documentation after 1992 acknowledged the challenges posed by the rapidly expanding use of computers, and sought ways of responding to the two areas identified as being of most concern: the effect of information technology on the language and the issue of the characters and the dictionaries within the software (see Gottlieb 2000 for details).

Policies relating to other languages

Ainu

Thus far we have seen how language policy is formulated with regard to Japanese as the national language and how the hot issues have linked to perceptions of national identity. We would be hard pressed, however, to find any country whose residents speak only one language to the exclusion of all others. Multicultural societies such as Australia and the United States have language policies which encompass or offer views on the use of languages other than the dominant English. How does Japan deal in policy terms with other languages used within its borders? We saw in Chapter Three that many minority language communities exist: Ainu, Korean, Chinese, English, Okinawan and others. I will concentrate in this discussion on Ainu and English, the first because it is the language of Japan's only indigenous minority and the second because it is the international language most influential in Japan's dealings with the world. Both of these make good case studies of the link between language and identity in contemporary Japan at policy level and are in fact the only languages other than Japanese for which policy has been developed.

Few things do more to destabilize a people's sense of cultural identity than to forbid the use of their native language and impose the language of another. Japan has implemented such a policy three times in its modern period, first with the Ainu people and then in its colonies of Taiwan and Korea, where – as we saw earlier – the teaching of Japanese was mandated as the appropriate language for subjects of the Emperor. In each case, the aim of the government was to assimilate distinct groups of people into a proposed seamless whole, i.e. the seamless whole of a unified nation with only one national language. Such a policy allowed for no linguistic variation, regardless of geographic location, racial difference or historical and cultural differentiation. To a lesser extent and in a different context, we can see the same motives at work in the Showa Period (1926–1989), when schools rigidly discouraged dialect use in order to facilitate the top-priority spread of the standard language. Japan's policy toward the Ainu language provides us with a case study of an attempt to eradicate the cultural identity of a people in order to create a culturally and linguistically unified homeland, in this instance to strengthen Japan's claim to its disputed northern borders (see Hansen 2001).

The Ainu people, as we saw earlier, today number around 24,000 and live mostly in the northern island of Hokkaido. Originally found also in the main island of Honshu, they were driven gradually northward over several centuries by the expanding Japanese, until in 1868 the government annexed the Ainu areas of Hokkaido. There followed a rigorous policy of assimilation aimed at strengthening Japanese sovereignty in the vulnerable and disputed peripheral regions. When Hokkaido's population increased after settlers from other parts of Japan were offered homesteads there, the Ainu became a minority. In one of the clearest possible acknowledgments by government of the link between language and identity, the assimilation policy, which also forbade them to practice their customs, compelled them to learn and speak Japanese and to take Japanese names. Many Ainu lost their livelihood as a result of the annexation and lived in poverty. Later laws such as the 1899 Hokkaido Former Natives Protection Law aimed to address this situation by granting Ainu land free of charge to be used for farming, but they were only marginally effective, as what land remained after settlement was often not fit for agriculture (see Siddle 1996).

As a result of the mandatory use of Japanese, the Ainu language declined over time to the point where it was no longer in daily use but was preserved in an oral tradition of epics, songs and stories, as we saw in Chapter Three. In the 1980s, however, as a result of international attention to indigenous minorities, Ainu activists became increasingly vocal about the conditions their people faced and the threatened disappearance of their culture in all but economically useful tourism terms. Political associations were formed to urge the government to provide assistance. In 1995, a "Round Table on a Policy for the Ainu People" found that only an extremely limited number of people were still able to speak the language (MOFAJ 1999: 4); an unsourced article in the western press put the number at less than ten in 1999 (Large 2001), all of them older people. To address this situation, the Round Table's 1996 report recommended that legislative and other measures should be taken to conserve and promote Ainu language and culture. Not long after this, in May 1997, the Law for the Promotion of Ainu Culture and for the Dissemination and Advocacy of Ainu Traditions was passed. Under its provisions, prefectures were required to develop programs to foster Ainu culture.

International considerations also played a part in the passing of this law. As we saw in Chapter Three, when the Sapporo District Court brought down its judgment on the Nibutani Dam case, it found that – despite Prime Minister Nakasone's claim that Japan had no indigenous minority – the Ainu did in fact constitute a minority under the terms of Article 27 of the International Covenant on Civil and Political Rights, which Japan had ratified in 1979. This minority status entailed recognition of the rights of separate culture and language.

The Ministry of Education's budget for fiscal 1997 announced that in order to implement the provisions of the new law the Ministry, together with the Hokkaido Development Agency (located in the Prime Minister's Office), would set aside subsidies for the promotion of Ainu culture and related measures (Ministry of Education 1997: 19). Accordingly, a month after the law was passed, the two bodies jointly established the Foundation for Research and Promotion of Ainu Culture (FRPAC). As its name indicates, the Foundation's goal is to promote Ainu culture, including taking steps to see that the Ainu language does not die out. The Foundation trains Ainu language instructors and conducts Ainu language classes, both through classroom instruction at fourteen places around Hokkaido (*Japan Times* 9 June 2000) and through radio broadcasts. Its website (www.frpac.or.jp) provides information on where to hire tapes of the radio broadcasts or videos on Ainu life as well as information on events relating to various aspects of Ainu culture. The FRPAC's attempts to promote the study of the Ainu language represent a 180-degree about-face from the government's earlier attempts to stamp it out. It is still too early to evaluate how successful these initial measures have been, although Siddle (2002) and Maher (2002) indicate that they may have been a trifle misplaced in their emphasis on language rather than culture, as discussed in Chapter Three.

English

Government policy with regard to the Ainu language is, as we have seen, less than a decade old and is in large part a reaction to both international and domestic pressures. By contrast with its small-scale focus, the teaching of foreign languages, in particular English, has attracted vast amounts of attention and funding. The nature and future of English teaching in Japan has come under particularly sharp scrutiny in the last few years, as the Japanese government seeks ways to reposition itself in the world following the continuing economic woes of the 1990s. One of the spurs for this was a 1998 TOEFL ranking which listed Japan's score as 180th among the 189 countries in the United Nations (Inoguchi 1999: 1). Yet most Japanese secondary school students, as we know, study English for six years and often follow this with further study at university level. Furthermore, a large amount of money has been poured into the JET program since the late 1980s in the hope of fostering a more communicative approach to the teaching of English in Japanese schools, which are often criticized for their grammar-translation approach. Teaching English as a foreign language is of course not limited to Japan's schools and universities: it is also a major private industry, to an extent which makes Japan's TOEFL ranking all the more galling. One estimate put the annual amount of money expended on this private sector in the neighborhood of 3,000 billion yen (in 1995, equivalent to about 30 billion US dollars) (Koike and Tanaka 1995: 18).

Not surprisingly, therefore, the TOEFL report caused some soul-searching in a variety of quarters both official and private as to how Japan ought to respond to the increasing prestige of English as a world lingua franca. Should all Japanese learn English? A broad base of postwar-educated Japanese already do to some extent. Or should government spending focus on fostering a smaller number of very fluent speakers able to interact freely in international contexts? What sort of Japanese person does the increasingly globalized environment of the twenty-first century require? Ought Japan to cling to its relatively monolingual (at least in the international context) linguistic identity, or should renewed efforts be brought to bear on producing citizens who, though living in Japan, can interact freely in the global context fostered by the Internet?

These questions of linguistic identity have elicited varying and contradictory responses. Some favor the elites-only approach. Suzuki Takao, for example, outspoken professor emeritus of linguistics from Keio University whose book *Nihonjin wa Naze Eigo ga Dekinai ka* (*Why Can't the Japanese Speak English?*) attracted considerable attention in 1999, believes strongly that Japan should concentrate on fostering just a small group of advanced-level English speakers and at the same time defend its own "linguistic sovereignty." An advanced ability to interact in English is not altogether a good thing, he argues, if it means that on the international scene high-level Japanese politicians converse in English with their international counterparts rather than in Japanese through interpreters. To do this cedes power to the English camp rather than defending linguistic equality for the Japanese. Speaking Japanese and using interpreters may have other benefits, too, as an amusing sideline to the April 2001 change of political leadership shows: when Prime Minister Koizumi appointed non-diplomat and frank speaker Tanaka Makiko as his Foreign Minister, an official worried about the possibility of verbal gaffes commented "it will be a disaster if she mentioned them in her fluent English because we cannot then say they were mistakes by interpreters" (Osedo 2001).

These possibilities aside, Suzuki takes a firm stance in favor of retaining a clearly separate linguistic identity rather than attempting to meld in with the trend to use English in the international community. This is not to say, however, that he does not support English education for Japanese.

He does, but envisages an elite body of globalized Japanese capable of interacting at high levels of proficiency in English rather than a broader base of less-proficient citizens. Suzuki would restrict English-language education to those Japanese working in fields with a requirement for substantial international contact, such as politics, business, scientific research and engineering, who have a pressing need to speak English and ought to be able to speak it fluently. The majority of Japanese having no real need to speak English at all, government spending on English-language education could be more usefully diverted to other areas.

Well-known political scientist Inoguchi Takashi, from the University of Tokyo, agrees. As he sees it, to expect everyone in Japan to speak English simply because they live in an age of globalization is unreasonable and imposes an additional burden on students. A much better strategy would be to insist that those planning to become high-ranking officials in the civil service be required to demonstrate top-level English proficiency. In this he echoes Suzuki's belief that a core of really fluent English speakers is all that Japan needs for its future external interactions, but he does not share Suzuki's views on linguistic sovereignty. "It is because the nation's elite is not fit for the globalizing process that Japan these days is sometimes viewed as being relatively unrefined" (Inoguchi 1999: 4); to Inoguchi one proof of such fitness would be the fluent use of English rather than a reliance on interpreters, whether such reliance was kept to prove a point of linguistic equality by using Japanese on the international stage or not.

Academics are not the only ones to push for higher levels of English proficiency. The business world has also begun to link career progression with mastery of English. Since March 2001, for example, employees at IBM Japan have needed a minimum score of 600 points (useable business English) on the TOEIC (Test of English for International communication) in order to be promoted to section chief, while Assistant General Manager positions require a score of at least 730 (able to communicate in any situation). The company gave such employees a year to polish up their skills, with subsidized English classes provided (*ELT News* 7 March 2000). Nissan and Marubeni also assign different levels of English ability, based on the TOEIC, to different jobs in the company, depending on how much English is required by the position.

Concern about requisite levels of language competence are not uncommon when a society grapples with an issue of language policy important to its national interests. In Australia, for example, similar arguments were advanced with regard to the teaching of Japanese when national language policy was under discussion in the 1980s, at a period which coincided with large numbers of students rushing to universities to learn Japanese at the height of Japan's economic prosperity. A few questioned the mass spread of Japanese language education in schools and universities, calling instead for a more targeted distribution of resources into the training of a smaller number of really fluent Japanese speakers. Reactions like this can be symptomatic of an underlying concern with national identity in that debate commonly focuses on the kind of linguistic identity with regard to the other language which will best fit the needs of the country concerned. In Australia's case, at that time and to a lesser extent ever since, it was the fit between Australians and the Japanese language within the context of national economic and other priorities which was at issue; in Japan today, it is that between the Japanese and English in terms of the broad spectrum of international relations, including their economic aspect.

Views of the kind expressed by Suzuki and Inoguchi, however, and in particular Suzuki's belief that ordinary citizens without work-related international contact have no real need for English, conflict sharply in some respects with the main thrust of a report submitted to the Japanese prime minister in January 2000, while supporting it in others. In response to a perceived drop in morale caused by the economically troubled 1990s, the then Prime Minister Obuchi Keizo charged a panel of Japan's intellectual elite with devising an agenda relating to national goals for the twenty-first century. The panel formed subgroups to consider five themes, in the process consulting widely and using a website to post minutes of meetings and solicit public input through e-mail and fax. The resulting report (see The Prime Minister's Commission, 2000) laid emphasis on empowering the individual and making strength of diversity. It recommended sweeping changes to a number of cherished Japanese ways of doing things, and was roundly criticized in some quarters on that account while being hailed in others.

Among the issues addressed was that of "global literacy," under the heading of promoting a pioneer spirit for Japan's twenty-first-century frontier. To qualify as possessing "global literacy," the Commission suggested, people would need a mastery of information technology such as the Internet and "the mastery of English as the international lingua franca." Referring in passing to the 1998 TOEFL ranking mentioned above, in which Japan's score was the lowest in Asia and not far off the lowest of all the countries included, the report argued that by mastering English, the people of Japan would be able to convey information about themselves and their country to the rest of the world, a point also stressed by Suzuki and Inoguchi in their writings but at a different level. Whereas Suzuki and Inoguchi would restrict that ability to transmit information from Japan in English to a limited number of fluent English speakers, the Commission viewed the ordinary Japanese too as requiring English proficiency in order to operate effectively in the new world of fluid boundaries enabled by the Internet. "Achieving world-class excellence demands that, in addition to mastering information technology, all Japanese acquire a working knowledge of English – not as simply a foreign language but as the international lingua franca. English in this sense is a prerequisite for obtaining global information, expressing intentions, and sharing values."

To do this, the report continued, would not of course devalue the role of the Japanese language, which as the national language was "the basis for perpetuating Japan's culture and traditions." Nor would it detract from the importance of studying other foreign languages, in particular those of Japan's nearest and most historically significant Asian neighbors, China and Korea. The Commission recommended as a strategic imperative that all citizens should be equipped with a working knowledge of English by the time they left school. Further, all government departments and other public institutions at both national and local level should be required to produce web pages and publications in both Japanese and English. It even flagged future discussion on the long-term possibility of designating English as an official second language.

How was this aim of universal English literacy to be achieved? Among other things, the Commission recommended an expansion of the number of native-speaker teachers of English in Japan. This is the usual response to discussions of English teaching and had already been happening to some extent for around fifteen years. As far back as 1984, the Ad Hoc Committee for Education Reform included among its recommendations a call for a move to a more communicative approach in teaching English, to be achieved in part by the increased employment of native English speakers as teachers. Three years later, in 1987, the government – under the general umbrella of "internationalization," then a prominent buzzword – initiated a two-pronged program intended to revitalize the teaching of English and other foreign languages. One prong would be to import native-speaker assistant language teachers to act as living resources in foreign language classrooms in schools. The other would be to adopt (in theory, at least, if not in actual practice) a communicative approach to language teaching aimed at fostering oral competence.

This program, known as the JET (Japan Exchange and Teaching) Program, has greatly expanded since its inception. The original intake of 848 participants in that first year rose to 6,078 by 2000 (MOFAJ 2000), and the program has now been running long enough to have been evaluated in a recent academic book (see McConnell 2000). The Council of Local Authorities for International Relations (CLAIR) administers it at the national level, together with the three Ministries of Foreign Affairs, Home Affairs and Education. These bodies between them carry out recruitment, training and placement activities, while host institutions under the control of local government bodies receive the participants and carry out the grassroots activities of the program. As a deliberate attempt by government to improve the teaching of foreign languages, in particular the strategically significant English, the JET program clearly comes under the umbrella of language planning as defined by Fishman and Eastman earlier in this chapter.

English teachers on the JET program have come from Great Britain, the USA, Australia, Canada, New Zealand, South Africa and Ireland. In fiscal 2000, following a report from a panel formed in January that year to advise the Education Ministry on ways to improve English education, citizens of Singapore, the Philippines and Jamaica (all countries where English is an official language) also became eligible to participate, in a bid to increase the number of EFL teachers in Japan. Whether this influx of extra teachers will have any appreciable effect on the English curriculum in schools remains to be seen. As long as the system of university entrance examinations remains geared to written English with a focus on grammar, the more academic high schools may not have the time to devote to communicative oral activities led by ALTs in the classroom, as borne out by the experience of JET participants even now (e.g., Bartlett 2000).

Some moves have been made, though, toward opening up further avenues in the education system for developing oral proficiency. A 1998 midterm report from the Ministry of Education's Curriculum Council stressed that the primary purpose of its national curriculum standards reform, which promotes the study of foreign languages, is "to help a child cultivate rich humanity, sociality and identity as a Japanese living in the international community" (Ministry of Education 1998). This clearly reflects the commitment to internationalization which has driven foreign language education policies since the late 1980s. Japanese elementary school students have been able since 1997 to choose English conversation as an after-school activity; once they reach third grade, they can also study English as an option in a "period for integrated study" which offers educational activities outside the normal curriculum. Oral Communication was introduced into the secondary English curriculum in 1992, but only as an elective; the major thrust of the curriculum, as noted above, continues to rest on the teaching of written English. The expansion of the Internet, however, has opened up new opportunities for communicative activities in English, and this may be one avenue which can be actively utilized for teaching as the Education Ministry works to improve the number of schools on-line. Students can use e-mail to communicate with English-speaking students elsewhere; and teachers can access the resources and discussion lists on the Web to improve both their English skills and their English teaching skills (Kitao and Kitao 1997).

In 2003, the Ministry of Education, Culture, Sports, Science and Technology announced a new action plan to cultivate "Japanese with English Abilities." Minister Toyama Atsuko said in her statement announcing the Action Plan that "English has played a central role as the common international language in linking people who have different mother tongues. For children living in the 21st century, it is essential for them to acquire communication abilities in English as a common international language. In addition, English abilities are important in terms of linking our country with the rest of the world, obtaining the world's understanding and trust, enhancing our international presence and further developing our nation" (MEXT 2003). The goals of the plan are to ensure that all Japanese citizens will be able to communicate in English upon graduation from middle and high school, and that university graduates will further be able to use English in their work. Strategies to achieve these goals are clearly outlined in the Plan, as discussed in Chapter Three.

The nature and extent of English teaching in Japan are bound to remain a focus of language policy for the foreseeable future. We turn now to its inverse, the teaching of Japanese to others.

Teaching Japanese as a foreign language

The third major aspect of Japan's language policy important to this chapter concerns the spread of Japanese as an international language in the loosest sense of that term, i.e. as a language taught to non-native speakers who seek such instruction from a variety of motives, whether related to business, education or culture. Earlier attempts at large-scale teaching of Japanese outside Japan, as we have seen, took place in the colonial contexts of Korea and Taiwan, or in the wartime context of occupation of other parts of Asia. Not surprisingly, then, when Japan sought to assert an equivalent cultural identity to match its economic strength during and after the 1970s by promoting the study of Japanese abroad, allegations of cultural imperialism were frequently heard from its neighbors and from further afield; a common theme of the "Japan-bashing" of the 1980s was that what had not been able to be achieved by force was now being pursued through economic imperialism. These somewhat extreme views, predicated upon loss and fear, did not gain common currency. The strength of Japan's economy was such that not just the Japanese government but other governments as well eagerly took up the challenge of increasing the number of foreign learners of Japanese, frequently interweaving economic benefits with notions of internationalization and grass-roots cultural exchange.

The major government player in the external arena here is, as might be expected, the Ministry of Foreign Affairs, which has expended vast sums of money on promoting knowledge of Japan and its language around the world through the activities of the Japan Foundation. Much of this has to do with Japan's perceptions of its identity as a citizen of the international community and the nature of its cultural and linguistic presence on the world stage. Funds have been pumped into promoting the teaching of Japanese as a foreign language, resulting in an increase in the number of overseas learners since the 1970s: over two million at last count, up from just over 127,000 at the time of the first Japan Foundation survey in 1979 (Japan Foundation 2000). The Japan Foundation runs a major language institute in Urawa which holds training programs for teachers of Japanese, develops and provides educational materials and acts as a clearing house for information. Other language institutes perform similar educational functions in Kansai and overseas.

Yet despite these expensive activities, Japanese is still nowhere near reaching the international status of English, owing both to the relatively small population of Japanese speakers and to its restricted geographical range compared to that of English or Chinese. Many have noted, and sometimes complained, that its standing as an international language is certainly not commensurate with the strength of its economy and that this ought to be rectified by some form of international recognition. The status of English as a lingua franca on the world scene, of course, arises not from economic power (or at least, not today) but from historical and cultural factors. Nevertheless, an attempt was made in the late 1980s to have Japanese adopted as one of the languages of the United Nations in order to reflect the size of Japan's economic contributions to that body. The attempt failed, but the issue has not been shelved; the National Language Council's 1995 report indicated that it remains on the agenda (Kokugo Shingikai 1995: 450).

On the one hand, then, Japan's policy regarding the teaching of its language to others is clearly tied to considerations of its status as a member of the international community, in terms of economic and political identity. But Japanese is not just taught overseas; it is also widely taught as a foreign language within Japan itself and in this regard it is the government's push toward internationalization which drives the policies. It is not sufficient for Japan to construct an international linguistic identity on the external stage; it must also be seen to act as a responsible member of the global community by encouraging internationalization within its borders. One aspect of this – the other side of the push to teach English – is to teach Japanese to non-Japanese studying or working there. Here again, as so often, international pressure has played a part: in 1983, when

Japan was found to host the lowest number of foreign students among the advanced industrial countries, the then Prime Minister Nakasone initiated a plan to have 100,000 foreign students studying in Japan by the early twenty-first century. Teaching Japanese was to be an essential cog in the success of this undertaking and many universities put great emphasis on recruiting TJFL-trained staff for their overseas student centers. Largely because of the economic difficulties of the 1990s, however, the target proved difficult to attain. A 1997 Advisory Committee on Foreign Student Policy proposed three priority programs to help: higher education programs should be made more attractive to foreign students, access to Japanese universities improved and Japanese language instruction incorporated into exchange programs (Kanisawa 1999). By the end of 1999, however, only 57, 555 foreign students were enrolled at Japanese universities. A Group of Eight ministerial meeting held in April 2000 showed that of the eight member nations, Japan still had the lowest percentage of foreign students (Koh 2000).

Other initiatives coming under the Ministry of Education's policy umbrella of teaching Japanese to others include teaching Japanese to refugees and to returnees from mainland China, and sending Japanese high school teachers to teach the language in other countries under the Regional and Educational Exchanges for Mutual Understanding (REX) program. The National Institute for Japanese Language, set up in 1948 to provide the National Language Council with data on which to base its policy decisions, incorporates a Japanese Language Education Centre which trains instructors, conducts research on pedagogy issues and develops teaching materials.

The tension between the two arms of internationalization policy – teaching English and promoting the spread of Japanese – was taken up in the 1995 National Language Council report referred to above. Like many government publications and reports, not just in Japan but around the world, which took the end of the twentieth century as a landmark in their areas of responsibility, this document took as its theme the development of national language policy for a new era. Its major thrust was that Japan's language policy vis-à-vis the international scene ought to be two-pronged: while English is increasingly important for international communication, the world also needs the diversity and richness of individual languages. Japanese language policy in the area of internationalization should therefore center on the Japanese language itself but incorporate other languages as well. This was unsurprising, given that the brief of the Council was to formulate policy and to deal with issues relating to the national language.

The Council outlined several strategies relating to teaching Japanese as a foreign language within Japan. For instance: TJFL institutions both at home and abroad should seek to collaborate in order to develop long-range strategies. The public should be educated about the value of teaching Japanese to others (presumably to overcome that cherished belief that Japanese is a "special" language impossible for non-Japanese to learn properly). Since many foreigners live and work in areas of Japan outside the major cities, language education should be promoted at regional level to help the disparate bodies engaged in meeting their linguistic needs. In addition to noting the need for ongoing research and development into pedagogy and print resources, the report also recognized the importance of technological support, suggesting a TJFL information database and promotion of multimedia teaching methods capable of reaching a wide audience (Kokugo Shingikai 1995: 449–450).

Conclusion

We have looked in this chapter at how Japan's language policy has been developed and continues to develop in three main areas: the management of the Japanese language for native speakers; the development of policies relating to the preservation of an endangered indigenous language and to Japan's engagement with the foreign language most important to its international dealings; and finally, government-supported activities relating to the teaching of Japanese to others. These are, of course, not the only language policy issues discussed in Japan today, but they serve to illustrate three major themes of language and identity taken up by the government as reflecting concerns about identity important to the diverse sectors of Japan's society. Looking back over the discussion, we can clearly see how notions of language and identity have informed Japan's debate on language planning and language policy.

We can also see, from the heavy emphasis on script-related issues in twentieth-century language policy, that enduring tendency to equate language and script referred to in earlier chapters. In many instances during the course of that debate, when someone said "language," they really meant "script"; perhaps nowhere is that more clearly seen than in the conflation of characters with national spirit during the ultranationalist years. What this underlines for us is the enduring role played by the Japanese writing system in that construction of national identity referred to above, over the last hundred years in policy debates and long before that in intellectual circles. Not that the script has always been viewed in the same way, of course; it has not. To many, it has served as a marker of cultural identity, intensified as such during time of war. At the same time, others have seen in it an exemplar of the urgent need to democratize the written language in order to develop a modern linguistic identity freed from feudal-period literary conventions. In today's computer age, the nature of the writing system continues its strong link with identity as the substantial Japanese-language presence on the Internet continues to expand rapidly despite the dire predictions of some that such technology would force Japan to adopt the alphabet (e.g., Hannas 1997), as we shall see in Chapter Seven.

As well as providing a historical perspective, this chapter has allowed us a window on the language-related issues which are of concern today in this nation with a rich cultural history and a strong but linguistically subdued presence on the international scene. By looking at what the Japanese government chooses to emphasize as important in its view of language, we can see what issues concern people and how they see themselves in language terms, from the small-scale area of Ainu-language policy to the larger issues of the international profile of the Japanese language and the engagement of its speakers on the international scene in languages other than their own. We have seen that the Japanese writing system has been and continues to be a particular focus of attention in language policy debates. The following chapter will show us how this system functions in Japan today.

5 Writing and reading in Japan

If we conflate the prevailing stereotypes relating to reading and writing in Japan, we come up with an image of a "typical Japanese" who is highly literate, has mastered the complexities of Japan's writing system with ease (and may wear glasses or contacts because of it), reads *manga* (comics) on trains when young and pocket paperbacks or newspapers when older, and writes with a brush and/or draws characters in the air. Some of these are merely comical; others contain a grain (or more) of truth. In this chapter we will look at whether these typical views stand up to scrutiny and why things might be changing. The *manga*-reading student on the train is these days just as likely to be staring at the screen of a mobile phone instead, either chatting with friends through SMS or downloading i-mode Internet pages, before going home to type assignments on a computer: reading and writing still, but in a form mediated by contemporary multimedia technologies.

We begin this chapter with a general description of the Japanese writing system, maligned and praised by Japanese and non-Japanese alike as possibly the world's most complex orthography.

The Japanese writing system

The Japanese writing system has been variously described as innately superior to all other writing systems (Suzuki 1975), inordinately difficult, complex and "perversely involved" (Miller 1982: 172 and 178) and a whole range of things in between, but usually with an emphasis on its complexity and, by extension, difficulty. To understand why this should be so, we need to look at how today's writing system functions in Japan and how it came to be the way it is.

Japanese today is written using kanji (Chinese characters as used in Japan), two phonetic scripts (hiragana and katakana, collectively known as kana), Arabic numerals, the roman alphabet in certain contexts, and any number of cute little symbols in computer chatroom communication.

The complexity of this script came about because, as we saw in an earlier chapter, characters were borrowed from China around the sixth century in the absence of any script of Japan's own. For a long time kanji were used to write Chinese as a foreign language in Japan, much as the roman alphabet is used to write English as a foreign language in Japan today. In time, however, people began to look for ways of using the characters to write Japanese, but here they struck trouble: the two languages are very different in structure and pronunciation, Chinese being uninflected whereas Japanese is inflected (e.g., for tense). Because of the lack of a Japanese writing system which had brought about this problem in the first place, the only possible means of writing down Japanese would therefore be to adapt the Chinese script in some way to the task. After various early attempts by different schools of Chinese studies and Buddhist sections involving diacritics or rebus writings (see Twine 1991a: 36–39 for details), phonetic scripts had been developed in different parts of the country by around the ninth century, and this enabled for the first time the written representation of the pronunciation of Japanese words and of Japanese inflections and other manifestations of grammar such as postpositions. Each flowing and graceful hiragana symbol was developed as an abbreviated form of a character as a whole, whereas the angular katakana were derived from only one section of a character, e.g. the character 加 yielded both the hiragana か and the katakana カ (*ka*). Both hiragana and katakana originally had several hundred symbols, owing to the existence of variant forms representing the same sound; these are reduced today to a basic forty-six symbols which can be manipulated to represent other sounds by adding an extra small mark, e.g. た (*ta*) becomes だ (*da*) by the addition of a small diacritic in the top right corner.

In writing modern Japanese, hiragana and katakana are combined with characters to show those things which characters cannot show: Japanese pronunciation in places, grammatical inflections and postpositions, and some words that by convention are always written in kana (e.g. some pronouns and the copula). Many thousands of characters are available, but the government's current script policy recommends 1,945 of the most commonly occurring for general use, and these are the guidelines followed in schools. In practice, around 3,000–3,500 characters are needed to read newspapers, advertisements and other sources of text encountered in daily life (Seeley 1991: 2).

The normal practice in writing since the end of World War Two, when the series of script reforms we saw in Chapter Four was enacted, has been to supplement kanji with hiragana to represent features of Japanese and katakana for foreign loanwords, foreign names (except for those of Chinese origin, which are written in characters), domestic telegrams (when these still existed) and as a form of italicization. There are of course exceptions to this rule; the visual properties of the script are often tweaked to create certain desired impressions, which may involve breaking with convention in how each script is used in, say, advertisements or *manga*. On the whole, though, if we pick up a Japanese newspaper, journal or book, we will find the combination as described.

A simple example will illustrate how this system works

東京はブリスベンより人が多いです。

Tōkyō wa burisuben yori hito ga ōi desu.
Tokyo has a larger population than Brisbane.

Here *Tokyo* and *Burisuben* are proper nouns giving the names of two cities; *hito* is a noun meaning "people"; *wa* is a case marker indicating that the word which precedes it is the topic of the sentence; *ga* marks the word before it as the subject; *yori* is a particle meaning "than"; *ōi* is an adjective meaning "numerous"; and *desu* is the verb "to be," meaning in this context "is." As can be seen from the Japanese version, *Burisuben* is written in the angular katakana script because it is a foreign place name; the Japanese place name *Tōkyō* and noun *hito* are both written with characters; and the grammatical particles and the copula are written in hiragana. In order to write this sentence by hand, we have to remember and correctly reproduce four characters interspersed with hiragana as appropriate; write one word in katakana; and remember that the particle *wa*, in a hangover from prewar usage, is traditionally written with the symbol for *ha*.

Let's look at a sentence which contains a verb other than the copula, for example:

よくすしを食べます。

yoku sushi o tabemasu
I often eat sushi

Here, the *ta* of the verb *tabemasu* (I eat) is written with the character for eat and the remaining *bemasu*, the Japanese present-tense inflection, is written in hiragana. The adverb *yoku* (often) is these days also written in hiragana. So is the object-marker postposition *o*, although it is written with the symbol for *wo*, the only use to which this particular symbol is now put. These two very simple examples demonstrate what has become the clearly defined pattern for the interwoven use of the three scripts in postwar Japan. Navigating the interplay between the three scripts in writing by hand, complex though it seems to onlookers, poses no particular difficulty for Japanese people themselves once they have learned the system.

Hiragana and katakana are easy to learn and to use. The nature of the kanji character set, however, represents a great burden on memory when we take into account not only the number of characters to be learned but also the fact that one character may have several different pronunciations depending on the context in which it occurs: these are known as its *on* and *kun* readings.[1] A person writing by hand has to remember the correct number of strokes in a character in the correct spatial relationship to each other and often has to differentiate between which of several similar characters is required for a particular word. These tasks have been made very much simpler these days by being able to use word processing software to supply the correct kanji without fuss when writing, instead of having to rely on memory, as we shall see in Chapter Seven.

Learning to read and write: kanji

Education in reading and writing officially begins in elementary school, although many children enter school already able to read hiragana, just as many children in other countries can already read their alphabets before they start school. Kindergartens generally do not provide explicit instruction in hiragana, although unstructured exposure to reading and writing activities takes place in which children can write if they wish (Mason *et al.* 1989: 392 and 395). Parents also buy a large number of books for preschoolers; while they may not explicitly teach the child to read, exposure to the script in the books leads to familiarity over time. One study, a large-scale survey by the National Language Research Institute in Tokyo between 1967 and 1970, found that 95 percent of five-year-olds could read hiragana five months before they started school (Sakamoto 1981, cited in Sheridan 1993). Two-thirds of the five-year-olds, i.e. still preschool,[2] surveyed could read sixty or more hiragana; most could also write around twenty-one hiragana; and only one in a hundred could read no hiragana at all. Ten years later, this level had increased to an extent whereby all preschoolers surveyed were able to read most of the hiragana and write about fifty of them just before entering school. The 1967–1970 study further found that, a month before school started, five-year-olds knew the meanings and at least one pronunciation of fifty-three of the kanji taught in grades one and two (Taylor and Taylor 1995: 342).

If hiragana were the only script used in Japan, children would learn to read very quickly, given the strong sound-to-symbol correspondence; but they must also learn both katakana and kanji, starting with eighty of the latter in the first grade. By the end of their first year of school, children have been introduced to all three scripts in their *kokugo* class. Over the following five years, they learn a further 926 characters, giving them in

Year	Number of kanji taught
One	80
Two	160
Three	200
Four	200
Five	185
Six	181

Source: *Gakushū Shidū Yōryō: Kokugo* (Ministry of Education 1998)

Figure 5.1 Number of kanji taught per year at elementary school.

total the 1,006 characters designated as Education Kanji (*Kyōiku Kanji*) by the time they finish elementary school. These characters account for about 90 percent of the characters used in a newspaper.

The matter of how many kanji should be taught in schools had exercised the minds of those interested in script reform for many years before the postwar reforms eventually enabled action. During the Meiji Period, the Ministry of Education set the number to be used in elementary-school textbooks at 2,000 in 1887 and later lowered this to 1,200 in 1900 (Twine 1991: 250). In 1945, the List of Kanji for Interim Use (*Tōyō Kanji Hyō*) was promulgated, containing 1,850 characters which henceforth were to be the only ones used in government-related documents, which of course included school textbooks. Three years later, after much deliberation by various committees (Gottlieb 1995: 143–145), the Separate List of Characters for Interim Use (*Tōyō Kanji Beppyō*), known in common parlance as the *Kyōiku Kanji* (Education Kanji) list, was announced. It contained 881 of the most common characters which were to be taught during the period of compulsory education, selected on the basis of relative simplicity, relevance to daily-life functioning and ability to form compounds. This number was revised to today's 1,006 after the revision of the kanji list resulted in today's recommended *Jōyō Kanji Hyō* (List of Characters for General Use) consisting of 1,945 characters, a slight increase over the earlier list (for details, see Gottlieb 1995). All 1,945 of the Kanji for General Use are to be learned by the end of the period of compulsory education, i.e. by the end of middle school.

Kanji are taught using a variety of methods, including writing in the air, colour charts showing radicals (the common elements under which characters are grouped), rote practice on squared sheets of paper, build-up methods and a range of other techniques (Bourke 1996: 167–174). At each year level, a segment of the time allotted to learning to write script is set aside for calligraphy practice. As we can see from the table below, the kanji to be introduced in Year One start from those with simple shapes with meanings most relevant to the daily lives of the students, e.g. numerals from one to ten and above, colours, words to do with school (e.g., book, school), the first characters of the days of the week, and natural phenomena (e.g., rain, flower, dog, hand, foot, mouth). The complexity of the characters jumps sharply in Year Two, where we can see that not only is the number doubled but most characters contain a much higher number of strokes; this continues up the year levels. Year Two contains 曜 (yō, day of the week), with a particularly high stroke count; however, this character is included because of the frequency with which students will need to read and write it. In Year Three, students begin formal learning about the different types of radicals which make up kanji. In Year Four they are introduced to reading and writing simple everyday words in the roman alphabet. Their education has thus by this time encompassed mastery of the two phonetic scripts, a good start on learning the characters, and a familiarity with writing in the roman alphabet which, while not a Japanese script, is nevertheless encountered widely throughout Japan in various contexts such as signs, advertising and magazine titles.

Taylor and Taylor (1995: 347–348) examined one of the introductory textbooks used in schools to teach Japanese and found that the first seventeen pages contained only basic hiragana in simple phrases, the next forty-nine added secondary and small-sized hiragana in simple sentences (with words separated by spaces) and stories, a few kanji were introduced over the following thirteen pages and in the last five pages a few katakana words appeared. The kanji were the numerals one to ten and names for natural phenomena (e.g. mountain). Kanji were taught with only one reading, usually the *kun* reading, or the way the word is pronounced in Japanese, e.g. *yama* and not *san* or the other possible *on* readings for 'mountain'). "More than the simplicity of shapes, it is the single reading, usually Kun, associated with a Kanji that eases initial learning."

A survey report published in 1988 looked at children in Tokyo, Akita Prefecture and Nara Prefecture and attempted to determine both the rate at which characters were acquired and the number of characters which children did actually acquire. The results showed that at both elementary

第一学年 Year One	一右雨円王音下火花貝学気九休玉金空 月　　　犬　　　　　　　　　　　　見 五口校左三山子四糸字耳七車手十出女
	小　　　　　上　　　　　　　　　　森 人水正生青夕石赤千川先早草足村大男 竹　　　　　　中　　　　　　　　　虫 町天田土二日入年白八百文木本名目立 力　　　　　林　　　　　　　　　　六 （８０字）
第二学年 Year Two	引羽雲園遠何科夏家歌画回会海絵外角 楽　　　　　活　　　　　　　　　　間 丸岩顔汽記帰弓牛魚京強教近兄形計元 言　　　　　原　　　　　　　　　　戸 古午後語工公広交光考行高黄合谷国黒 今　　　　　才　　　　　　　　　　細 作算止市矢姉思紙寺自時室社弱首秋週 春　　　　　書　　　　　　　　　　少 場色食心新親図数西声星晴切雪船線前 組　　　　　走　　　　　　　　　　多 太体台地池知茶昼長鳥朝直通弟店点電 刀　　　　　　　　　　　　　　　　当 東答頭同道読内南肉馬売買麦半番父風 分　　　　　聞　　　　　　　　　　米 歩母方北毎妹万明鳴毛門夜野友用曜来 里　　　　　理　　　　　　　　　　話 （１６０字）
第三学年 Year Three	悪安暗医委意育員院飲運泳駅央横屋温 化　　　　　荷　　　　　　　　　　界 開階寒感漢館岸起期客究急級宮球去橋 業　　　　　曲　　　　　　　　　　局 銀区苦具君係軽血決研県庫湖向幸港号 根　　　　　祭　　　　　　　　　　皿 仕死使始指歯詩次事持式実写者主守取 酒　　　　　受　　　　　　　　　　州 拾終習集住重宿所暑助昭消商章勝乗植 申　　　　　身　　　　　　　　　　神 真深進世整昔全相送想息速族他打対待 代　　　　　第　　　　　　　　　　題 炭短談着注柱丁帳調追定庭笛鉄転都度 投　　　　　豆　　　　　　　　　　島 湯登等動童農波配倍箱畑発反坂板皮悲 美　　　　　鼻　　　　　　　　　　筆 水表秒病品負部服福物平返勉放味命面

Figure 5.2 Table of kanji to be taught by year level at elementary schools

	問 役 薬 由油有遊予羊洋葉陽様落流旅両緑礼列 練 路 和 （２０００字）
第四学年 Year Four	愛案以衣位囲胃印英栄塩億加果貨課芽 改 械 害 街各覚完官管関観願希季紀喜旗器機議 求 泣 救 給挙漁共協鏡競極訓軍郡径型景芸欠結 建 健 験 固功好候航康告差菜最材昨札刷殺察参 産 散 残 士氏史司試児治辞失借種周祝順初松笑 唱 焼 象 照賞臣信成省清静席積折節説浅戦選然 争 倉 巣 束側統卒孫帯隊達単置仲貯兆腸低底停 的 典 伝 徒努灯堂働特得毒熱念敗梅博飯飛費必 票 標 不 夫付府副粉兵別辺変便包法望牧末満未 脈 民 無 約勇要養浴利陸良料量輪類令冷例歴連 老 労 録 （２００字）
第五学年 Year Five	圧移因永営衛易益液演応往桜恩可仮価 河 過 賀 快解格確額刊幹慣眼基寄規技義逆久旧 居 許 境 均禁句群経潔件券険検限現減故個護効 厚 耕 鉱 構興講混査再災妻採際在財罪雑酸賛支 志 枝 師 資飼示似識質舎謝授修述術準序招承証 条 状 常 情織職制性政勢精製税責績接設舌絶銭 祖 素 総 造像増則測属率損退貸態団断築張提程 適 敵 統 銅導徳独任燃能破犯判版比肥非備俵評
	貧 布 婦 富武復複仏編弁保墓報豊防貿暴務夢迷 綿 輸 余 預容略留領（１８５字）

Figure 5.2 *Cont.*

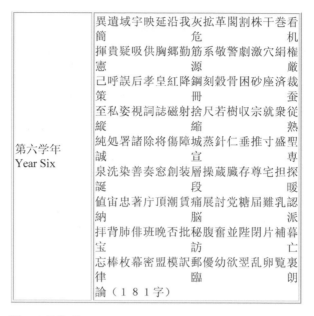

Figure 5.2 *Cont.*

and high school levels students were better able to read than to write kanji, and that knowledge of *on* and *kun* readings fluctuated, with students able to read one or the other better than both (National Language Research Institute 1988: 389–391). It would be interesting to know if other factors than school instruction and student motivation contributed to this discrepancy between recognition and reproduction, given that by 1988 the use of personal word processors had become widespread (see Chapter Seven): perhaps students, at high school level at any rate, were using them outside school and as a result had lost some of their facility in writing by hand, as was widely reported at the time. Various other studies which have examined the kinds of errors students make in reading and writing kanji are also discussed in Taylor and Taylor (1995: 349–351). The findings may best be summarized as follows: reading skills become stronger than writing skills as the number of kanji learned increases; homophone substitutions are common errors; and not as many shape-based errors relate to complexity as might be expected. Overall, the authors conclude, "the mastery of Kanji by Japanese students and adults is far from perfect, despite the effort and time expended on it. Kanji are extraordinarily complex and confusing, in shape, meaning, and especially in sound. All the same, Kanji are learned and used because they are useful." (353)

Learning to read and write: non-kanji aspects

If we compare the *Gakushū Shidō Yōryō* (Course of Study Outlines) for *kokugo* put out by the Ministry of Education and revised seven times since 1947,[3] we can see that the number of hours allotted to *kokugo* classes in elementary school has varied over the years at different year levels. In 1960, for example, the annual allocation to *kokugo* in the first year of elementary school was 238 hours; today it is 272 hours, much more than the number of hours allocated to other curriculum areas (e.g., the 114 allocated to maths). Subsequent years, however, have shown a marked decrease; today's sixth-year students study *kokugo* for only 175 hours compared to 245 in 1960. In middle school, the number of *kokugo* hours in the first year remained constant at 175 from 1960 until the 1998 revision which dropped them to 140; the same change is reflected in the other years, so that a student in the third year of middle school today (the last year of compulsory education, by which time all the Kanji for General Use must be mastered) spends 105 hours on *kokugo* compared to 175 in 1960. This reflects the necessary adjustment brought about by the recent decision to close schools on Saturdays,[4] but also provides fodder for the many who, as we shall see later in this chapter, attribute a decline in language ability to these cutbacks. Nevertheless, at each year level in elementary school *kokugo* classes account for the largest number of hours. Clearly, learning to read and write are prioritized. These skills are still taught by the whole-class method observed by Mason *et al.* in 1982, despite the often quite large class sizes, with an emphasis on oral reading as well as silent reading and on teacher-centered practices.

The overall objectives for the subject are multifaceted: to teach children to express themselves appropriately and understand others accurately; to facilitate the ability to communicate with others; to foster thinking, imagination and language awareness; and to nurture an attitude of respect for and interest in language. The phrase *tsutaeau chikara o takameru* (increase the ability to communicate with each other) appears for the first time in the current guidelines issued in 1998. Specific objectives are set for different year levels in two-year bands; words such as *aite* (counterpart, the other person) and *kikite* (listener) appear frequently, further underlining the shift of emphasis from language as skill to language as means of communication. In Years One and Two, the objectives focus on speaking about, listening to, writing and reading about things the children have experienced or imagined: specific strategies are set out for each objective. With regard to writing, for example, students are asked to collect material in order to fulfill a particular writing task, to keep the reader and purpose of their writing in mind, to pay attention to making sequence clear and so on. They are taught about the relationship between subject and predicate in a sentence and how to use punctuation, and are introduced to the difference between ordinary language and honorific language. By the time they reach Years Five and Six, the objectives have progressed appropriately in depth and breadth and we find that students are now taught to read simple *bungochō* (literary style) passages, be familiar with different types of sentence construction, use simple everyday honorifics and understand the difference between dialects and standard Japanese, speaking in the latter (Ministry of Education 1998).

In middle school, *kokugo* is taught for 140 hours in the first year, much more than the 105 allocated to maths, science, society and foreign languages, and then drops back to be on a par with those subjects at 105 hours in the second and third years. The objectives for the subject overall are almost identical to those for the primary school curriculum, with only a couple of words being changed to indicate a higher level. The emphasis is again very much on communication and reception of ideas through the four skills. In writing at first year level, for example, students are to research topics from life and study and present their own ideas on the issues clearly and accurately; to check over their own writing's expression, orthography and description to ensure that it is easy to read and understand; and to read each other's written work to promote cross-fertilization of ideas about research. In Years Two and Three, the focus on putting the student's own viewpoints forward is sharpened; the purpose of reading classmates' work is no longer just to discover different ways of collecting material but to check for logical development of ideas as well. By this time students are expected not just to be able to tell the difference between dialects and standard language but to have an understanding of the role of each in society. They are also expected to be able to use honorifics appropriately in their daily lives (Ministry of Education 1998). The time allocated for writing (*kaku koto*) within the overall *kokugo* allocation at primary school is ninety hours in Years One and Two, eighty-five hours in Years Three and Four, and fifty-five hours for Years Five and Six. At middle school, where students are taught to write essays, letters, reports and other genres, the allocation is "around 20–30%" of the time.

In high school, objectives step up another level. Now language awareness is to be polished, interest in the culture of language is to be deepened, and *hyōgen* (expression) is very much the focus. The curriculum is divided into various subjects: Kokugo Hyōgen I (Japanese Expression I), Kokugo Hyōgen II (Japanese Expression II), Kokugo Sōgō (Integrated Japanese), Gendaibun (Modern Literature), Koten (Classical Literature) and Koten

Kōdoku (Translating the Classics). Kokugo Hyōgen I deals with issues such as expressing the student's own thoughts logically, speaking with others with respect for their views and understanding the characteristics of language in terms of expression, phrasing and lexicon. It focuses on balanced attention to speaking, listening and writing skills. Kokugo Hyōgen II takes the skills of Kokugo Hyōgen I to a more advanced level in the same manner. Kokugo Sōgō includes along with the other three skills a focus on reading, through summary writing, textual analysis of structures and expression, and general appreciation of the details of a text in terms of characterization and ideas expressed. All four skills are to be developed in an integrated manner. Gendaibun focuses on the reading of texts of various kinds, including literary texts, written since the Meiji Period. Koten, as its name suggests, teaches *kambun* and other older styles necessary for reading classical texts and contrasts them with modern written Japanese so that students develop an awareness of how the language has changed. Finally, Koten Kōdoku aims to develop a lifelong love of the classics through applying the knowledge gained in Koten to reading them. Given the dramatic changes that have taken place in written Japanese since the Meiji Period in both stylistic and orthographic terms, as we saw in Chapter Four, special training in reading prewar material of any kind is necessary if school children are to be able to develop a sense of their cultural heritage in literary terms. It is not necessary to do this in any general sense, of course, since the classics have long since been translated into modern Japanese and sets aimed at a high school readership have been on the market for many decades. However, the hands-on training in high school classes teaches students just how the language has changed and enables them to discover for themselves the beauties of the original texts (much as if Old or Middle English were taught in high schools elsewhere).

Dyslexia

What of the child who cannot keep up with the usual pace in language classes? Dyslexia has for a long time been an unrecognized problem in Japan. Makita (1968:599) concluded that reading disabilities are extremely rare in Japan, based on the fact that in ten years not a single child with dyslexia had been brought into his university's children's psychiatric service, that reports on the topic had been "almost non-existent" at Japanese child psychiatry conferences and on a survey he had conducted. He attributed this rarity to the properties of the Japanese writing system, concluding that "reading disability . . . is more of a philological than a neuro-psychiatric problem" (613). Twenty years later, Hirose and

Hatta (1988) challenged this finding,[5] based on the observations of elementary school teachers and on their own research which administered a standardized reading ability test developed in Japan. Their findings put children with reading disabilities at 11%, which put paid to Makita's theory of the significance of orthography: cognition, they argued, and not orthography was the major determinant of dyslexia.

Children with dyslexia experience difficulty in acquiring reading and writing skills. The characters in the Japanese word for dyslexia, *shitsudokushō*, literally mean "loss-of-reading syndrome." The children may reverse the positions of kanji elements; assign mistaken pronunciations when reading aloud based on semantic similarities to another character; or have trouble writing small-sized kana symbols (Taylor and Taylor 1995: 352). Unlike other countries, Japan has no separate category for the condition, which is bundled together with a number of others under the rubric of "learning disabilities" (*gakushū shōgai*), defined as "not lagging in overall intellectual development, but having various conditions which lead to demonstration of marked difficulty in learning and use of specific aspects of the ability to listen, speak, read, write, calculate or infer" (MEXT 2004, my translation). Parent-inspired groups such as NPO EDGE (Japan Dyslexia Society)[6] have been largely responsible for pushing the issue with the Ministry, which carried out a survey in 2002 aimed at finding out what support was needed in classrooms for the education of children with learning disabilities (see MEXT 2002) and in 2004 announced guidelines for putting the support in place (MEXT 2004). On the basis of teacher responses, the survey identified 4.5% of children who, though not intellectually impaired, nevertheless had marked difficulty with "listening, speaking, reading, writing, calculating or inferring" as posited in the definition of learning disabilities above. Japan's best-known expert on dyslexia, Dr. Uno Akira, reports that only 1% of Japanese students have dyslexic problems in reading kana and 2% in reading kanji. For writing, 2% have trouble with hiragana, 3.8% with katakana and 5% with kanji, although these figures are low by comparison with America (Spaeth 2003). Parent groups such as EDGE would argue that the rates are low because the problem still remains largely undiagnosed.

Literacy rates

Whether literacy rates are indeed as high as the over-99% claimed by the government is open to debate, given that a certain proportion of any population will have learning or other developmental disabilities that inhibit reading. The 4.5% of schoolchildren identified by the survey above alone put paid to that figure, but of course the definition of literacy is key here. The United Nations Development Office Human Development Report for 2003 assigns Japan and nineteen other countries an adult literacy rate of 99%, where adult literacy is defined as "the percentage of people aged 15 and above who can, with understanding, both read and write a short, simple statement related to their everyday life" (United Nations Development Programme 2003). Such a definition is of course a base level and does not take cognizance of the gradations in between that ability and full literacy of the kind exercised on a daily basis by sophisticated readers and writers. It proved impossible in the course of this research to find definitions of levels of literacy for Japan.

The first national survey of literacy in Japan was conducted in 1948 by the Civil Information and Education section, a subdivision of General Headquarters (GHQ) during the Allied Occupation. Testing 17,000 men and women between the ages of sixteen and sixty-four throughout Japan, it found that while the rate of complete illiteracy, i.e. being unable to read or write anything at all, was very low, only 6.2% of the population were fully literate, defined as being able to answer all the (quite simple) survey questions correctly. A later, smaller survey in 1955–1956 by the Ministry of Education found even greater rates of lack of functional literacy (Unger 1996: 36–37).

On one level it has been argued that once a child can read hiragana they can read anything and that therefore Japan's literacy rate is almost 100%, as in the following example:

We can show the reading of kanji by writing hiragana at its side. If children can read hiragana, they can read all books, because, they need not know the spelling. Therefore it is easy for Japanese, including children, to read books and, as a result, Japan is a nation with a high literacy rate (almost 100%). (Adachi 2001)

This, of course, ignores the fact that books and newspapers in Japan are never just written in hiragana; nor do they usually place *furigana*[7] glosses beside kanji. If texts were written in hiragana alone, then it is true that children would be able to understand everything once they had mastered that script, or at least, that they would be able to read out the words. To suggest that it is easy, therefore, "for Japanese, including children, to read books" is to obscure the fact that no such books (except for early grade school primers) exist. As Unger (1987: 84) notes:

There is an important distinction to be made between literacy as usually defined in technical studies (minimum ability to read and write) and literacy as a vehicle for full and free participation in society. The use of kanji makes the distinction crucial:

one might be able to write and read kana and know the principles underlying the use of kanji yet be unable to read texts without furigana or write an acceptable petition to the authorities.

Taylor and Taylor (1995: 364) take as their definition of functional literacy the following:

People can read such everyday reading materials as newspapers and manuals, and also can fill in forms and write memos or simple letters. In addition, they have basic numeracy skills; and some can use a computer. They are likely to have finished at least middle school education.

As we have seen, attaining this level of functional literacy in Japan involves a long, hard grind at school and not everybody succeeds in terms of fulfilling the expected outcomes perfectly. Although young people finish their period of compulsory education supposedly able to read and write all the Kanji for General Use, in practice that is often not the case. Neustupný (1987: 137) tells us that "it can be assumed that even today at least ten percent of the total adult population is likely to suffer from serious problems in the use of written documents in their daily life." Nevertheless, the rates of functional literacy by the Taylor and Taylor definition above are undoubtedly high, a fact that supports a large publishing industry as we shall see. If the holdings of public libraries, books sold and newspapers and magazines read are indeed an indicator of a nation's literacy activities (Taylor and Taylor 1995: 369), then Japan is doing well.

What people read in Japan

Japan publishes the world's largest number of daily newspapers, many of which have millions of readers and put out both morning and evening editions. In 2002, total newspaper circulation was over 71 million, compared with over 55 million in the United States and nearly 18 million in Britain (Nikkei 2003b). A comparison of major Japanese and British broadsheets for the same period shows that the circulation of the top five papers combined in Japan worked out to one copy per 4.6 people, whereas in Britain it was one copy for 25.7 people (Nikkei 2003a).

Outside the newspaper world, publishing and printing are major industries but have been experiencing a prolonged period of recession. The bookshop business has entered upon hard times in recent years, with sales figures falling in 2002 for the fifth year in a row, although the number of new titles published has increased (Kiyota 2002: 7). Part of this may be due to the popularity of second hand bookshops, discount bookshops at which nearly-new books are sold cheaply. Sales of magazines, which had expanded in the booming 1980s while book sales did not keep up, dropped in the mid-1990s and those of comics grew. Even so, today, magazines account for about 60% of sales and books for 40%. As in other countries, many smaller bookshops have gone to the wall, with large chains taking their place.

The ever-popular *manga* and its many sub-genres form an important component of what Japanese read, as any trip on a Japanese train will show. Kinsella (2000: 21) shows the exponential growth in the annual circulation figures for all *manga* between the years of 1979 and 1997, during which period sales doubled.[8] "The actual readership of *manga* magazines however is approximately three times as high as their circulation figures," (43) thanks to the practices of standing reading in bookshops, leaving *manga* lying around for others to read, recycling and passing on to friends and family. *Shukan Shonen Jump*, which has been published for almost forty years, publishes 3.4 million copies a week (Japan Information Network 2003). Other good sources of comment on circulation trends include Schodt (1996:9), who puts *manga* sales in 1995 (i.e. actually sales, not counting returns) at nearly 40% of Japan's total circulation of books and magazines, up from 27% in 1984 (Schodt and Tezuka 1986:12). A list provided by the Japan Magazine Publishers Association (2003) includes current circulation figures for the major *manga* aimed at young men. *Manga* clearly still have a substantial profile in Japanese reading habits, particularly among younger people, but the abbreviated language they employ does little to develop better language skills in their readers. Nevertheless, their text does contain kanji, which may encourage younger readers to apply themselves harder to study in order to be able to understand.

A drop in book sales overall, however, does not necessarily correlate with a decline in interest in language matters. Despite the extended recession in the book publishing industry, one area showing lively sales activity is that of books relating to the Japanese language, in particular guides to correct usage. Tokyo University Professor Komori Yōichi observes that sales figures for books on Japanese tend to increase during times of recession, a phenomenon he attributes to the fact that during these periods readers fall back on pride in their language as a substitute for pride in the economic prowess which fuels sales of different sorts of books in better times. Nostalgia, too, plays a part, with many books on language being compilations of quotations from famous literary and other works (Komori 2002: 1–2).

The overall drop in sales figures, while perhaps recession-related to a certain extent, may also be due to a general decline in the amount of time spent on reading by older students. Every year the Mainichi Shimbun publishes the results of two national surveys of reading habits, one targeting those over sixteen (*Dokusho Yoron Chōsa*, Survey of National Attitudes to Reading) and the other, conducted with the National Association of School Libraries, looking at children in the fourth year of elementary school and above (*Gakkō Dokusho Chōsa*, Survey of School Reading). The 2002 survey showed that in the month of May elementary students read an average of 7.5 books each, middle school students 2.5 and high school students 1.5. By the following year, this had increased slightly to 8 and 2.8 for elementary and middle schools, but decreased to 1.3 for high school students. The popularity of the Harry Potter books[9] and the school-based "morning reading time" which many schools had adopted were thought to be in part responsible for the increase among younger readers. Worryingly, though, 58.7% of high school students listed themselves as "non-readers," i.e. they had not read a book (apart from schoolbooks, reference books, *manga* and magazines) during May (J-SLA 2004), no doubt due to the competing attractions of study, television, the Internet and their cell phones. The last of these particularly worries the book world, in terms of the effect the increasing use of handheld devices is likely to have on book sales (Nagasaki Industrial Promotion Foundation 2002).

The Organization for Economic Co-operation and Development (OECD) released a 32-country survey in 2000 which showed Japan to be the country with the highest number of middle and high school students reporting that they did not read for pleasure.[10] Subsequently, in December 2001, a cluster of eleven laws relating to the promotion of reading activities in children[11] was passed by the Diet (the Japanese parliament): among other things, these specified April 23 as Children's Reading Day. An action plan based on the laws was put in place the following year,[12] aiming to establish the habit of reading in children at elementary school so that it will have a flow-on effect to later years.

Reading and writing are popular topics for surveys of all kinds. Yet another survey, conducted by the Fukui Chamber of Commerce and Industry in 2001, indicates that the decline in reading is not limited to schoolchildren. Questionnaires were sent to 250 adult company workers. Of the 146 (58%) of those who responded, 70% reported that they bought between one and three books each month; only 30% were satisfied with the amount they were currently reading. They would like to read more, they said, but could not. The reading rate had fallen since a similar survey three years earlier, showing that adults too, and not just schoolchildren, were evidencing a *katsujibanare* (moving away from print) trend because of being busy (the reason given by 80% of those who said they were reading less). In their case, although their sources of information had diversified to include the Internet and mobile phones, this did not seem to have as much influence on their reading habits as pressure of work (Fukui Chamber of Commerce 2001). The 2002 version of the annual Agency of Cultural Affairs survey of language, a much bigger survey than the local Fukui one, also included, for the first time, a question on reading habits which found that 37.6%, of respondents said that they did not read at all, a response particularly marked among men in their teens through to their forties (Kawaijuku Educational Information Network 2003).

Evidence from this range of disparate sources, then, shows us that the postwar self-image of Japanese as avid readers has begun to falter in recent years. Unlike the pre-Internet years when sales, particularly of translations and of the small *bunkobon* and *shinsho*[13] boomed, people riding the subway these days are as likely to be staring at the screen of their cell phone or playing with a handheld game as to be reading something in print form. While literacy rates are high, then, reading (or at least, reading in its traditional forms) may be beginning to decline as other activities encroach upon the time available to indulge.

One area in which writing and reading remain a particularly powerful means of disseminating information is that of citizens' movements. Local interest groups always have a newsletter to circulate to members and others they think will be interested in the issue they are pushing. These days many know how to set up home pages and shift their newsletters to the Internet. As we shall see in Chapter Seven, with the Internet penetration rate now at one in two, this is a viable means of communication, depending on the area and the wired status of members. Until the Internet arrived, it was all done on paper. Citizens groups who for one reason or another found access to the mainstream media difficult utilized a variety of what were known as *minikomi* (mini-communications media, as opposed to *masukomi*, mass-communication media): alternative media, self-produced materials which could be cheaply and easily reproduced without having to approach mainstream publishers. Groups and individuals of all persuasions were able to print and distribute material through small publishing companies specializing in *minikomi*, in a non-regulated structure similar to that of the Internet twenty years later (Kinsella 1998: 294).

The *minikomi* gave literacy a powerful role to play in activism. Many of them targeted political hot topics, as in the case of *Kokuhatsu* (*Indictment*), published by a group set up to denounce the Chisso chemical company over its role in the environmental pollution disaster of the 1960s and 1970s which led to Minamata disease. By facilitating wider debate at the level of individual contribution through reading and writing, they extended the commonly-held view of the public sphere, creating "an independent space for critical public discourse not readily available in the mass media" (Sasaki-Uemura 2002:90). The women's movement used *minikomi* with titles such as *Feminist, Agora, Onna Eros* and *Ajia to Josei Kaihō (Asian Women's Liberation)* in the 1970s to protest against the stereotyping of women in the mass media; they also distributed a wide range of handwritten and machine-duplicated newsletters and broadsheets (Buckley and Mackie 1986: 181). In the case of the Burakumin, one of the main *minikomi* activities has been the newsletters published by the Buraku Liberation Research Institute: *Buraku Kaihō Kenkyū* in Japanese, published bimonthly since 1977, and the *Buraku Liberation News*, its English counterpart, published bimonthly since 1981.

Perceptions of language use related to reading and writing

The 2002 Mainichi national reading survey showed that 78% of respondents believed a decline in people's ability to use their own language to be due to a corresponding decline in print-based reading (Mainichi 2002a). The perception that people are no longer able to use Japanese correctly is not new: the topic of *kotoba no midare* (disorder in the language) has been a frequently recurring theme in discourse about language since the late eighteenth century. Older people are particularly prone to thinking (and saying) that a departure from earlier language norms is something akin to a breakdown of the moral fabric of society, i.e. of the accepted ways of doing things which have brought comfort to them in their lives. These complaints have been heard in many language contexts for at least the last two thousand years. As Jorden (1991:3) points out, people who complain about *midare* in Japanese "overlook the fact that the 'pure' language they miss is simply the *midareta nihongo* of another generation."

In postwar Japan the term *midare* was used on occasion in relation to honorifics and script issues; after the early 1990s, when the focus of language policy investigations broadened to include the spoken language, and as a result of the language awareness activities undertaken during the preceding decades by the National Language Council, the concept became more entrenched in the public consciousness. NHK surveys carried out in 1979 and 1986 on public attitudes to language revealed concerns about spoken language, honorifics and greetings among other things; subsequent newspaper articles by readers in the Asahi Shimbun in 1992 focused on disorder in spoken language, and the National Language Council's discussions of *kotoba no midare* also zeroed in on this area (Carroll 2001: 81–85).

More recently, an Agency for Cultural Affairs survey on language attitudes in 2002 showed that 80.4% of the 2,200 respondents believed that the language was either "very disordered: or disordered to a certain extent" (Agency for Cultural Affairs 2003). Perceptions of disorder were not, however, limited to spoken language. Close to 90% of respondents believed that the ability to write good Japanese had declined either "very much" or "somewhat," compared to a 69% belief in a decline in reading ability, 59% in speaking and 57% in listening.[14] These perceptions of declining ability in all categories continued a trend which had been apparent since the surveys began in 1995. Many blamed the gaps in today's abilities on the erosion of time allotted to study of honorifics, proverbs and *kango* since the introduction of the new Courses of Study aimed at a more relaxed curriculum (Kawaijuku Educational Information Network 2003), a complaint often heard in other countries as well since the 1980s.

In response to the findings of this survey, the government announced that it would put in place measures to address the perceived decline in capabilities through the selection of 200 schools at all three levels across Japan to be flagship language education providers. Students at these schools would be required to improve their reading and writing skills, to learn about Japanese literary classics and to engage in debates to foster communication skills (Mainichi Shimbun 2002b). Advanced schools with model Japanese programs of this sort form one arm of the strategic plan to cultivate "Japanese with English abilities," Goal Six of which states that "in order to cultivate communication abilities in English, the ability to express appropriately and understand accurately the Japanese language, which is the basis of all intellectual activities, will be fostered" (MEXT 2003a). A good command of one's own language is here seen as a prerequisite for successful acquisition of a foreign language, and that good command includes knowledge of common proverbs and literary allusions.

Playing with writing

No discussion of reading and writing in Japan today would be complete without reference to the nuances of difference which manipulating the writing system can give. One of the great benefits to come from the complexity of the system is the playfulness it allows, the way in which simply by changing the expected use of script (by using katakana, for example, instead of kanji) a novel and interesting impression can be created. This finds expression in the creation of individual touches in, say, the text of wedding or other invitations, as well as in eye-catching flyers and advertisements. It goes further than the manipulation of different fonts, to the deeper level of playing with society's expectations of how writing is managed and creating (usually) pleasant variations through the unexpected.

A further manifestation of play in the writing system is the use of emoticons (*kaomoji* in Japanese) in both handwriting and in online communication, whether accessing the Internet through computer or mobile phone. These often substitute for words, and can convey information that the sender may not want to articulate explicitly. "By inserting an illustration, the sender can depict heartbreak, happiness, loneliness, or love: s/he can modify the impact of words, or even nullify earlier damaging statements – all of this without having to actually write words." (Holden and Tsuruki 2003: 41). At least twenty dictionaries of *kaomoji*, either hard-copy or online, have been published since 1993; some can be downloaded from websites directly into the user's computer (Katsuno and Yano 2002: 211). *Kaomoji* use is rampant in online chatrooms; once the preserve of computer geeks, these little symbols now pop up everywhere to express ideas or (usually) emotions either in conjunction with everyday text or as a substitute. Katsuno and Yano liken them to the language of *manga*, now used in cyberspace, and point out the rich field of cultural intertextuality which has led to the phenomenon:

These include the conventions of play and aesthetics in traditional writing systems in Japan; the modern embracing of technology and gadgetry in part for its own sake, in part for its very newness; the pattern of "boom"/fad culture in Japan; the development of an *otaku* subculture; the rise of *shōjo* "cute" culture in Japan from the late 1970s and 1980s through to the present; and *manga* [comics] with their highly codified visual language. (2002: 213)

And finally, on the subject of written language play, a recent newspaper article (*Mainichi Daily News* 2004) drew attention to the phenomenon of online "gal talk," or *gyaru moji*. Gal talk divides up the component segments of kanji and arranges them in a vertical line, with punctuation marks to show where a word ends, or uses characters which are almost but not quite correct but whose meaning can be understood anyway through context. This kind of text manipulation functions almost like a code which excludes those not familiar with it. Websites have been set up to translate ordinary Japanese into "gal talk," e.g. http://mizz.lolipop.jp/galmoji/ (accessed 27 February 2004). The site gives three options for conversion: "a little bit," "in a hurry" (sokosoko) and "the whole hog." Another site, http://members.jcom.home.ne.jp/cmx/tx/gal.html, lists various versions of hiragana options.

The use of language play of this sort functions to create virtual identities for online users who may find it too difficult or may not wish to invest the time in writing out messages that can be condensed into one visual symbol, or who just want to have some fun with their friends.

Writing and reading in Japan, as we have seen in this chapter, offer all manner of links to personal identity. That identity may be defined in terms of habits ("we are what we read," or don't read), abilities ("I can read more kanji than you can") or disabilities ("I have a learning disability, therefore I am 'different'"). Language play may identify the user as a member of a particular subculture; emoticons can be used to enhance or conceal identity. As with any other language, the way we write and what we choose to read is governed to a large extent by personal choice.

6 Representation and identity: discriminatory language

One of the strongest indicators of a society's attitudes to language and identity is the kind of language used to refer to those of its members who are seen as in some way disadvantaged or outside the mainstream. The last thirty years of the twentieth century saw a heated debate on inclusive language in most of the world's advanced industrial societies, as ethnic and other minority groups protested against the use of language which labeled them as in some way inferior to other members of those societies. This was fuelled in part by international movements on minority rights such as the United Nations International Year of Disabled Persons in 1981 and Decade of Disabled Persons (1983–1992), the United Nations Decade for Women (1976–1985), and the United Nations Year for Indigenous People in 1993 and Decade for Indigenous People (1994–2004).

Japan was no exception, although the debate on "political correctness" (a backlash from people who did not wish to restrain the speech they used in referring to others) which resulted came rather later than in other countries like Australia or the United States. The push for language change in Japan came not from a strong civil rights tradition as in the United States but from a combination of international pressure and a strongly developed domestic sensitivity to public embarrassment on the part of the media and government. The prime movers in the debate, as we shall see, have been the Burakumin community, or more specifically, the Buraku Liberation League (BLL), an organization which supports and is the main representative for Japan's largest minority group, the descendants of people who in the pre-modern period were hereditary outcasts because of the nature of their occupations (see Weiner 1997, Pharr 1990, Neary 1989 and Upham 1987).

Debate over whether certain terms are discriminatory or not is one area in which the prevailing narratives of power and control within a society are most readily visible/identifiable, and is certainly the one often least voluntarily recognized by majority interests. Before we can delve into this issue, however, we must first define what we mean by calling language discriminatory. Some would argue that whether a certain term or description is discriminatory or not depends wholly on the attitude of the user and the perceptions of the audience. The former is not too difficult to determine: when a word or phrase is meant to convey an attitude of contempt or ridicule, as in "nigger," "gimp" or, in Japanese, *eta*,[1] that intention is usually quite clear. As to the latter, an audience is not a monolithic entity; some people may find the term offensive, others may not. In any case, whether the audience expresses resistance to the use of such a term or not does not render it any less discriminatory when the intent of the speaker is to denigrate. Certain words and expressions crystallize societal and personal anxieties and fears. These act as lightning rods for tensions and fractures within the social fabric of Japan.

Sometimes expressions are used which, while they do not express outright hostility as in the case of the terms illustrated above, nevertheless are felt by those to whom they refer to patronize them or to lower their status in the perceptions of the community at large, as in the case, for example, of the *shokuba no hana* (office flower) expression used of female company employees. This sort of description, or any kind of description which depicts certain types of people performing stereotypical roles not necessarily in line with the facts, might more accurately be referred to as linguistic stereotyping rather than discriminatory language.

Problematic expressions are usually identified as discriminatory by the targets themselves, whose protests draw the attention of the wider community to the matter. In Japan, most complaints have come from those minority groups which have experienced discrimination on the grounds of difference, weakness or social background: Burakumin, women, Koreans born in Japan, foreigners and those with physical or mental disabilities. Ainu people have also experienced this kind of linguistic bombardment, as have the gay community. In recent years, the issue has moved online, with the emergence of online hate speech in certain bulletin boards and chatrooms in Japanese cyberspace.

Burakumin

The Burakumin are Japan's largest minority group (between two and three million, exact figures unclear). Although they are Japanese, physically indistinguishable from other Japanese, they have traditionally suffered badly from status discrimination and continue to suffer prejudice today because in feudal Japan their families were outcasts, excluded from the four-tier class system because their occupations involved activities considered polluting, usually (though not always) having to do with places of blood and/or death, such as meat works, tanneries, cemeteries and garbage dumps. The term *Burakumin*, which replaced the previously mentioned *eta*, means "people of the village," and refers to the fact that they were forced to live in small communities separate from nearby mainstream communities. In 1997, however, when the Buraku Liberation League rewrote their manifesto for the first time in years, they replaced the term *burakumin* (hamlet people) with *buraku jūmin* (hamlet residents), to try to debunk the false but enduring belief that Burakumin are a different race from other Japanese (see De Vos and Wagatsuma 1966).

Members of this group today continue to face discrimination in finding employment and marriage partners if they are known to come from a Burakumin background. In the 1970s, employment blacklists containing details of known Burakumin communities were found to be circulating among companies in Osaka; the resulting outcry led to applicants no longer having to give full details of where they were born. The lists were banned in Osaka, but similar lists have begun circulating on the Internet in recent years. In cases of arranged marriages, parents or their go-betweens may hire personnel to perform background checks on their offspring's prospective marriage partners, searching for evidence of Burakumin or other undesirable background.

The Burakumin minority has been particularly vulnerable to both outright unpleasant description and linguistic stereotyping and has been proactive in fighting back. In 1922, the first national Burakumin organization, the Suiheisha (Levelers' Society), forerunner of today's Buraku Liberation League, was formed and adopted a strategy of *kyūdan* (denunciation) to target instances of discrimination. The first campaigns, in the same year the group was formed, involved protests about the use of such derogatory words as *eta, doetta* and *yottsu*. During the 1920s and 1930s, this strategy "was a form of organized protest which was as specific to the Suiheisha as the withdrawal of labor of the industrial union or the refusal to pay rent of the tenants' union . . . *Kyūdan* was not just the only Suiheisha activity that most Burakumin took part in but was also the only manifestation of the movement's activity that the majority population encountered" (Neary 1989:85). During this period protests were made to newspapers which carried articles including discriminatory language in reference to Burakumin, a trend which was to become more pronounced postwar.

The kind of words they targeted fell into three main groups: historical terms of contempt such as *eta* and *hinin*; words used allegorically to indicate inferiority or ostracism, such as the use of the term *tokushu buraku* (special village) to equate to "ghetto"; and expressions relating to social status, parentage/family and lineage (Takagi 1999: 31). A further example of the first of these was the term *shinheimin* (new commoner). This was the term used to refer to those formerly known as *eta* when the government abolished the four-tier class system in 1871 and replaced it with a scale of "aristocrat, commoner, new commoner." While the highly derogatory *eta* was at least replaced, in practice the outcast origin of those whom it had designated was still marked out by the presence of the character for "new" (shin) in front of the word "commoner" on their family registers.

The major newspaper *Asahi Shimbun* featured in a series of incidents during the 1950s and 1960s, most of them involving the use of *tokushu buraku* to describe some sort of unacceptable behavior or social ostracism. Although this term was taken out of official documents from the beginning of the Taisho Period (1911–1926), it remains in general society as a synonym for outcast villages, and until recently was also commonly used allegorically to indicate inferiority or worthlessness. In a column about the arts in the *Asahi* of 9 January 1956, for example, literary circles were described as displaying a *tokushu buraku-teki* narrow-mindedness (the sort of narrow-mindedness one finds in a ghetto). The manner in which this incident was handled subsequently became the model for later censure of the media by the Buraku Liberation League (Takagi 1999: 35–36). The League lodged a complaint with the *Asahi*'s Osaka office. The editor-in-chief then apologized, admitting that the paper had been careless in using the expression and would be more careful in future. The League, however, announced that an apology in itself was not sufficient; they wanted in future to see reporting of a kind which would eradicate discrimination. As a result of this incident, the *Asahi* thereafter for a time adopted a policy of writing openly about discrimination rather than treating it as a taboo, in order to foster awareness of Burakumin problems. A special unit dealing with the selection of material on Burakumin topics was set up in the "social issues" section of the Osaka office and seven articles were featured in December that year. Even so, the *tokushu buraku* term was used on a total of seven more occasions in the *Asahi*, resulting finally in a full-scale *kyūdan* by the BLL in November 1967. The expression also cropped up in other newspapers, magazines and books, on television programs, in political press releases and even during a 1982 lecture at a school Parents and Teachers Association meeting, on each occasion drawing complaint from the BLL.

During the 1970s the scale of the denunciations increased; some cases in Osaka and Kyushu involved semi-violent threats and unusual intimidation, the case of Terebi Nishi Nihon (TV West Japan) in Kyushu in 1973 being an example of this. Large groups of League members calling themselves *kakuninkai* (confirmation tribunals) would ask offenders whether they thought certain words they had used were discriminatory or not. If they agreed that they were and apologized, they were asked whether they thought an apology was sufficient, and the threats continued until further redress was promised. If they maintained that their words were not discriminatory, they were subjected to several hours of grilling until they accepted that they had been at fault (Yōgo to Sabetsu o kangaeru Shinpojiumu Jikkō Iinkai 1989: 8–9). In the Terebi Nishi Nihon case, this station broadcast as its late night movie the 1959 Daiei film "Ukigusa" (The Floating Weed), in which the hero is a wandering performer whose son wants to marry a woman in the troupe but is advised not to as he and she are "of different races" (*jinshu ga chigau*). The local branch of the Buraku Liberation League complained about the references to "traveling player" (a traditionally Burakumin or Hinin occupation) and "of different race."[2] The channel management argued that as the film was an artistic work from an earlier time, complaint on the grounds of discrimination was inappropriate, but the League would not accept this, and its members bombarded everyone from the company president down with complaints. Finally, after an all-night meeting, the channel capitulated and agreed to five promises: that a letter of apology would be issued, a thirty-second television apology would be broadcast, the company would carry out research on Burakumin issues for an hour a week, it would broadcast a program twice a month aimed at enlightening viewers on these issues, and staff would participate in study and training meetings run by the League.

These sharper-edged tactics grew increasingly more common during the 1970s and 1980s. From the mid-1970s on, fearing the public embarrassment that inevitably resulted from large groups of disaffected readers demonstrating outside company offices, both print and visual media resorted to practicing self-censorship in order to avoid such discomfiture. This took the form of in-house collections of words to be avoided (*kinkushū*) and alternative expressions which were to be substituted (*iikaeshū*), similar to those used in English by newspapers such as the *Los Angeles Times* and by university equity offices in Australia and overseas. After this practice became generally known, however, criticism of another sort, to the effect that the companies involved were engaging in unacceptable *kotobagari* (word-hunting), led most companies to conceal the existence of the lists. Apart from the collection of NHK, the national broadcaster, which is also used as a reference by other organizations, only the Kyodo News Service and the Jiji News Service published their guidelines (Sukigara 1995), although Japanese books discussing discriminatory language have excerpted those of other companies.

Takagi (1999), for example, includes those of TV Asahi and the *Asahi Shimbun*.

The 1974 NHK program standards handbook (excerpted in Yōgo to Sabetsu o kangaeru Shinpojiumu Jikkō Iinkai 1989: 307–323) divided the issues into categories, including human rights, character and reputation/dignity, race, ethnicity and international relations. Colloquial terms referring to people with physical or mental disabilities, such as *bikko* (cripple), *mekura* (blind) and *tsunbo* (deaf) were to be avoided except under special circumstances, as were derogatory references to certain occupations, such as those of servant or manual laborer and references to Burakumin. Names of occupations such as *inukoroshi* (dog killer) and *onbō* (cremator), for example, were to be replaced with the less emotive *yaken hokakuin* and *kasō sagyōin* respectively. Racial descriptions such as *kuronbo* (blacks) and *ketō* (whites) were to become *kokujin* and *hakujin*; blind/deaf/lame were changed to *me/mimi/ashi no fujiyū na . . .* , and so on. In the guidelines developed by the *Asahi Shimbun* the following year, *tokushu buraku* was to be replaced with *hisabetsu buraku* (discriminated-against villages), *mikaihō buraku* (unliberated villages) or *dōwa chiku*, while the word *buraku* itself, where it indicated a "village community," should be changed to *shūraku* or *chiku* so as not to give the reader the impression that it was a Burakumin community (Yōgo to Sabetsu o kangaeru Shinpojiumu Jikkō Iinkai 1989: 324–326). Other organizations' guidelines[3] followed similar principles, with some slight differences in coverage but all encompassing the broad areas relating to race and ethnicity, social status and health differences. Private sector television took the lead from NHK.

The main arguments against such self-censorship, as debated over the ensuing twenty years, may be summed up as follows.[4] First, language controls do nothing to eradicate discrimination itself but merely push it further underground by hiding the sort of language which best manifests the discrimination while at the same time making people feel inhibited about expressing themselves freely. To single out words formerly used and replace them with other equivalents is really to deny history; in particular, authors of literary works such as historical novels or even contemporary novels which deal with topics such as Burakumin or in which characters have some sort of disability should not be constrained in their choice of language if the sanitized alternative takes away from the immediacy of the novel's dialogue. Subtle nuances of expression may no longer be possible. Overall, the whole debate about whether certain words should be replaced, and if so with what, has been carried on only between those who lodge the complaints and the publishers and writers involved, without any formal input from the general public (who constitute the reading public at which the words are aimed). If that public only ever sees censored texts, people will not be able to develop any real awareness of the realities of discrimination.

What happened here is that in a sense the media became its own best watchdog, and to a large extent ceased what little coverage there was of Burakumin-related items, in particular, for fear of provoking unwelcome retaliatory publicity. This in turn provoked criticism from writers in particular in the 1990s who claimed, not without justification, that attempts by publishers to enforce conformity with the lists constituted an unacceptable infringement of freedom of literary expression. Such lists of substitutions, insofar as they focus on the symptom and not the cause, are ineffectual in dealing with the wider social discourse of discrimination, it has been argued; they are simply there to protect the media from embarrassment. It is certainly true that while the emergence of such lists is on the surface of things a victory for the Burakumin Liberation League and other groups in controlling the kind of language used about them, on a deeper level it is a defeat, since rather than risk infringement the media have chosen to stop discussing issues of discrimination almost entirely. Kawamoto (1995: 46–47) classifies responses to complaints about discriminatory language and the Burakumin since the late 1970s into three broad types: positive acceptance of the substance of a complaint and an attempt to find new ways of talking about Burakumin issues; emergency evasive measures on receipt of a complaint; and criticism of the complaint itself, after which people continue to do as they wish, citing freedom of speech as their justification. He positions the media collections under the second of these headings, i.e., as emergency measures taken to avert criticism and to paper over a difficult issue rather than coming to grips with the substantive matters of discrimination which lie behind the complaints. They are in no sense a solution to the problem.

People with disabilities

The movement against discriminatory language really thus began with the activities of the Buraku Liberation League and its predecessor, the Suiheisha, which were specific to Japan. During the 1970s and 1980s, however, in line with developments in other countries and often with support from the BLL, other groups began to protest as well. Among them were support groups of or for people with physical or mental disabilities, who targeted the use of expressions related to disability.

The word *kichigai* (madness, a lunatic) was, not unexpectedly, a particular focus of complaint when it was used in relation to behavior considered abnormal (but not usually the outcome of mental illness). In 1974, *kichigai* was used in a broadcast of "The Lordless Retainers of Arano" to describe rowdy antisocial behavior, whereupon the Osaka Association of Families of the Mentally Disabled complained to Mainichi Broadcasting that medical evidence showed that exposure to such words could cause medical treatment to be retarded, families to endure stress and recovering patients to experience a relapse. Following a second complaint later the same year, Mainichi Broadcasting decided that *kichigai* would from then on be a prohibited word, and thereafter a movement began to ban the use of this word in all areas relating to people with mental disabilities. Less straightforward, however, was its metaphorical application to other situations where no disability was involved, e.g. *beesubōru-kichigai* (mad about baseball). The early 1980s saw a succession of complaints about its use on television in similar contexts such as *sakka-kichigai* (soccer-mad), *kuruma-kichigai* (car-mad), *tenikichi* (a contraction of *tenisu-kichigai*, tennis-mad) and others in the same vein. The television stations concerned apologized and cut the offending material (Takagi 1999: 110–113).

Terms related to physical disabilities also became problematic. *Bikko* (lame) and *katawa* (cripple) were replaced by *ashi no fujiyū na kata* (people whose legs do not work freely) and *shōgaisha* or *shintai shōgaisha* (person with a physical disability) respectively. Protests were also lodged in situations where no explicit word such as "deaf" or "cripple" had been used but where the inference to be drawn from ordinary language was considered offensive, as in the advertisement which appeared in the *Asahi* on 3 November 1988 under the heading *aruku kara, ningen* (I'm a human being because I walk), prompting letters of complaint from people unable to walk who asked if they were therefore not considered to be human beings (Takagi 1999: 120).

Not only words such as *mekura* (blind), *tsunbo* (deaf), *oshi* (mute) drew complaint, but also expressions which contained them, such as *tsunbo sajiki* (upper gallery/blind seat) and *mekuraban o osu* (to stamp one's seal on documents without reading the contents). The Japan PEN Club, a literary society whose membership encompasses playwrights, poets, essayists, editors, novelists and non-fiction writers as well as broadcasters and video producers, reported on this trend in the mid-1990s: *mekujira o tateru* (to carp) and *mekuso ga hanakuso ga warau* (the pot calls the kettle black) were acceptable, but *mekusare* (a bleary-eyed but not alcoholic person) and *mekura ni chōchin* (a lantern for a blind person) were not. *Mekura meppō* (recklessly/blindly) was to be changed to *detarame* (random, hazard) or *yamikumi* (at random, rashly). *Tsunbo sajiki* was out of favor, even though it just meant a seat where one could not see the actors (Nihon PEN Kurabu 1995: 4–5).

A movement to remove from legal statutes terms which might be offensive to people with disabilities (what was called *fukai yōgo*, displeasing terminology, or *futekisetsu yōgo*, inappropriate terminology) began in Nagano prefecture in October 1980, at the suggestion of a disabled city councilor there. The council concerned put out a *Yōgo Kaisei no Ikensho* (a written opinion on revision of terminology) and requested that national and prefectural legislation be revised as well. With 1981 being the United Nations International Year of Disabled Persons, the national government turned its attention to terminology reform. Various acts covering aspects of health services, such as the Medical Practitioners Law and the Dental Practitioners Law, were overhauled to replace terms such as *fugu* (cripple) and *haishitsu* (deformity). *Tsunbo, mekura* and *oshi* were replaced with *mimi ga kikoenai mono, me ga mienai mono* (a person whose eyes cannot see) and *kuchi ga kikenai mono* respectively. *Hakuchi* (idiot) was later also changed, to *seishin no hatsuiku no okureta mono* (a person whose mental development lags behind others) (Takagi 1999: 130). Similar changes were also made at prefectural and local government levels.

A very famous incident involving disability and language, which relates to the issue of media self-censorship described earlier involved novelist Tsutsui Yasutaka in 1993. Tsutsui's science-fiction story (*Mujin Keisatsu*, The Robot Police) was to be included in a high school textbook published by Kadokawa in 1994, but the choice was criticized by the Japan Epilepsy Association on the grounds that the story disparaged epileptics. It was set in a police state of the future, where police routinely scanned brain waves and prohibited the driving of vehicles by anyone with signs of epilepsy (the passages are reproduced in Namase 1994: 97–100). The Association, fearing that students would gain a poor impression of epileptics from the story, requested that the offending passage be cut. The publisher in this instance sided with the author and refused to make the cuts; Tsutsui, however, announced that he would give up writing altogether in protest against what he saw as unacceptable restrictions on freedom of speech and the sanctity of literature by advocates of political correctness, a decision he rescinded several years later. This incident, however, prompted a heated debate about "word hunts" and media self-censorship, with other prominent authors springing to the defense of freedom of expression (see Gottlieb 2001 for further details).

Women

A reconsideration of language relating to women also flowed on from the attention drawn to language issues by the activities of the Burakumin Liberation League. Other factors were at work here, too: the guaranteed equality of men and women in the postwar constitution; the women's liberation movement overseas from the 1960s on and the growth of its Japanese counterpart in the 1970s (see Muto 1997); the 1985 United Nations Convention on the Elimination of All Forms of Discrimination Against Women; and, in Japan, the passing of the Equal Employment Opportunity Law in 1986. This last was particularly influential: the move-ment to delete discriminatory terms and references to women grew with their increasing participation in employment.

Terms traditionally used to refer to women often saw them lumped together with children (*onnakodomo*, women and children). Actions per-ceived as being weak were described in terms of women, e.g. *onna no yō ni* (like a woman) and *onna rashii* (like a woman). The word *shujin* (where the characters mean "main person"), for "husband" and *okusan/kanai* (inside the house) for "wife," not to mention *mibōjin* (not yet dead person), for "widow" were particular targets of feminist complaint. A 1985 book by the Kotoba to Onna o kangaeru Kai (Women and Lan-guage Research Group) set out to draw attention to the derogatory atti-tude towards women of dictionary makers by examining words relating to men and to women in eight Japanese-language dictionaries published in the previous five years. The 1980 third edition of the *Iwanami Kokugo Jiten* (Iwanami Japanese Dictionary), for example, defines the word *umazume* (stone woman, a derogatory word referring to a woman unable to bear children) as "a woman without the ability to conceive; a woman who can-not give birth to children." There is no corresponding word for a childless man; despite the fact that the cause for infertility often lies with the man, it is the woman who is referred to as cold and hard as stone (Kotoba to Onna o kangaeru Kai, 1985: 15–16).

Depictions of women which did not necessarily use sexist language but portrayed them in highly stereotypical fashion were also contentious, with advertising being a particular offender. A 1983 advertisement for instant noodles which ran *watashi tsukuru hito* (I am the one who makes them, said by the woman), *watashi taberu hito* (I am the one who eats them, said by the man) was withdrawn after complaints from the women's movement, as was a 1988 Eidan subway poster which was withdrawn a month earlier than planned after women's groups complained that its close-up of a woman's legs emphasized women as sex objects. In the same year, the Ministry of Postal Services withdrew from post offices around the nation pamphlets featuring women in aprons after complaints from an Osaka women's group that it was no longer appropriate to equate women with housewives (Takagi 1999: 136).

As had happened in the case of people with disabilities, interna-tional movements relating to women played a large part in the growing awareness of sexist language, as did the larger social debate relating to the status of women in Japan itself. Certain government organs began to examine their documentation with a view to removing inappropriate terminology relating to women. In 1984, for example, the Kanagawa prefectural government instituted the Kanagawa Women's Plan, predicated on improving expressions and content relating to women in prefectural publications, in particular with reference to gender-determined divisions of labor. Its overall aim was to address and countermand the belief that house and family were the responsibilities of women alone and were the sole areas to which they could be expected to contribute. Women were to be portrayed as having a fundamental human right to work. Each prefectural organization was requested to examine its publications in order to detect and remove traditional gender-role stereotypes and views of male-female relations (particularly in the family context) which were remnants of the patriarchal feudal system and words which expressed bias or contempt towards women. Among the expressions removed were: *shokuba no hana* (office flower, a term used to denote young, decorative female employees who performed only the lightest of office duties and whose term of employment was short); *ikka no daikakubashira wa yahari chichi oya* (the most important member of a family is the father); *fukei-shijo* (fathers and brothers, children and women); *onna no kusatta yō ni* (like a rotten woman); and character-stereotyping expressions such as *josei wa judōteki* (women are passive). Just as in other countries the women's movement campaigned to have "lady" replaced with "woman," so in Japan the word *fujin* (lady) was also replaced in many government contexts with *josei* (woman) (Takagi 1999: 145–149).

Ainu

As we saw in Chapter Two, language played a crucial part in defining boundaries or creating similarities between Ainu and Japanese in terms of the language the Ainu people were permitted to use in different historical periods. Derogatory terms and stereotypical portrayals also functioned to create and perpetuate images which kept Ainu stigmatized as Other regardless of the policy of assimilation. "The history of the Ainu people has been, in part, a struggle over their discursive representation" (Siddle 2002: 405). The terms regarded as discriminatory by Ainu people are thus inextricably related to the history of their colonization and exploitation, and in particular to their racialization within the terms of empire and their portrayal by both government and academe as an ethnic group on the verge of extinction.

Even the word *Ainu* itself, which in the Ainu language means "human being," was for a long time regarded by many Ainu people as a term to be avoided because it had become inextricably bound up with the derogatory connotations given to it by non-Ainu Japanese. "Ainu" dolls sold in shops had "inhuman, exaggerated features" (Totsuka 1993: 13); children were taunted with shouts of "Ainu!Ainu!," so that they learned that "'Ainu' was not a word to be proud of" (Chiri 1993: 19). The name alone lent itself to puns, as *inu* means "dog." *Ainu* could therefore equate to *A-inu!* (look, a dog!). As late as April 1986, a social studies comic book published by a Tokyo press and used as a teaching aid in schools depicted children saying "Look, a dog is coming!" when an Ainu child approaches (Roscoe 1986:67).

One of the popular racial jokes used against the Ainu is a pseudo-etymological explanation of their origin. In Japanese the phoneme "a" can indicate "second best," while "inu" is the Japanese word for "dog." It is therefore not difficult to see how the Ainu were denigrated by the Japanese through this pseudo-etymological link with dogs and how this deliberate misinterpretation of a foreign language could then be used by the dominant power group as a rationalization for relegating the Ainu to an inferior status (Taira 1996).

Others equated the word *Ainu* with poverty and stupidity; "primitive," too, has been a favored connotation and remains so even today. Because of the weight of historical discrimination which surrounded the term, therefore, the newly reconstructed Ainu Association of Hokkaido (AAH) decided in 1961 to change its Japanese name to the Hokkaido Utari[5] Association. "Utari," notes Sala (1975: 56) in relation to this decision, "thus became a euphemism, an indication among other things that the term Ainu (which means 'man' or 'human being') had become an unendurable burden in a highly prejudiced society." The Japanese name remains Hokkaido Utari Kyōkai today. During the 1970s, however, a number of new movements reclaimed the term *Ainu*, incorporating it into their names, among them the Nibutani Ainu Cultural Resource Museum, the Yay Yukar Ainu Minzoku Gakkai (Acting Ainu Ethnological Society) and a "National Meeting of the Talking Ainu" in 1973 (Koshida 1993: 5).

One noticeable indicator of the influence on Ainu groups of the Buraku Liberation League was the formation in 1972 of the similarly-named Ainu Liberation League by young Ainu activist Yūki Shōji. Impatient with the assimilationist emphasis of the Hokkaido Utari Kyōkai of which he had been a member of the board of directors, Yūki sought more direct action which would foster Ainu minority politics and pride in Ainu identity. Perhaps this group's best-known activity was the Burakumin-style denunciation it carried out at an academic conference of anthropologists and folklorists in Sapporo in August 1972, when Yūki and others unexpectedly commandeered the podium to take issue with the academic practices of treating Ainu as relics of a dying race and ignoring the way they lived in modern Japan.

Takagi's wide-ranging study of discriminatory language and minority groups lists a few instances of Ainu protests against derogatory language in the following decade. In July 1981, for example, the Japan Travel Bureau (JTB), in an advertisement in the English-language *Japan Times* for travel in Hokkaido, used the word *kebukai* (hairy) to describe Ainu people, prompting local Ainu people to convene a Burakumin-style denunciation meeting and protest to the JTB. The JTB inserted an apology in the newspaper, removed all derogatory references to Ainu from its Hokkaido guidebook and agreed to educate all staff (again, a Burakumin-style pattern). This incident was further referred to in a submission by the AAH to the Sixth Session of the Working Group on Indigenous Populations in Geneva in 1988 (Ainu Association of Hokkaido 1988) and is often referred to in scholarly literature on the Ainu (e.g. Siddle 1997:32; Hanazaki 1996:127–128).

The significance of the insult "hairy," which refers to the fact that pure-blooded Ainu people have more body hair than do Japanese, lies in its animal associations: taunts of "monkey" were often to be heard on that account. Writer Ishimori Nobuo's *Kotan no Kuchibue* (A Whistle in the Ainu Village) includes a scene in which an Ainu child agonizes over having to expose her hairy body to her Japanese friend in the bath and eventually attempts to kill herself before her father's grave on account of it (Yumoto 1963, cited in Taira 1996). Victorian writers perpetuated the linked use of the words "hairy" and "Ainu" in English as well: Christian missionary John Batchelor who worked in Hokkaido published *The Ainu of Japan: The Religions, Superstitions and General History of the Hairy Aborigines of Japan* in 1892, and adventurer A. H. Savage Landor published a travelogue with the title of *Alone with the Hairy Ainu* the following year.

"In every rural district, there are still Japanese who make derogatory comments or show contempt for their Ainu neighbors. Nineteenth-century images of the 'hairy, dirty, shōchū-drinking natives' still are widespread" (Sala 1975: 49). A 1986 list of anti-Ainu discriminatory incidents compiled by the AAH included information about Ainu women who wanted to become nurses being told to shave their hairy arms when they applied for hospital jobs (Roscoe 1986:67). Body hair, then, was not a good thing to have in Japan, and the word *kebukai* and other associated words when applied to Ainu people came to encapsulate all that was undesirable in terms of both physical and mental characteristics. "This reputed duality [of hairiness vs. comparatively non-hairy Japanese] is turned into the relative worth of each race by the ideology of the dominant" (Taira 1996). The association between hairiness and barbarian status played an important historical role in delineating Japanese from barbarians (see Morris-Suzuki 1998). That the term "hairy" today is offensive to Ainu people, therefore, stems not only from its association with dogs and other animals but also from its role in delineating them as barbarians beyond the civilized pale.

The 1990s saw a series of incidents in which Ainu groups complained to publishers about stereotypical or discriminatory depictions of Ainu. In this they were perhaps encouraged by the 1993 United Nations International Year of Indigenous People and following the example of the Buraku Liberation League's denunciation tactics, which by that time had achieved considerable success in bringing the press into line as far as the language used to refer to Burakumin (and indeed other minority groups) went. One incident involved the republication of a 1942 novel by Osami Gizō called *The Ainu School*; it described the everyday experiences of Ainu people at that time, using a primary school attended by Ainu children (and intended for assimilation) as its setting. The AAH complained to publisher Kobunsha that the novel contained many expressions insulting to Ainu people. When an Ainu baby was born, for example, the text said: "It wasn't a devil's child, it wasn't a monkey's child, it was an Ainu child." After a month of discussions, the publisher apologized, stopped printing the book and recalled those copies already distributed (Yamanaka 1995: 70–71).

This incident followed closely upon a complaint made by three Ainu rights groups about a New Year's Day 1994 variety program hosted by well-known personality Beat Takeshi, in which a dance to the song "Night of the Iyomante"[6] was seen as parodying and demeaning this very significant Ainu traditional ceremony. Nihon Terebi (TV Japan), which had screened the program, broadcast an apology several months later (Takagi 1999: 176–179). Other incidents followed, signaling a willingness to fight that had earlier been to a large extent lacking in the assimilationist stance of the AAH. In particular they took issue with portrayals of Ainu people as barbaric, spurred by the activism of the 1980s consequent on the rise of concern for minority rights and indigenous interest around the world. "Entering the modern period as 'barbarians', the Ainu have transformed themselves into an 'indigenous people'"(Siddle 1996: 2) and have demanded the respect due to them as a result.

Ethnic Koreans in Japan

The Korean community in Japan, referred to in Japanese as *zainichi kankokujin/ chōsenjin*[7] or *zainichi* for short, as we saw in Chapter Two, numbers over 625,000, most of whom are third and even fourth generation descendants of people who stayed on in Japan after the Japanese colonization of Korea ended in 1945 and have permanent residence. The official count of Korean permanent residents has been decreasing steadily as Koreans either take Japanese citizenship or marry Japanese partners, so that their children are automatically Japanese citizens.

This continuing integration through citizenship, however, has not brought any noticeable lessening of anti-Korean discriminatory practices, and discrimination against the Korean community regularly features in reports of various bodies on human rights in Japan. For example: "Despite improvements in legal safeguards against discrimination, Korean permanent residents (most of whom were born, raised and educated in Japan) still are subject to various forms of deeply entrenched societal discrimination" (Bureau of Democracy, Human Rights and Labor 2001). Sociologist Fukuoka Yasunori conducted in-depth interviews with around 150 *zainichi* youths in the early 1990s and found that "the vast majority of *zainichi* youths we interviewed had an experience of being exposed to some forms of discrimination and prejudice, either direct or indirect, either overt or covert, against themselves as Koreans by the majority Japanese, and have had or have identity crises" (Fukuoka 1996).

Discrimination takes many forms, but the manifestation of most interest to us in this chapter is the type of language directed against Koreans. Three of the most contested expressions have been *baka-chon, senjin* and *sangokujin*, all of which carry the baggage of discrimination originating from events during the period when Korea was a Japanese colony. The first of these, *baka-chon*, combines the word for "fool" (*baka*) with an abbreviation of a word for "Korean" and is used to describe very simple things, such as point-and-click cameras, which was where the term originated: so easy to use that even a "stupid Korean" can do it. The term is heard much less often now than earlier, possibly because it originated at a time when most cameras were complicated and took a lot of special knowledge to operate correctly and the point-and-click cameras were much easier to use by comparison. Many cameras since then have become automatic and much simpler to use, so that the term has dropped out of use, although negative publicity as to the truly derogatory implications of the expression has no doubt helped. Many of those who continue to use it do so without being aware of the historical baggage it carries or even that it refers to Koreans, and are surprised to have this pointed out. An example: on a Linux users' online discussion group in 1999 (the thread may be found at http://search.luky.org/fol.1999/msg00627.html, accessed 1 March 2004), when one contributor commented that TurboLinux, used every day, was *bakachon* easy, another took issue with the use of the word, and yet a third argued both with the second's interpretation of it and with his chiding the first person for using it. To Koreans themselves, however, the term is naturally insulting and demeaning.

Senjin is a contraction of the word *chōsenjin* which was used to display a contemptuous attitude to Koreans during the colonial period. *Senjin* is listed as "not to be used" in NHK's list of taboo words, in the Nihon Minzoku Hōsō (National Association of Commercial Broadcasters in Japan) taboo list,[8] and in another online list of taboo words put together by an online Japanese-English dictionary project.[9] The last of these warns that "the term *senjin* and other words that abbreviate *chōsen* (Korea) as *sen* are . . . regarded as discriminatory," which explains the upset experienced by a Korean resident present at a trial when a judge asked whether his son's nationality was *kankoku* (South Korean) or *kitasen*, instead of *kita chōsen* (North Korean). Who would believe, he asked, that fifty years after the war, in a Japan at last beginning to show recognition of its invasive activities in Asia, a Supreme Court judge in charge of a trial dealing with the rights of resident Koreans would use the word *kitasen*, a highly discriminatory term used against Koreans by Japanese government personnel during the colonial period in Korea and premised on the fact that since Koreans had no brains, it was appropriate therefore to drop the first syllable of the name of their country?[10]

The derogatory term *sangokujin* (third country people)[11] caused deep offence in April 2002 when Tokyo governor Ishihara Shintarō used it in a speech to the Ground Self-Defense Forces, warning of the likelihood of riots by such people in the event of a major natural disaster such as an earthquake. What he said was "*sangokujin* and foreigners who have entered the country illegally" (thereby equating those of Taiwanese or Korean descent living in Japan with undesirable illegal immigrants). Members of the Korean community were particularly angry, since large numbers of Koreans living in Japan had been massacred after the 1923 Tokyo earthquake. A flurry of newspaper and journal articles and online chat ensued. Ishihara's use of the word was censured by the ethnic groups concerned, by members of labor unions and NGOs who assist foreign workers and residents (McLaughlin 2000), by groups of scholars[12] and by the Japan Committee of the Buraku Liberation League's international arm, the International Movement Against All Forms of Racism and Discrimination (IMADR-JC),[13] which sent a letter pointing out the international conventions to which Japan was a signatory and that Ishihara's remark had contravened and demanded a retraction and apology.[14]

Governor Ishihara himself, several days later, expressed regret (though not apology) if he had offended Koreans and foreigners in general living in Japan. Explaining that he had not meant to cause offence with the term *sangokujin*, he blamed the media for focusing on that particular word and overlooking the fact that he had also been speaking about illegal immigrants as sources of crime, particularly snakeheads from China. Ishihara is well-known to be right-wing and anti-foreigner and is often in the news for making contentious comments of the type illustrated here. Morris-Suzuki (2000), analyzing the response of right-wing academics and commentators who defended Ishihara as a victim of *kotobagari* following the incident, notes that a consistent theme in their arguments was that the word *sangokujin* is not discriminatory because "it was introduced during the postwar occupation period as a technical term to describe people from 'third countries' other than Japan and the occupying powers," thereby ignoring the historical freight which words acquire depending on the circumstances in which they are used. What Ishihara is doing by using this word, she contends, is adopting (either consciously or unconsciously) an old strategy beloved of politicians of all stripes everywhere, i.e. tapping into xenophobic fears to divert attention from other issues at hand by eliding the old term *sangokujin* with the more recent phenomenon of "illegal immigrants" to create one threatening foreign face which the Japanese would be well advised to buffer themselves against.

All these words carry historical baggage from the colonial period which Koreans resident in Japan find deeply inappropriate and offensive and which have no part in the "third way" identity they are forging for themselves as Japanese Koreans, i.e. as neither Japanese nor Korean, but a third way in between the two.

Others

The list of groups who have been insulted by the use of derogatory language in reference to them could go on and on; given the space restrictions, not everyone can be included here. The above detailed case studies give a good idea of what the problems have been and how they have been handled. I shall finish this discussion with a necessarily brief mention of three other groups who have complained about stereotyping and abuse: the Chinese community, foreigners and gays. For each of these groups we shall single out one of the major expressions used to refer to them.

As we saw in Chapter Two, Chinese communities in Japan are located mainly in large urban centers, reflecting the historical waves of merchant and labor immigration. Language used about the Chinese community covers the usual gamut of outright discriminatory terms and also linguistic stereotyping in advertisements and other publications or depictions. Of particular concern is the well-documented tendency on the part of the authorities to equate rising crime rates with foreigners and in particular with Chinese, reflecting Governor Ishihara's conflation, discussed above, of Korean and Chinese residents with illegal immigrants and with criminal activity. In December 2000, for example, an uproar ensued when it was found that police stations in Tokyo had been issued with posters (ultimately not used) urging citizens who heard people speaking in Chinese on the street to call the police. The poster gave as justification for this the fact that crime among foreigners, particularly Chinese, was on the increase. In February 2004, the Ministry of Justice's Immigration Bureau homepage attracted widespread complaint from human rights groups such as Amnesty International Japan when it added a link to its homepage enabling anonymous tip-offs about illegal immigrants, a move labelled as xenophobic but defended vigorously by the Ministry (Mainichi Shimbun 21 February 2004).

The use of the word *shina* for China caused a fuss at Reitaku University in 2000 when the university felt constrained to issue a counterstatement to a report in the *Nippon Keizai Shimbun* on July 17 that year which had said that a lecture critical of the Nanjing Massacre had been abandoned as a result of a complaint from an international student in a political science class. The university's rebuttal stressed that the class in question had eventually been taken away from that particular staff member, not because of disputes about the veracity of the Nanjing Massacre, but because the staff member had consistently refused, despite repeated requests from the university, to stop using the word *shina* in class, which the student claimed was discriminatory. *Shina* has been described as encapsulating a worldview of "the superiority of a modern Japan over an unchanging China" (Tanaka 1993: 9), which modern Japan still holds today. The staff member argued that *shina* was a contemporary word which was in no way contemptuous of China or Chinese people, but the university authorities, unconvinced, replied that their practice had always been to follow the Ministry of Education's request that *shina* not be used and thus removed the staff member from control of the class. The newspaper report, the official statement assured the public, had wrongly given the reason as being a dispute over the Nanjing facts, but the university upheld the principles of academic freedom and would not remove a lecturer on those grounds; it was rather the language itself that was at issue.

Foreigners in Japan complain about the use of the term *gaijin* to refer to them, and have done since at least the late 1980s. When Japanese use this term to mean "foreigner," they often mean specifically western foreigners rather than other Asians or Africans. The two characters of the word mean "outside person"; it is a contraction of the word *gaikokujin*, literally "person from another country." *Gaikokujin* is uncontroversial and simply means a person who does not hold Japanese citizenship; it is the more common contracted version that has been the subject of irritated complaint. Sometimes this is because of the manner in which it is used: people may be pointed at by children and have the word *gaijin* either shouted or whispered, though this behavior is much less common in Japan today than it was thirty years ago. At a deeper level, though, it is the connotation of exclusion and oddity that irks, particularly when the term is combined with the adjective *hen na* to mean "peculiar foreigner," a term once often heard on Japanese TV shows. Valentine (1997a:96, 98) points out that this term is not used of foreigners who stay outside of Japan, but only of foreigners within Japan, where their failure to conform to Japanese norms is perceived as peculiar rather than being put down to everyday intercultural differences. At any rate, the term *gaijin* itself is included these days by most broadcasters on their list of terms best avoided. The website of Issho Kikaku, an NGO established in 1992,[15] contains much information on the debate over this word, as does that of David Aldwinckle (Japanese name Arudō Debito), a long-term resident of Japan who has taken Japanese citizenship.[16]

And finally, a few words on discriminatory language and gays. Most of the terms referring specifically to gays and lesbians are imported and written in katakana as *gairaigo*, signaling that these are alien forms of sexuality. *Rezu*, *homo* and *gei* are examples of this, although the last of these is reserved for foreigners rather than Japanese. "In terms of identification, *gei* carries implications of a political stance or movement, of sexuality defining self, and hence of coming out." In terms of Japanese words, men are referred to as *okama* (literally "a pot", referring to the shape of the buttocks and thereby anal intercourse as well as associating gay men with the kitchen) and women as *onabe* (literally "a pan," shallower than a pan and with a wider opening), among other things (Valentine 1997: 99–101; see also McLelland 2000). *Okama* usually intimates that the man is effeminate in behavior and *onabe* that the woman is masculine in dress and demeanor. Opinions differ among gay activists themselves on whether *okama* is actually discriminatory or not; Itō Satoru, for example, from gay rights group OCCUR, considers the word to be highly so, while another equally experienced gay rights campaigner does not (McLelland 2001, note xxi). There is little doubt, however, given the stereotypical and offensively amusing portrayals of gays on television, that the term is not meant to signal inclusiveness but rather to exclude and stigmatize.

Clearly the issue of discriminatory language and its regulation is just as contentious and has inflamed tempers on both sides just as much in Japan as in other countries. Both sides approach the issue as one of identity formation, each group seeking to construct its own desired identity as

Japanese: the targeted groups through the abolition or defiant reclaiming of terms marking their members as different and a large group of writers through asserting their right as literati to use the language for literary purposes without regulation. In the middle sit the media, attempting to please everybody by censoring certain expressions without, in most cases, admitting that this is the case, or, in the case of Governor Ishihara and the *sangokujin* reference, zeroing in on the term itself in the manner of word police. The recent resurgence on the Internet of expressions no longer found in the print and visual media and the efforts of Burakumin groups such as IMADR to combat this indicates that far from being a dead issue, the fight has merely shifted to a new arena, that of cyber-identities.

7   Shifting electronic identities

One of the major twentieth-century developments affecting the Japanese language, at least in its written form, was the development around 1980 of character-capable software. Although, as we saw in Chapter Five, Japan has not been noticeably handicapped by the intricate nature of its orthography, until the invention of this technology the complexity and size of the character set meant that it had never been able to have a successful "typewriter age" as in the west, so that most office documents and of course personal documents were still written by hand at a time when printed documents had become the norm elsewhere. The new technology therefore carried wide-ranging implications for writing. In the business domain, of course, it expedited office automation. In the personal domain, it brought about changes both in the way people wrote when they used it and in the nature of interpersonal relations mediated through print. Japanese consumers made of it a powerful expression of individual identity during the 1980s and 1990s, a trend which continues and today finds an extra dimension of expression in the messaging capability of mobile phones.

In addition to revolutionizing the way people thought about document production both in the office and at home, word-processing technology also then enabled Japan to construct a Japanese-language presence on the Internet. After a slow start relative to other countries, Japanese rose quickly to become the second most common language on the Internet, a position from which it was only edged out by Chinese in September 2000; it is currently sitting in third place. Japan is now seeing the emergence of a rich and vibrant range of cybercultures as the ability to write in Japanese online enables subcultures of various types (including those previously marginalized) to communicate in ways not previously possible. Today we sit at our computers or hold our mobile phones and easily type in kanji and kana, not perhaps realizing that this only first became possible just over twenty years ago. This chapter will show how and why this technology evolved and what its social and cultural consequences have been so far.

A Japanese typewriter (at first for kana only but later including characters as well) had been developed in 1929 but was bulky and slow, requiring specialist training for effective use. Instead of being able to key in text quickly as on an English-language typewriter using the QWERTY keyboard, a Japanese typist first had to locate the desired character in a matrix of metal characters on a large tray in front of (usually) her and then retrieve it by positioning a round metal eyelet on an arm above it and pressing a lever, a much more time-consuming process. Because of the number of pieces of metal type needed, the typewriter could not be easily moved around. To return to one of our example sentences from Chapter Five:

東京はブリスベンより人が多いです。

Tōkyō wa burisuben yori hito ga ōi desu.

Tokyo has a larger population than Brisbane.

To type this using a Japanese typewriter would involve finding and retrieving a total of sixteen symbols from three different matrices and would take much longer to type than the romanized version of the sentence. Handwriting was much faster and therefore remained the norm in the Japanese office until the early 1980s. The fax machine was developed as one way around the problem of input (Unger 1987: 165; Kodama 1991: 13), but not, of course, of output.

It was precisely the fact that the romanized version of our sentence could be typed more quickly than Japanese that led some to argue that Japan would be better off getting rid of characters and adopting the alphabet as its script. This was not a new idea, as we have seen, although it now emerged in a different context. In the modern era of internationalization and increasing globalization of many aspects of life, people such as Yamada Hisao, for example, former director of the research and development department of the National Center for Science Information Systems, argued strongly in favor of romanization, believing that the information era required language which was simple to read and write and that characters could not meet these needs (Yamada 1984: 10–14). For a while it seemed as though this might be the only way Japan could enter the computer era, but this argument became redundant with the invention in the late 1970s of technology enabling rapid character retrieval.

Development of the technology

Word-processing technology developed earlier in western countries, where the alphabet posed no significant difficulty, but was for a long time thought impossible in Japan because of the nature of the Japanese writing system. In 1978, however, Toshiba succeeded in producing a word processor capable of handling both input (typing in) and output (printing) using characters, with a keyboard of forty-six kana keys and a conversion system which entailed the user pressing a button to have the kana converted into Chinese characters brought from storage in memory. Again returning to our example sentence: to type this on a word processor is much faster and simpler than on a Japanese typewriter (although still not as fast as if the typing were done in English or romanized Japanese). The text can be input in either hiragana or rōmaji which are automatically converted to hiragana, and then converted to the correct character equivalents where necessary simply by pressing the conversion key (called the *kana-kanji henkan* key) (see Lunde 1993 for details). Sometimes a character which has the same reading but is not the correct one in that context is displayed, in which case it is necessary to keep pressing the key until the right one appears. This can be done easily on the screen as many times as necessary before the document is printed out, unlike a typewriter's instant output where a mistake results in having to redo the document or blemish it in some way to correct the error.

The invention of this technology was clearly a major breakthrough for machine production of documents. The earlier constraints on the capacity of the writer to remember and to use large numbers of characters were now lifted, though those on the capacity of the reader to recognize them were not. It had always been the norm to be able to recognize more than one could reproduce, however; the real hardship lay in the difficulty of remembering how to write a large character set correctly. This had been one of the underlying arguments in favor of the postwar script reforms which resulted in limits being placed on the number of characters to be taught in schools for general use. Newspapers also, for fifty years prior to those reforms, had been vocal advocates of character limits in the interests of increasing their circulation and of production economy during the era of movable type, when large boxes of type had to be carried about by hand. The adoption of word processing technology by the press and its rapid uptake in society at large therefore implies that two of the major pillars supporting Japan's present policy on script have now been removed.

The early word processors were very large and cost millions of yen, but in the early 1980s smaller versions were developed, prices began to fall and the technology eventually came within the reach of the average consumer. As a result, sales of machines to be used both in offices and in homes rose sharply. Ministry of International Trade and Industry (MITI)[1] statistics show that annual sales figures for stand-alone word processors[2] rose from 30,728 in 1982 to 2,237,333 in 1986,[3] with notable peaks in 1984, 1985 and 1986 as advances in computer technology and the economies of scale made possible by mass production combined to lower prices (Tsūsan Daijin Kanbō Chōsa Tōkeibu 1987: 226). As well as making inroads into the non-business realm, the technology continued to consolidate its hold in offices: by 1986, 90% of businesses were using word processing in one form or another to produce Japanese-language documents (Tsūsan Daijin Kanbō Chōsa Tōkeibu 1986: 448), although of the total number of stand-alone word processors in circulation in 1987 close to 90% were for personal as opposed to office use. A few years later, a 1991 survey by the Economic Planning Agency found that one in four people possessed a word processor (Aoyama 1991: 217).

In 1992, the opening of the Japanese market to American computer companies meant that clones made by Compaq arrived in Japan at half the price of the local NEC machines. As a result, the number of people who preferred to use word-processing software on a personal computer (PC) rather than on the earlier stand-alone machines increased, both because of the wider range of applications a PC offered and, later, because PCs allowed Internet access. In 1991, only 12.2% of all households had personal computers, compared to 32.6% for stand-alone word processors; in 1993, this changed to 13.9% and 37.8% respectively (Japan Statistical Association 1992: 548 and 1995: 588). In 1994, however, PC sales soared and surpassed word processor sales for the first time by a large margin; the following year, annual sales of stand-alone word processors dropped below two million for the first time in ten years (1996: 25). The 1990s saw the release of Japanese versions of operating systems and word processing software such as Word for use on PCs, starting with the release of a Japanese version of Windows 3.0 in 1991.

A new technology very seldom comes into common use without debate, particularly when it impinges upon something so fundamental as the way people write. Even the simple fountain pen was compared unfavorably with brush writing when it first appeared. In like manner, debate about the pros and cons of word processing accelerated along with the sales, usually in terms of whether people ought to use a machine to produce their personal correspondence or not. In the early 1980s, terms like personal computer, word processor and database came into common use; the word *waapuro* or *wapuro* (short for *waado purosessaa*, the Japanese pronunciation of "word processor") began to appear everywhere in advertisements and in the press. Certain terms which reflected the cultural consequences of the technology also began to appear in the language. The word *waapurohorikku*, for example, a pun on "workaholic" indicating a person who was always using his/her *waapuro*, came into use as early as 1984, along with terms such as *wapuro ningen* or *kiibōdo ningen* (keyboard person, meaning somebody who hardly ever writes by hand). Converts loved the cleanliness of the process (no more eraser shavings or ink-stained fingers) and the greater productivity and speed that on-screen editing allowed them. Not everyone was convinced, though; some viewed the rise of the *waapuro ningen* as a potential social disaster, fearing that lazy over-use of standard formulaic expressions used in correspondence and now made available in word processor memories, for example, could lead to a loss of the personal touch in letters (Andō 1988: 102).

Considerations of time, space and economy had a great deal to do with the enthusiastic uptake of the technology. Word processors, and later PCs, contributed to saving labor, time and space in the home, the main objective of household information technology. They enabled large amounts of information to be stored comparatively rapidly and easily on disk rather than on paper requiring storage space and produced less paper rubbish compared to making handwritten drafts and discarding unwanted documents. Best of all, the information was completely portable; a disk could be slipped into a pocket or a handbag. The incorporation of the technology into people's daily routines, particularly once Internet access and email became available (now on mobile phones as well as computers), indicates that it has become fully functional, for "to become functional a technology has to find a place within the moral economy of the household, specifically in terms of its incorporation into the routines of daily life" (Silverstone, Hirsch *et al.* 1992:24).

Above all, in all of this, convenience has been a prime mover. Convenience, as the 1990 White Paper on Living Conditions remarked, is the primary reason why the entry of the microprocessor into household appliances has changed people's lives (Keizai Kikakuchō 1990: 175). If we think back over the earlier chapters in this book, we can see how ironic it is that convenience is advertised as one of the great virtues of the word processor: this technology makes available easy access to vast numbers of characters stored in memory, far more than are needed (or indeed, recommended) for daily use. In the script policy debates discussed in Chapter Four, it was the very same concept of convenience when related to orthography which was so harshly attacked by right-wing conservatives. Convenience was also put forward by those who eventually succeeded in bringing about those postwar script reforms as one of their main reasons for doing so. The word processor now appears to have gone some way towards overturning their efforts, in theory if not yet actually in practice, in the name of convenience. We can clearly see, then, that this concept has played an elastic and multi-faceted role in debates over writing in Japan.

Icon of identity

Just as important to word processor uptake were issues of identity creation through consumerism; being up to date with the latest gadgets established the owner as a person of style, at least in his or her own mind. In the 1980s, the word processor became an icon of chic, a symbol of the information society which marked its owner as a citizen of the information age. To own a word processor, or so the advertisements implied, stamped a person as progressive, trendy, and in the know, as in some way "advanced." A brochure advertising Toshiba's Rupo JW88FX congratulated purchasers on their cleverness, describing buying a word processor as making an investment in themselves. Different advertising discourses offered different user identities: a 1995 Toshiba Rupo JW-V600 brochure showed four different types of professional user ranging from corporate types to a female chef producing printed menus, while a Casio Darwin G-770ZX brochure from the same year targeted home users, showcasing an older man sitting in a home library and a younger woman sitting casually in her lounge room. A 1996 brochure for the Casio Darwin G-900ST featured an older professorial type and displayed shots of the word processor among what were clearly meant to be scholarly surroundings. Something for everyone, the photographs tell us, bearing out what Jackson and Thrift have to say about the geographies of consumption:

There is no essential, one-to-one, correspondence between particular commodities and particular identities: the same commodity can have radically different meanings for different individuals and for the same individual over time. Advertising and marketing campaigns have begun to realise this in targeting their products to specific niches. But rather than targeting particular market segments by associating their product uniquely and unambiguously with a particular lifestyle, they are increasingly trying to position their products in order to take advantage of the ambiguous and shifting boundaries of people's identities. (Jackson and Thrift 1995:227)

If the rate at which sales increased can be attributed in part to the influence of this kind of advertising (always debatable), then it might be argued that in a sense word processor owners in the 1980s were constructing differentiated individual identities according to their own needs and desires but linked by the overarching identity of themselves as people in the vanguard of technology, unafraid of its demands, able to break free of the well known "keyboard allergy" of the Japanese and establish control of the new. The focus of the advertising may be seen as consumerism which allows control over one's own life, specifically over the construction of an orthographic identity and, by association, of their wished-for identity as ultra-modern individuals. "The consumption pattern that (individuals) select, whether represented by their choice of car or clothes, house, furnishings or leisure-time pursuits, can . . . be regarded as indicative not simply of their 'self-identity,' but of how they wish others to regard them"

(Campbell 1995: 112). The link between consumer and observer in this nexus, however, as Campbell points out, is problematic, as the intended message may not always be interpreted as the consumer desires. Nevertheless, when this particular form of information technology entered households, it provided "a means both for the integration of the household into the consumer culture of modern society – into a national as well as an international culture – and for the assertion of an individual's, a household's . . . own identity: a domestic as well as a local culture" (Silverstone and Hirsch 1992:4).

Despite warnings from pundits that more did not necessarily mean better in the matter of the number of kanji in the internal dictionaries, consumer preference was in large part the reason why manufacturers continued to give priority to characters in word processors and software. Had customers not wanted so many characters in the memory banks, the internal dictionaries might have been smaller, but in fact increasing demand led to the incorporation of not only JIS (Japan Industrial Standard) Level One but also eventually Level Two in the memory banks, a total of 6,353 characters. It became common for owners to brag about particularly arcane kanji that their word processors could supply. The content of dictionaries was in no way standardized and manufacturers in fact kept them secret to prevent the competition stealing their competitive edge, so that different machines could contain different characters around the edges of the main body of characters. Intending buyers would test for particularly unusual kanji at point of sale, either from a desire to identify themselves as super-literate persons or merely from a wish to possess a top-of-the-range status symbol and manufacturers exerted themselves to meet the demand.

Social consequences

Given this feature of the technology, i.e. that kanji which once were difficult to produce using a typewriter were now easily called up from the memory banks, it was only natural that changes in the way users wrote and thought about writing soon became evident. Whereas writing by hand was a formalized, private process of committing thought to paper where one began at the beginning and went on to the end and where the actual shape of one's characters on the paper was cause for either pride or shame, word processing allowed a much less structured mode of arriving at a final product where the physical manifestation of handwriting was no longer an issue. Rather than relying on individual characteristics of handwriting, users could experiment with layout and font to invest otherwise bland documents with "personality." To many people, particularly younger users, this freedom quickly came to equate to creativity in a visual sense.

In the literary and social arenas, word processing signaled the beginning of a profound change in the way in which Japanese writers engaged with text production in the intellectual as well as the mechanical sense of the term. Whereas the function of the typewriter is simply to produce clean copy, the word processor can be used at all stages of the writing process, from the rough notes stage through all intermediate stages to the final product. This capacity contributed to the widely-held 1980s view of the word processor not just as a typewriter which could handle characters but as a potential tool for intellectual production.

The affective arguments in the 1980s over the likely social impact of the technology were often quite vehement. Where one person viewed it as a means for enhancing communication, another saw it as converting one aesthetically and "morally" prized means of communication (handwriting) into something impersonal and mechanistic. Many people worried that they would no longer be able to tell a person's character from a piece of text which was not handwritten; in this sense the technology may be said to have negatively affected sociability. On the other hand, both its status as a consumer item and the convenience it afforded led to a documented increase in the amount being written (rather than just a transformation of the means); it therefore opened up lines of communication which the exigencies of writing by hand, in particular the "handwriting complex,"[4] might formerly have seen remain closed, resulting in generally wider interaction. Overall, within Japan, the technology acquired social significance as a reshaper of work and personal habits, a consumer icon, a focus of conservative criticism and a site of controversy in interpersonal interactions.

The social consequences which flowed from its introduction have included: the mass spread of printed documents, previously the province of a specialized class of operator in business, with consequent changes for the work force and for the nature of text in both business and non-business environments; an increase in *minikomi*, or desktop publishing; and a perceived cooling or distancing in certain social relationships when used for personal communications. To a certain extent this last exacerbated the generation gap, creating a cultural divide between accepted forms of social intercourse with the pen on one side and the word processor on the other. The technology has been a liberating force domestically in terms of document production. As well, on the international scene, after a slow start caused by competition and confusion among ministries involved with Japan's national communications policy, it has allowed Japan to construct a Japanese-language presence on the Internet.

In a sense, word processing technology represented an acceptable face of technology in a period where many perceived technological developments as the enemy, resulting in redundancies and uncertainty for the work force. It was an acceptable face because it reinforced cultural norms surrounding script (by coming up with a way to handle kanji electronically) and involved no dirt or danger for the user. Despite affective concerns surrounding script issues and interpersonal relationships, it proved on balance to be an empowering force, enabling at last a degree of freedom in relation to the restrictions imposed by Japan's writing system on the production of printed documents, and having the potential to bring about a change in the national script policy in the next century.

Changes in writing habits

As we have seen, the new technology was accompanied by a chorus of voices predicting disastrous consequences for written Japanese as a result. Not many of these have eventuated, however, and many were (naturally enough) predicated on the technology as it was then. Subsequent development, of course, ironed out many of the early deficiencies. Concerns ranged from the broad to the specific.

In the 1980s, for example, it was frequently argued that the limitations of the inbuilt dictionaries, which might not have contained the latest colloquialisms or offered the user's preferred choice of orthography on their conversion menus, could lead to personal style becoming a casualty of convenience: a kind of de facto "standardization" of writing resulting in uniform orthography and loss of individuality would occur unless users took the time to key in the extra strokes needed to arrive at their preferred version. Arguments of this kind rested on the assumption that users would be so dazzled by convenience (where convenience is defined as the minimum time and effort needed to achieve a result) and by the glamour of the conversion process that the effort of making a few extra keystrokes would assume an importance out of proportion to the extra time thus taken. And in fact the 1980s did see considerable criticism from users of the limited nature of the dictionaries then available, the most frequent requests being for the inclusion of more characters, more colloquialisms and greater choice of orthographic variants to allow people to play with the language as they pleased to the same extent that writing by hand allowed.

One important concern centered on the use of *okurigana*, the kana added to kanji to show inflection in verbs, adverbs and adjectives. Despite the existence of an official government policy designed to standardize usage ('Revised Rules for Using *Okurigana*' 1973), *okurigana* use in

practice varies from person to person, depending on individual preference, and it was feared that compliance with whatever version the internal
dictionaries of word processors first suggested would lead to a loss of that
individuality in writing. If the dictionary were to offer only one alternative,
e.g. only *no-ri-mono* (transport) and not *norimono*,[5] users preferring the
latter could enter their preferred variant by typing in the component parts
separately, but there was a strong tendency to accept what the conversion
key offered rather than take the extra time and trouble (Ogino 1987: 33*)*.
In early word processors, perhaps, when the novelty of the conversion
process dazzled many, when dictionaries did not offer as many choices as
later, and when the 'learning' function which remembers which form is
most likely to be used by a particular writer was not as developed, there
may have been some grounds for fearing such an outcome. As time went
on, however, and users became more experienced, they became adept at
instructing their machines in the kind of orthography they preferred.
During this first decade of widespread use, many writers, e.g. Atsuji
(1991: 224), warned that the word processor was nothing more than
a tool, a new writing implement, which it was now the duty of those
engaged in intellectual production to master without letting the use of
that tool become an end in itself and leach their writing of character. In
other words, the user must take responsibility for the final product of
his or her engagement with the word processor rather than being over-
influenced by the actual process of using the machine.

Apart from anxieties about the general nature of machine-produced
writing, perceptions of changes in the area of kanji usage formed the
most consistent theme of the material which appeared in the 1980s and
early 1990s. Critics complained that too many kanji were now being used
because it was so easy to call them up; that certain very complex older
characters which had been dropped from the official lists because of their
difficulty were once again appearing in print; that mistaken character
choices for homophones would proliferate; and that those who used word
processors would forget how to write characters by hand. It became clear
very early on that there was substance in these concerns. The novelty of
the kana-kanji process *did* lead people just for the fun of it to use kanji
they would otherwise have avoided, or to write words normally written in
hiragana in kanji, and they did call up older, complex kanji for the same
reason. For a time this led to documents appearing unacceptably "black";
the higher-than-usual proportion of kanji, most of which have many more
strokes than kana, looked denser on the page. As we saw earlier, the size
of the dictionary was a selling point for manufacturers, spurred on by
customer demand. Some feared that this heralded a return to the pre-war
situation when there were no lists of recommended characters for general

use. Others (e.g. Kida, Furuse *et al.* 1987: 148) saw it as a temporary phenomenon which would disappear as users became more adept, which was what in fact did prove to be the case. Journalist Tanaka Ryōta (1991: 133–135) recalled that, as a cadet journalist back in 1965, he had been instructed to keep the proportion of kanji in his writing down to around 30%. Journalists used a large number of proper nouns (written in kanji) in their articles and therefore needed to take care not to use too many other characters in the rest of the article; the common consensus was that too many characters made an article harder to read. Later, Tanaka calculated, had he accepted all the kanji the word processor threw up as first choice, the proportion of characters in his recent articles would have risen to between 60 and 70%.

A common example of older, more complex characters revived by word processor use is the word *kirei* (beautiful) 綺麗 where the two characters, with fourteen and nineteen strokes respectively, have been written since the war in kana. The word processor dictionary "reacquainted" people with characters they might otherwise have forgotten or, more likely with this example, never knew in the first place. The only way to avoid the appearance of these characters, which still pop up from time to time, occasioning sarcastic laughter on the part of some readers, is to take steps to see that they are not converted from kana. I had no trouble at all in typing in the characters for *kirei* above, since the Japanese function on my Word 2002 automatically provided them for me to select if I so desired. And of course, for the purposes of this discussion, I did so desire. Otherwise, however, if I were typing a Japanese sentence in which the word *kirei* appeared, I would have signaled "no conversion" by pressing the space bar to accept the hiragana version.

Mistaken character choices for homophones did indeed proliferate, particularly among young people, until users grew more accustomed to the process of character conversion. Somebody would type in a word in hiragana; the word processor dictionary would provide a list of character choices with the same pronunciation as that word but each having a differ-ent meaning. If the user were careless about which button s/he pushed to select the desired alternative, a wrong choice could end up being accepted in the document. To give an example: the word written *kōshō* こうしょう has twenty-eight homophones (Yokoyama 1984: 65). Somebody writing in a hurry and wanting the characters meaning "negotiation" 交渉 would have to be careful not to accidentally push the key selecting those mean-ing "refined" 高尚 or some other homophone. There is a lot of scope for this sort of mistake in Japanese, as statistically, about one third of the words in the dictionary have homophones (Nomura 1986: 69). It is thus not surprising that all word processor users, including myself, have stories to relate about problems in this area; younger users in particular might simply not have known the meanings of all the options. In time, users became more experienced and careful, and artificial information technology became more advanced after 1987 so that word processor dictionaries offered at the top of their list of choices the one most likely to fit the context. The number of homophone errors in documents declined thereafter, though such errors have never quite disappeared.

The deeper fear underlying all the other concerns about changes in kanji use was that people might forget how to write kanji altogether if they stopped writing by hand. Surveys (e.g. Atsuji 1991, Ogino 1994) have found that this does in fact happen and widespread anecdotal evidence backs them up. An article in the *Asahi Shimbun* on 23 September 1985, for example, reported that since the full-scale introduction of word processors on a university campus in Isehara, more and more students were finding it increasingly difficult to write even quite simple characters by hand. There was believed to be a causal relationship at work here, with the kanji skills students had possessed at high school exit level being eroded by their use of the word processors during their university studies. Not everyone agreed with this deduction, though; some argued that the specific kanji errors mentioned in the article were more likely to be the result of generally poor kanji skills among the student body at entrance level (Katō 1985: 33).

Not everyone saw the loss of kanji writing skills as a matter for unalloyed dismay. The small interest groups which advocated the abolition of characters, of course, such as the Kana Club and the Japan Romanization Society, viewed the prospect with equanimity, not to say joy. Others (e.g. Kida, Furuse *et al.* 1987; Ogino 1987) without such a specific aim in mind argued that the use of word processing, even if it did result in people forgetting how to write characters to some extent, would free up time now spent on character drills for learning other language skills such as expressive writing, even from the early primary school stage. Since it is the writer who does the thinking and not the machine, however, it seems difficult to sustain the argument that the simple act of using a word processor, which – like a pen – is no more than a conduit, would necessarily help composition ability. It must also not be forgotten, when considering the argument above, that writing on a word processor might substitute for kanji instruction, that the actual process of learning to write through extended practice plays an important role in fixing characters in memory so that they can later be recognized. And it is important that they can be recognized, because if a word processor user cannot distinguish between the alternatives offered by the kana-kanji conversion process, mistakes will, as we have seen, occur very easily.

An automotive metaphor put forward in the literature debating the impact of the new technology in the 1980s encapsulates the kanji skills issue very neatly. A car is a product of technology which undergoes constant improvement and which enables easy and rapid movement of people and materials. In just the same fashion, using a word processor lets people write quickly, which in turn circulates information more quickly. On the other hand, the invention of the car led to an increase in traffic accidents. Likewise, the invention of the word processor has brought with it the risk of an increase in poorly written documents. Using cars means that our legs are not as strong as they once were; using a word processor might reduce the ability to reproduce or remember difficult characters. Nevertheless, the continuing invention of machines and human dependence on them is part of the march of progress, and should not be denied (Fujisaki 1984: 115). The invention of calculators brought fears of a decline in arithmetical skills which to some extent were realized, but the counter argument is that machines can now do mechanical work which people no longer need to do for themselves.

Implications for language policy

People began to think differently about how they used kanji once this technology became available and its possibilities became clear. Not surprisingly, therefore, some began to consider whether a revised approach to script policy and character education might be appropriate, given that current script policy is premised on the fact that characters are handwritten. The argument ran like this: characters can easily be called up on a word processor without imposing a memory burden on their user. More characters than formerly are being used in word-processed documents. Would it not make sense, therefore, to change the policy so that a greater number are taught for recognition only and a reduced number for reproduction, rather than placing equal emphasis on both skills? Osaka academic Kabashima Tadao, for example, argued that Japan's large character set with its many complex forms was more suited to production by machine than by human beings (Kabashima 1988: 25). Many others agreed with him. The consensus appeared to be that the List of Characters for General Use should be expanded from its present 1,945 characters to around 3,000 characters, with the majority to be taught for recognition only and a small number taught for reproduction. A typist who knows the pronunciation of the characters can input that pronunciation in kana or rōmaji; the conversion process takes care of the output, as long as the typist is able to distinguish between homophones. Reading comprehension is assured so long as the reader can recognize the characters. People do not need to learn to write all the characters by hand.

Some of the pillars which had supported postwar script policy, such as newspaper requirements, office automation difficulties and the predication upon a culture of handwriting, have certainly been made redundant by word processing technology and the JIS standard characters contained in the memory banks. The newspapers voluntarily adopted the character limits in the main, despite being private businesses not bound by the government declaration, in order to make savings in time and labor. Advances in computerized typesetting since then, however, have done away with the problem of movable type and with it the need to stick to a reduced character set.

The National Language Council was not eager to rush into any precipitate reconsideration of script policy, given the years it had taken to arrive at today's character list. It did, however, recognize the issues and called in the 1990s for large-scale surveys to be carried out to estimate what the impact of the new technology was likely to be. Much of its work during that decade, however, focused on standardizing the variant shapes found in word processor memories and not on the implications for script policy. In 2000, the Council released *Hyōgai Kanji Jitaihyō* (Proposal for Character Shapes outside the List of Characters for General Use), in an attempt to establish a standard for variant shapes used for characters not already covered by the official list and to bring a measure of uniformity to the character-shapes issue. In 2001, the Council was abolished during a period of restructuring of advisory councils and language matters are now dealt with by the language section of the Culture Advisory Committee within the Agency for Cultural Affairs. It is therefore unlikely that any putative change to current script policy will occur for some time.

Japan and the Internet

We have seen that the capacity to handle characters electronically led to an Internet presence for Japan. The trajectory of Internet access went like this: first, in 1984, the Japan University/Unix NETwork (JUNET), a research network linking Keio University, the Tokyo Institute of Technology and the University of Tokyo, was launched. In 1988, a project in which the private sector also participated, known as WIDE (Widely Integrated Distributed Environment), set out to develop network technology. Private and commercial use began some time later, in 1993. That was the same year that the development of the versatile and user-friendly MOSAIC graphic-interface WWW browser appeared in the USA, leading to a surge in Internet use outside Japan.

In Japan itself, Internet take-up was relatively slow at first. This was due in part to conflict between MITI and the Ministry for Posts and Telecommunications[6] over policy; the comparatively high cost of land-line phone calls in Japan; and the slower diffusion rate of personal computers, due perhaps in part to the preference until 1992 for the use of stand-alone word processors. Once PCs were more readily available, though, statistics show that the number of Japanese Internet users grew rapidly, as shown by the growth in the household penetration rate during the late 1990s. By the end of fiscal 1998, it was 11%; by March 1999 it had risen to 13.4%. It had taken only five years after the Internet became commercially available in 1993 to attain a household penetration rate of 10%, compared to thirteen years for the PC, fifteen years for the mobile phone, nineteen years for the fax machine and seventeen years for the telephone (Ministry of Posts and Telecommunications 1999). Even allowing for the fact that the social, political and cultural environment of the late 1990s was very different from that of some of those earlier technologies, in particular the telephone, this is a remarkable statistic. By the end of 2002 the Internet penetration rate was 54.5%, i.e. one in every two Japanese used the Internet (Ministry of Public Management, Home Affairs, Posts and Telecommunications Japan 2003).

While the rapidity of the Internet penetration rate has been remarkable, that is not to say that the actual PC penetration rate for Japan is high. It remains lower than for some other developed countries. This has no bearing on Internet access, though, because Japan has led the world in the use of mobile phones to access Internet sites using wireless technology. I-mode service providers, chief among them NTT's Do-Co-Mo which had grown to be Japan's leading Internet Service Provider (ISP) in terms of number of contracts only a year after the 1999 launch of the i-mode technology (Ministry of Posts and Telecommunications 2001), allow users to access the Internet through a wide range of text-based information sites accessible only by mobile phones. It is also possible to convert standard PC websites to i-mode reception in some cases, as was done by Rikkyo University in Tokyo when it established its student communication site in 2001. At the end of 2002, more than 80% of all phone subscribers were subscribers to the mobile Internet, the highest rate of any country (Ministry of Public Management, Home Affairs, Posts and Telecommunications Japan 2003).[7]

The rapidity with which the Japanese language established an online presence despite a comparatively late start may best be illustrated by the fact that the Ministry of Posts and Telecommunications reported in September 1998 that the number of web pages in Japan had risen from 10 million to 18 million over a seven-month period and that working from the assumption that each page contained 2,000 characters, this meant that the number of characters online exceeded the total number published in Japanese newspapers and magazines for that year (Japan

Online Language Population
Total: 680 Million
(Sept. 2003)

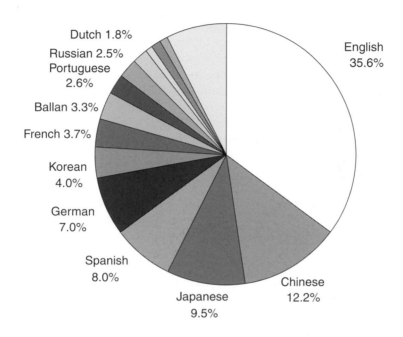

Source: Global Internet Statistics by Language,
www.glreach.com/globstats/index.php3, accessed 7 March 2004.

Figure 7.1 Online language populations September 2003

MarkeTracker 1998). Thanks to *keitai* (mobile phone) Internet access, the domain of on-screen Japanese now also includes the tiny *keitai* screen as well as desktop and laptop computers and other devices. Also in 1998, Japanese became the second most widely used language after English on the Internet, a position which it held until Chinese overtook it at 9% in March 2001. While the relative percentages for Japanese and Chinese were only marginally differentiated for some time after that, by October 2003 Chinese had increased its lead to 12.2%, with Japanese coming in at 9.5%. Japanese nevertheless remains well ahead of Spanish, which despite its greater number of speakers currently accounts for 8% (Global

Internet Statistics by Language 2003). Japanese-language pages are not often accessed by non-Japanese, however; other than scholars, students of the language and those few professionals able to read them, most Japanese-language pages on the web are accessed by Japanese.

Given that the Internet is often hailed as a globalizing technology and a forum for discussion among people who would never otherwise meet or even know of the others' existence, does use of the Japanese language online function to subvert this to some extent by virtue of the fact that it is not yet a world language? Castells (2000) has argued that it is the contradiction between local identities and global networks that more than anything else shapes international media and communication today. In the case of Japanese on the Internet it is the local linguistic identity which wins out in Japan's interactions with this technology. For very widely used languages such as French, Arabic, Spanish, Chinese and English, online communication between people of different races or ethnic groups living on different continents is enabled because of the historical specificities, usually colonization, which have led to their using those languages. This is not the case with Japanese, despite the increase in the number of overseas learners during the last twenty years. English is not an official language in Japan,[8] but most official web pages have both Japanese and English versions, with the former of course carrying much more information than the latter. Minority groups such as the Burakumin community who wish to garner international recognition of and support for their activism use English strategically on web pages for this purpose (see Gottlieb 2003), as do organizations with international affiliations. Japanese is therefore one case among many where a borderless technology is nonetheless restrained within national boundaries by linguistic usage – unless, of course, the user chooses to communicate in English or some other language.

As we have seen in this chapter, technological advances affecting language use have had a strong impact on users' perceptions of identity. From avant-garde word processor user to techno-literate Internet user, with perhaps the latest mobile phone with its online capabilities, electronic Japanese has changed the image of writing and writers in a way unimaginable fifty years ago. Identity is always multi-faceted and in a state of constant fluidity and technology of this sort adapts itself well to such conditions. The rapidity of the changes already experienced in the interface between technology and the Japanese language indicate that a symbiotic relationship is likely to exist between technology and linguistic identity far into the foreseeable future.

8   Conclusion

In the chapters of this book, we have seen the many levels on which language in Japan functions today and has functioned in the past: to include and to exclude, to confirm national identity and to impose it on others, to encapsulate both prewar and postwar ideas of what it is to be Japanese, and to mediate a personal identity in a multitude of different ways. The widespread belief that only one language is spoken in Japan is confounded by the diversity of other languages used within the borders of the archipelago, a diversity long ignored, denied or unrealized.

We are now beginning to see a delayed but nevertheless deeply encouraging recognition that Japan has become a multicultural society through both the specifics of its history and the effects of globalization. The presence of the established ethnic communities, the indigenous Ainu people, the many overseas students, scholars and business people and the large numbers of illegal immigrants working in the areas where Japanese themselves are not keen to work points to a rich and colorful linguistic fabric.

The question now arises, where to from here? The diverse sections of the community referred to above have special language needs which need to be addressed: the education of the children of migrants, both legal and illegal, for example, and the provision of Japanese language classes for their parents. The Ministry of Foreign Affairs in early 2004 ran a conference to address the educational needs of the children of returnees from Brazil, for instance. We can expect to see this sort of activity increase rapidly in the future as the proportion of non-Japanese-speaking children in Japanese classrooms also increases. A major internal task for Japan, then, is to service the linguistic needs of its constituent communities properly.

On the external scene, the big issue is whether or not Japanese has the potential to become an international language at some time in the future. We have seen that this question has exercised the minds of politicians and intellectuals for some time and that money was even allocated with this in mind to develop the ill-fated and much criticized *Kan'yaku Nihongo* project when Japan's economic power was at its height. The argument was, quite reasonably, that the languages of other, earlier empires had attained world language status through the economic activities of their metropolitan powers; why, then, should the language of Japan, whose economic status was indubitably that of a superpower, not follow the same trajectory, in particular with regard to becoming an official language of the United Nations? Ought not the increasing influence of globalization on many aspects of life in Japan also extend to its language?

Before we look further into this issue, we should pause to consider what the terms "globalization" or "internationalization" mean in relation to language. When these expressions are used, people usually have one of two particular meanings in mind. One is the increasing influx of foreign loanwords into particular languages, which is often held up as a highly visible proof of an increasing internationalization of languages, at least at lexical level. We saw in Chapter One that in Japan, concern with the apparently endless influx of loanwords from other languages into Japanese recently translated into the formation of a panel at the National Institute for Japanese Language at the Prime Minister's request in order to provide some suggestions on stemming the flow. The second is the belief that "globalization of language" means that a single language, which in today's world – though not necessarily tomorrow's – is English, dominates linguistic interactions in business, education and many other fields as a lingua franca through which speakers of other languages can find common ground for communication. Proponents of this view, which is supported by many governments including some in East and South East Asia, argue that English-language skills are an essential part of a twenty-first century citizen's education and are pouring significant amounts of money into ensuring that English is taught well in their countries alongside the national language(s).

Since the 1999 session of its General Conference, UNESCO has advocated a policy of trilingualism, recommending that its 181 member states promote linguistic pluralism such that "when pupils leave school they have a working knowledge of three languages" – their own language, the language of a neighboring country and an international language such as English – "which should represent the normal range of practical linguistic skills in the twenty-first century" (UNESCO 1999). The concept of international languages is therefore well entrenched, not in the sense of an artificially-constructed attempt at a solution such as Esperanto but in the sense that certain languages, for reasons rooted in history, have achieved the status of languages of wider communication on the international stage and may be considered dominant in these terms today.

Such a view (perceiving, e.g. English as dominant), of course, underlines the importance of intercultural communication skills: two non-native speakers of English whose own languages are, say, French and Japanese, may be achieving surface communication in English, but they are speaking from two different cultural frames of reference which are at odds with that of the language in which they are speaking and which may influence the intended outcome of the communication event. Intercultural communication is thus likely to become increasingly important as a discipline in the future if the dominance of international languages continues, and there is no reason to suppose that it will not (although it may not always be English which leads). If Japanese were to become an international language, the demand for intercultural communication training which we see in Japan today with reference to English would be mirrored in other countries with reference to Japanese.

Graddol (2000: 59) considers the issue of what makes a language a world language today. It is clearly not the number of its speakers alone; nor is it the military power of its users, as suggested by Crystal (1997: 7). The model Graddol discusses "weights languages not only by the number and wealth of their speakers, but also by the likelihood that these speakers will enter social networks which extend beyond their locality: they are the people with the wherewithal and ambition to 'go about' in the world, influence it and to have others seek to influence them." He speculates that, on the basis of projections generated by this model, Spanish will rise quickly but the nearest rivals to English in the table – German, French and Japanese – will grow much more slowly. Japanese ranks fourth on his table of global influence of major languages with a score of thirty-two, where 100 represents the position held by English in 1995.

What would be needed to take Japanese out of its local sphere of influence and make it a global language? The following are a few possible scenarios.

The United Nations route

Japan has been trying for some time to have its language accepted as a UN official language along with English, French, Spanish, Chinese, Russian and Arabic. In the late 1980s the question of whether this should happen, in view of the size of the Japanese financial contribution to that body, was raised but not resolved. The item was still on the agenda of the National Language Council at the time of its 1995 report, which listed the promotion of Japanese as a language to be used at international meetings and conferences as an important means of reflecting Japan's standing in the world and again flagged the issue of whether Japanese should be adopted as an official language of the UN (Kokugo Shingikai 1995:449–450).

The best-known advocate of this proposal is linguist Suzuki Takao, who addressed the question in his 1995 book *Nihongo wa Kokusaigo ni nariuru ka (Can Japanese become an International Language?)*, his main thrust being that Japanese should be promoted as a world language for intellectual exchange and that the push to make it an official language of the UN had been ignored (20). Various arguments advanced in favor of the proposal in a short survey of Internet references to the issue are: that this would mean an advantage for Japanese nationals in acquiring positions in the UN in numbers more consonant with Japan's contributions to that body (Shu n.d.); that if Japanese were made an official language all treaties would automatically be produced in Japanese as well (Kokugo Shingikai 1999); and that unless this happened Japanese would never become an international language (Noyama 1998). The implication of this last point, that Japanese would become an international language simply by being made a UN language, is debatable. The official languages of the UN were chosen because they were *already* international languages, used widely outside the borders of their country of origin. To say that adding Japanese to their number purely in recognition of Japan's contributions would automatically confer upon it the status of an international language imputes an importance to the association with the UN that would not be borne out in reality.

Increasing the number of official UN languages is no easy task. Others feel they have equal claims (India, for example, wants Hindi adopted), and Esperanto advocates still point in vain to the cost of UN interpreting into those languages which, they argue, the use of Esperanto as a common language could avert. I quote an Esperanto-advocacy website on this point:

The cost for translation and interpretation into the six official languages of the General Assembly (Arabic, Chinese, English, French, Russian, Spanish) already represents around a fifth of the budget of the United Nations. Given the experience of the European Union and its institutions, where those costs reach up to two fifths of the total budget, one can imagine how the costs for the United Nations would further increase if other languages were adopted, as some might have the right on the basis of the number of people, or countries, using them (for instance Hindi, German, Indonesian, Italian, Japanese, Portuguese) . . . Adopting an international language like Esperanto by the United Nations - initially complementary to the six official languages and gradually expanding its use until all documents are stored in Esperanto and only certain documents are translated into other languages -, would require a modest up-front investment compared with subsequent enormous cost savings, and would mean growth in efficiency and, above all, equality as the major outcome. (Transnational Radical Party and Esperanto International Federation n.d.)

When Arabic was added as the sixth official language in 1973, it was because of its numerical (spoken by 220 million people), political (official language of twenty countries), cultural and religious significance. The number of native speakers of Japanese in 2000 was given in the Ethnologue top twenty list as 125 million. Japanese, of course, is profoundly significant in economic and cultural terms, if not in political (being restricted mainly to Japan itself). If UN official languages are chosen because they are the most widely spoken, however, that puts Japan into a chicken and egg situation, as we saw above: Japanese *may* become more widely spoken, perhaps, as a consequence of being chosen as one of the official languages, but cannot be chosen because it is not already widely spoken. This leads us now to the second scenario, a much greater increase in the overseas study of Japanese.

Greater uptake outside Japan

David Crystal's 1987 *Cambridge Encyclopedia of Language* listed Japanese in ninth place in a list of the top twenty languages, with the number of mother-tongue speakers, the official language population figure and the estimated number of speakers worldwide all coming in at 120 million, the then population of Japan (Crystal 1987: 287). Since then, as we have seen, the number of non-native speakers has increased due to the activities of the Japan Foundation and of governments which since the 1980s have devoted policy activity and funding to increasing the number of people learning Japanese in other countries. The number of overseas learners of Japanese worldwide more than doubled between 1988 and 1993, and by 1998 had reached approximately two million.

We saw in Chapter One that Weber (1997) lists the number of secondary speakers of Japanese (defined as those who use the language regularly or primarily even though it is not their native language) as eight million. Even adding to that the two million students identified by the Japan Foundation survey only brings the total of secondary speakers to 10 million, compared to 190 million secondary speakers of French, 150 million secondary speakers of English and 125 million secondary speakers of Russian. On the list of languages ranked in terms of the number of countries where each is spoken, Japanese comes in at number 11, with only one country listed, compared to English (115), French (35), Arabic (24), Spanish (20) and Russian (16).

Combining his various lists, Weber lists Japanese eighth in a list of the world's most influential languages, based on the following six criteria: number of primary speakers; number of secondary speakers; number and population of countries where used; number of major fields using the language internationally; economic power of countries using the languages; and socio-literary prestige. The total number of points Japanese scored across these categories was 10, compared with English (37), French (23), Spanish (20) and so on. Economic power in this equation was apparently not enough to lift its rating. Clearly, on these quantitative measures alone, Japanese does not yet fulfill the criteria for an influential international language and will not until the number of speakers around the world increases.

A change of thinking about Japanese by Japanese

Greater proactivity from Japan itself is needed in thinking of Japanese in international terms rather than in the previously prevailing Nihonjinron terms of the language as belonging to Japanese alone and being too difficult for non-Japanese to master. Significant steps have already been made in this direction, of course, through the activities of the Japan Foundation, and a few official-sounding reports have also raised the issue. A 2000 report from the then National Language Council, *Kokusai Shakai ni okeru Nihongo no Arikata*, for example, suggested several strategies for the internationalization of Japanese, which it defined as both having the use of Japanese spread by achieving recognition of the value of Japanese language to more people around the world and also having the way that Japanese is used become more suited to international communication. The strategies suggested, couched in very general terms in the manner of policy documents, were:

a. promoting knowledge *about* Japan and the Japanese language and also knowledge *through* the medium of Japanese.
b. Providing very finely tuned support for learning of Japanese in line with the diversity of learners' needs.
c. Clarifying what needs to be done to make Japanese an instrument suited to international communication and thereby extending the ability of the Japanese themselves.

Structural changes in the world resulting from globalization, the report asserted, are bringing about changes in the relationships between languages and the roles each language plays. Although movements for the protection of national and minority languages are widespread, English is currently dominant, both as a language of wider communication and on the Internet. The report called in high-flown terms for positive steps to promote the use of Japanese overseas to counter this, as well as fostering proper language use at home.

So far so good, although immediately after that the National Language Council was dissolved and the body charged with oversight of language policy issues was downgraded to a subsection of an overarching Culture Advisory Committee. What is really needed, however, is a different mind-set in relation to the requirements of global use of language rather than local. We saw in Chapter One that the Director of the Japan Foundation's Urawa Language Institute, Katō Hidetoshi, suggests that the total number of people able to speak Japanese as a foreign language worldwide is likely to be around ten million, and that he argues that native speakers of Japanese should begin to acknowledge the fact that the language is used by non-Japanese and be tolerant of imperfections in the interests of communication.

Katō is right. It is communication that takes precedence when a language takes on greater international prominence, not slavish adherence to prescribed norms which not even native speakers, diverse as they are, observe. Lo Bianco, discussing globalization as a frame word for discourses on human capital and other issues, makes the point that one approach to globalization theory sees nationality as something transient which will inevitably be overwhelmed by globalization. This view "assumes that although under the pressures of globalization multilingualism may remain, language is essentially about communication (not solidarity). In other words, most languages will fade away, minority languages in particular will pass away, and people will be linked by common economic interests. Languages are, by this approach, essentially distractions, remnants of past times when wider communication systems were not possible" (Lo Bianco 1999: 10–11). He then goes on to present alternative views under which nations are seen as "useful, necessary and mostly benign" and national languages provide a sense of identity and belonging. The interesting point about the first approach, however, is that it views language as being for communication rather than national solidarity and implies a future wherein only a few languages remain as vehicles of intercultural and international communication. In the case of Japanese, while national solidarity (however that is defined in the face of incontestable diversity) will of course remain important to a large extent, it cannot take precedence over communication in the international context.

The romanization scenario

Should Japan adopt the roman alphabet instead of its present character-based writing system in order to become an international language? Romanization advocates have been arguing for this outcome since the Meiji Period on a variety of platforms ranging from educational convenience to technological imperatives. The latter, as we saw in Chapter Seven, were routed by the invention of character-capable input technology which enabled Japanese-language word processing of documents and, eventually, Internet pages. The success of this invention did not, however, put an end to arguments by Japanese scholars such as Yamada Hisao and western scholars such as J. Marshall Unger and William Hannas that before Japanese could become a successful global player online it would need to abandon characters in favor of the alphabet. Yamada (1994) consistently argued that the use of characters prevents completely satisfactory communication between computers at international level, despite the adoption of the Unicode and other systems; Japan ought therefore to bow to international convention and adopt romanization in this era of increasingly globalized electronic communication. Hannas (1997) posits that the performance gap in terms of speed, applications, storage, retrieval and input between computers using alphanumeric systems and those using characters is such that it is only a matter of time before East Asian language users rebel and adopt the alphabet.

To a certain extent their arguments have weight: it *is* undeniably faster for an experienced user to type in the alphabet than it is to input Japanese, in a variety of ways. What would be lost by switching to the alphabet, however, is probably much greater than what would be gained. Hannas' argument does not take into consideration the infrastructure considerations of a move towards romanization in a highly industrialized and, as we have seen, highly literate society such as Japan. The implications for education and the publishing industries in particular are such that I do not think this will happen, especially when combined with the likely affective or emotional resistance to such a change.

The influence of kanji on international perceptions of Japanese is not negligible, however. Katō argues that having to learn 2–3,000 kanji contributes to the perception of Japanese as too difficult, puts people off studying it and indeed may actually be used as an argument against studying Japanese by student advisors. Many people with an interest in studying Japanese are therefore discouraged from doing so, or fall by the wayside if they start. We saw in Chapter Seven that the development of word processing capability has contributed to a recent increase in the numbers of kanji seen in use. Katō accuses the developers of the kana-kanji conversion facility of a grave cultural crime against the way Japanese ought to be – even his voice recognition software, let alone his keyboard conversion software, throws up an unacceptably large number of kanji (Katō 2000: 22–25). While he does not, of course, argue for the abolition of kanji, he does see their proliferation as a major factor impeding the use of Japanese as a global language. Alfonso (1989: 76) also predicts that were Japanese to become an international language there would be increasing pressure for a simplification of the writing system.

The above scenarios are all meditations upon what might be necessary to make Japanese an international language. Supposing that *were* to happen, what would be some of the consequences? Student numbers would soar as more and more people tuned in to the benefits of studying Japan and its culture and as Japanese itself began to function more as a lingua franca alongside English both in the region and the rest of the world. Native speakers of Japanese would experience a boost to national pride and prestige; increased confidence in being able to make themselves understood during travel and study abroad; and probably a falling off in the urgency of English-language education. Japan would no longer have to refer apologetically to the poor language skills of its people. Trade negotiations could no longer use language barriers to obscure or explain difficulties. The influence of Japan's pop culture icons would spread even further than it already has. And Japanese-language pages on the Internet would no longer be accessed by Japanese people alone, although the present tension in cyberspace between a global network and local online identities would never fade entirely, even if it blurred a little. In every case, the identity of the speaker or the learner would be enhanced in some intangible but important way.

We have seen in this book the multiple and fluid identities language in Japan has been used to confer upon its users throughout the modern period, and the multiple and constantly shifting identities people proactively use language to construct for themselves. Future developments in this area of language and identity are bound to emerge as multiculturalism and technology continue to evolve. One thing we can be sure of, however, is that a major proactive mindset shift will be needed to deal with changing conceptions of how language should function in Japanese society and, in the case of the Japanese language, outside the borders of Japan for the remainder of this century. It is heartening to see evidence of this sort of thinking already emerging.

Notes

1 THE JAPANESE LANGUAGE

1. Nationality, ethnicity, language competence (in Japanese), birthplace, current residence, subjective identity and level of cultural literacy.
2. Theories on being Japanese. Nihonjinron have been one of the conspicuous features of Japanese intellectual production since the 1960s, presenting an officially promoted and now widely contested ideology of a harmonious and uniform society, a view which the Japanese language itself is used to sustain. This view emphasizes the uniqueness and separateness of Japanese society and presents Japan as a homogeneous whole untroubled by dissent, notwithstanding all evidence to the contrary. In recent years a growing body of scholarship disputing this view has been published both inside and outside Japan (e.g. Morris-Suzuki 1998; Sugimoto 2003 and 1989; Weiner 1997; Hicks 1997).
3. A body set up in 1972 within the Ministry of Foreign Affairs to promote knowledge of Japanese culture, including the study of Japanese language, abroad.
4. When the feudal system was abolished in 1871, the domains went with it. Today Japan is divided into forty-seven prefectures. For a map and list, see Sugimoto (2003).
5. http://nihongo.human.metro-u.ac.jp/long/maps/perceptmaps.htm, accessed 3 March 2004.
6. The word used to designate the Japanese language as used by Japanese.
7. Renamed the Ministry of Education, Culture, Sports, Science and Technology in 2001.
8. The three reports may be found on the website of the NIJL at www.kokken. go.jp.
9. A 1998 survey by the National Institute for Japanese Language on international views of Japanese (*Nihongo-kan no Kokusai Sensasu*) spanning twenty-eight countries had identified Japanese as the third most important language in the world after English and French, in answer to a question on which languages respondents considered would become necessary for world communication in the future. In Australia, Japanese came in second after English; in another six countries, including the United States and China, it ranked third (Kokugo Shingikai 2000); in England, Russia and five other countries, it ranked fifth (Imidas 2002: 1085).

146

10. The issue of the native-speaker myth has been widely debated in applied linguistics.

2   LANGUAGE DIVERSITY IN JAPAN

1. That is, officially registered as Ainu. As DeChicchis (1995: 106) notes, however, the denial ratio of those who will not admit to being Ainu or of Ainu descent is difficult to determine, so that the figure when such people are taken into account is likely to be much higher.
2. Lectures on the Ainu language were given there by Jinbo Kotora, who also collaborated to produce an Ainu conversation dictionary in 1898 (Siddle 1996: 83).
3. As of 1 April 2004; formerly called the Department of Asian and Pacific Linguistics.
4. See http://www.tooyoo.l.u-tokyo.ac.jp/ichel/ichel.html.
5. See   http://jinbunweb.sgu.ac.jp/~ainu/biblio/european.html#section1   and http://jinbunweb.sgu.ac.jp/~ainu/biblio/japanese.html.
6. See http://www.hku.hk/rss/res_proj/21/21.htm for a description of past and planned projects.
7. http://www.frpac.or.jp/
8. A Google search for the term "Okinawan language" on 19 February 2004, for example, showed it as categorized under "Japanese dialects."
9. As the islands to the south of Japan, of which Okinawa is the largest, were collectively known owing to the earlier Ryukyuan kingdom which had existed there between 1429 and 1609.
10. Naha is the capital of Okinawa.
11. E.g. Eric's Okinawan Language Lessons at http://nvokinawa.net/facesvoices/hougen/
12. http://www.okinawan-shorinryu.com/okinawa/uchina.html.
13. Although they could and did apply to private and prefectural/municipal universities (Fukuoka 2000:26).
14. See Okano and Tsuchiya 1999 for details.
15. See, for example, http://www.themodelminority.com/ for a discussion of this. Another useful website, http://racerelations.about.com/library/weekly/blmodelminority.htm, reports that the term "model minority" was coined by an American journalist in a 1994 article for *The New York Times Magazine*. "The phrase has been used as a catch-all to describe Asian Americans as a hard-working, well-educated, successful minority race."
16. Test of English as a Foreign Language, a test compiled and administered by the US Educational Testing Service and used by institutions worldwide as an indicator of English proficiency.
17. This program is run jointly by the Ministry of Foreign Affairs, the Ministry of Education, Culture, Sports, Science and Technology and the Council of Local Authorities for International Relations, in collaboration with local authorities.
18. Archived in a database at the National Institute for Education Policy Research (http://www.nier.go.jp/homepage/kyoutsuu/index.html). I am deeply

indebted to my research assistant, Dr. Akemi Dobson, for her perusal and categorization of this large mass of documents.

3 LANGUAGE AND NATIONAL IDENTITY: EVOLVING VIEWS

1. For information on the varying forms of education available, see Mehl 2003, Passin 1982 and Rubinger 1982.
2. Subject-verb-predicate in Chinese as opposed to subject-predicate-verb in Japanese.
3. Words which form the end of one sentence or phrase and the beginning of another, usually with a different meaning.
4. Samurai, farmer, artisan, merchant, in descending order, with hereditary outcasts and other similarly ostracized not appearing on the scale.
5. E.g., the word for "butterfly," now pronounced *chōchō*, was still written *tefutefu* and the sound *hō* was written with the symbols *ha* and *fu*.
6. Members of the Kana Club advocated replacing kanji with kana, while members of the Rōmaji Club wanted the Roman alphabet for Japan's script (see Twine 1991a, Chapter Nine).
7. As it was then known. It has since changed its name to the National Institute for Japanese Language.

4 LANGUAGE AND IDENTITY: THE POLICY APPROACH

1. It was replaced in 2001 by today's Japanese language section of the National Culture Council.
2. E.g., physicist Tanakadate Aikitsu (1856–1952), supporter of romanization since the days of the Meiji Period Rōmaji Club and later president of the Japan Romanization Society, who in 1946 presented a petition entitled "Make Rōmaji Our Script!" to the National Language Council.
3. Distinctions between sounds which no longer existed in the modern language were eradicated, e.g. *wi* was written as it was now pronounced, *i*, but the symbols for *ha, he* and *wo* continued to be used for the particles pronounced *wa, e* and *o*, for instance.
4. Most of these policies may be found online at www.bunka.go.jp.

5 WRITING AND READING IN JAPAN

1. The *kun* reading is the pronunciation in Japanese, the *on* reading represents an earlier Japanese attempt to approximate the pronunciation of the character in Chinese. The character 人 (person), for example, has a *kun* reading of ひと (hito), and at least two *on* readings, じん (jin) when it is used after the name of a country and にん (nin) when it is used after a numeral.
2. Japanese children start school in the April following their sixth birthday.
3. Archived at http://nierdb.nier.go.jp. I am indebted to my research assistant, Dr. Akemi Dobson, for her excellent work in finding and synthesizing information from these documents.
4. Students formerly attended school on Saturday mornings as well as week days. This was phased out over a period extending from the mid 1990s to 2002.

5. As had an earlier international comparative study (Stevenson *et al.*, 1982).
6. See www.npo-edge.jp
7. *Furigana* is the name given to tiny kana used beside kanji (in vertical writing) or above them (in horizontal writing) to indicate the pronunciation of the characters.
8. Sales flattened out after 1997, however, as new computer-centered pursuits emerged.
9. The first printing of the Japanese translation of *Harry Potter and the Goblet of Fire* sold 2.3 million copies in 2002 (Kiyota 2003).
10. See http://www.gov-online.go.jp/publicity/tsushin/200304/pdf/qa.pdf, accessed 25 February 2004.
11. The laws may be found on the website of the Japan School Libraries Association at www.j-sla.or.jp/shiryo/s4.html, accessed 25 February 2004.
12. See home page at http://www.mext.go.jp/a_menu/sports/dokusyo/index.htm, accessed 25 February 2004.
13. Libraries of small pocket-sized paperbacks.
14. The perception of a drop-off in listening ability is a little puzzling: when asked what would be the optimal outcome in this category, nearly 60% of respondents replied "to understand what the person they were talking to was saying," but no further details were given as to why that was not happening now.

6 REPRESENTATION AND IDENTITY: DISCRIMINATORY LANGUAGE

1. A term in which the characters mean "great filth" (or as Sugimoto 2003: 189 terms it, "amply polluted" or "highly contaminated"), referring to the kinds of occupation traditionally undertaken by the Burakumin. Neary (1989:11) likens the use of this term to that of "nigger" in the USA.
2. A common argument in Japan, as we have seen, was that Burakumin were originally not Japanese at all but Korean.
3. Excerpts from those of the Mainichi and Yomiuri newspapers and some regional newspapers may be found in Yōgo to Sabetsu o kangaeru Shinpojiumu Jikkō Iinkai (1989).
4. The summarized arguments in this paragraph are based on a document found on a website which is no longer active, that of Professor Asaho Mizushima's seminar at the Waseda University Law School.
5. Meaning "fellows, friends."
6. A ceremony in which the soul of a bear is returned to the gods.
7. *Kankokujin* refers to South Korea, *Chōsenjin* to North Korea.
8. Online at http://home.att.ne.jp/wood/micci/WandC/TABOO.htm, accessed 1 March 2004.
9. At http://www.jekai.org/entries/aa/00/np/aa00np30.htm, accessed 1 March 2004.
10. At http://www.han.org/a/identity/adm2_lee_impeach.html, accessed 1 March 2004.
11. Used after World War Two to insult Koreans and Chinese from Japan's two former colonies who were forced to give up their Japanese citizenship and who

were often stigmatized as criminals, much in the way Ishihara has resurrected the term to imply (or state outright) that crime in Japan is often committed by *sangokujin*.

12. See, for example, http://www.geocities.co.jp/CollegeLife-Labo/8108/ishihara-e.htm, accessed 1 March 2004.

13. "The Japan Committee of the International Movement Against All Forms of Discrimination and Racism (IMADR-JC) is a national chapter set up in Japan in 1990 to promote collaboration with people working for the rights of Burakumin, Ainu, non-Japanese residents, people with disabilities and women. IMADR is an international organization devoted to the elimination of all forms of discrimination around the world. It is in the consultative status with the Economic and Social Council of the United Nations (ECOSOC)" (excerpted from the IMADR-JC letter of complaint found at the website given in the text above).

14. See http://blhrri.org/blhrri_e/news/new113/new11301.html, accessed 1 March 2004.

15. http://www.issho.org/

16. http://www.debito.org/

7   SHIFTING ELECTRONIC IDENTITIES

1. Ministry of International Trade and Industry, as it was then known. In 2001, following a reorganization of Ministries, its name was changed to the present Ministry of Economy, Trade and Industry (METI).

2. As distinct from word-processing software used on personal computers, which did not come until the early 1990s. Stand-alone word processors for personal use were slightly larger than today's laptop, and portable; they could be carried around in shoulder bags as are laptops today. Like the laptop, they incorporated a screen, processor and keyboard. Unlike laptops, however, they also incorporated their own printer.

3. Each year showed an exponential increase over the preceding one: the full set of figures for the intervening years is 88,986 (1983), 201,231 (1984) and 988,804 (1985).

4. Mentioned by many Japanese as inhibiting the frequency with which they write because of shame over poor handwriting.

5. The bold print indicates which elements of the word would be written in kanji.

6. This ministry in 2001 became part of the Ministry of Public Management, Home Affairs, Posts and Telecommunications.

7. For information on aspects of how mobile phones are used in relation to the Internet, see Holden (2003) and McVeigh (2003) in Gottlieb and McLelland (2003).

8. Although as we saw earlier, a 2000 position paper suggested that in time it might become the official second language.

References

Adachi, N. 2002. "Negotiation of speech style in Japanese women's language: vantage theory as cognitive sociolinguistics," *Language Sciences* 24 (5–6): 575–590.

Adachi, S. 2001. *The Growing Trend of Reading Movements in Japan: Animación a la Lectura, Ten-Minutes Reading in the Morning, and Reading Aloud by Parents*. Paper presented at International Reading Association 46th Annual Convention, New Orleans, Louisiana. Online at http://www.e.yamagata-u.ac.jp/~sachiko/pp200105/handout.htm, accessed 25 February 2004.

Agency for Cultural Affairs 2003. *Heisei 14nendo "Kokugo ni kansuru Seron Chōsa" no Kekka ni tsuite (Results of the 2002 Survey on Language)*. Online at http://www.bunka.go.jp/1kokugo/14_yoron.html, accessed 26 February 2004.

Aikyo, K. 1998. "Okinawa asks: what is the nation-state?" *Social Science Japan* 14: 6–7. Online at http://newslet.iss.u-tokyo.ac.jp/ssj14/ssj14.pdf, accessed 15 September 2004.

Ainu Association of Hokkaido 1989. *A Statement of Opinion Regarding the Partial Revision of I.L.O. Convention No. 107*. Online at ftp://ftp.halcyon.com/pub/FWDP/Eurasia/ainu.txt, accessed 2 March 2004.

Alfonso, A. 1989. "Nihongo ga kokusaigo ni naru ni wa (For Japanese to become an international language)," in Nihon Mirai Gakkai (eds.) *Nihongo wa Kokusaigo ni naru ka (Will Japanese Become An International Language?)*. Tokyo: TBS Britannica, pp. 63–90.

Andō, S. 1988. "Waapuro no fukyū to kokugo kyōiku: doko ga mondai ka (The spread of the word processor and Japanese language education: where does the problem lie?)," *Kokugo Kyōiku Kenkyū Nenkan*: 100–103.

Aoyama, Y. 1991. *Kaden (Domestic Appliances)*. Tokyo: Nihon Keizai Hyōronsha.

Atsuji, T. 1991. *Chiteki Seisan no Bunkashi: Wapuro ga Motarasu Sekai (A Cultural History of Intellectual Production: The World the Word Processor Will Bring About)*. Tokyo: Maruzen.

Baba, Y. 1980. "A study of minority-majority relations; the Ainu and Japanese in Hokkaido," *The Japan Interpreter* 13 (1): 60–92.

Backhouse, A. 1993. *The Japanese Language: An Introduction*. Melbourne: Oxford University Press.

Bartlett, A. 2000. "Foreign teachers find Japan a challenge," *Weekend Australian* 4–5 March: 12.

Batchelor, J. 1892. *The Ainu of Japan: The Religions, Superstitions and General History of the Hairy Aborigines of Japan*. London: Religious Tract Society.

Bourke, B. 1996. *Maximising Efficiency in the Kanji Learning Task*. Unpublished PhD thesis, University of Queensland.

Brown, R. 1985. *Orthography in Contemporary Japan: Reality and Illusion*. Unpublished PhD thesis, University of Texas at Austin.

Buckley, S. and Mackie, V. 1986. "Women in the new Japanese state," in G. McCormack and Y. Sugimoto (eds.), *Democracy in Contemporary Japan*, Sydney: Hale & Iremonger, pp. 173–185.

Bureau of Democracy, Human Rights, and Labor 2001. *US Department of State Country Reports on Human Rights Practices 2000 (Japan)*. Online at http://www.state.gov/g/drl/rls/hrrpt/2000/eap/index.cfm?docid=709, accessed 1 March 2004.

Campbell, C. 1995. "The sociology of consumption," in Miller, D. (ed.), *Acknowledging Consumption: A Review of New Studies*. London: Routledge, pp. 96–126.

Carroll, T. 2001. *Language Planning and Language Change in Japan*. Richmond: Curzon.

Carroll, T. 1997. *From Script to Speech: Language Policy in Japan in the 1980s and 1990*. Oxford: Nissan Occasional Paper Series No. 27.

Castells, M. 2000. *The Rise of the Network Society*. Oxford: Blackwell.

Chang, Y. 1998. *Japan Chinatown Changes, But Culture Lives On*. Online at http://huaren.org/, accessed 23 February 2004.

Chiri, M. 1993. "False images: the Ainu in school textbooks," *AMPO* 24 (3): 19–22.

Clarke, J. 1918. *Japan at First Hand*. New York: Dodd, Mead and Company.

Cominos, A. 1992. "Managing change in foreign language education: interview with Minoru Wada," *The Language Teacher* 16 (11): 3–7.

Cooper, R. 1989. *Language Planning and Social Change*. Cambridge University Press.

Crystal, D. 1997. *English as a Global Language*. Cambridge University Press.

Crystal, D. 1987. *The Cambridge Encyclopedia of Language*. Cambridge University Press.

Dale, P. 1986. *The Myth of Japanese Uniqueness*. London: Croom Helm.

De Vos, G. and Wagatsuma, H. (eds.) 1966. *Japan's Invisible Race: Caste in Culture and Personality*. Berkeley: University of California Press.

DeChicchis, J. 1995. "The current state of the Ainu language," in J. Maher and K. Yashiro (eds.), *Multilingual Japan*. Clevedon: Multilingual Matters, pp. 103–124.

Eastman, C. 1983. *Language Planning: An Introduction*. Novato, USA: Chandler and Sharpe.

ELT News 2000. Online at http://www.eltnews.com/eltnews.shtml, accessed 7 March 2004.

ELT News 2004. "Give us more English!" 24 February. Online at http://www.eltnews.com/news/, accessed 29 February 2004.

Ethnologue 2000. *How Many Speakers Do Various Languages Have?* Online at http://www.terralingua.org/Questions/QHowManySpkrs.html, accessed 8 March 2004.

Etō, T. 1943. "Tōago toshite no nihongo kyōzaikan (A view of materials for teaching Japanese as the language of East Asia)," *Nihongo* 3 (3): 66–68.

Fishman, J. 1974. "Language modernization and planning in comparison with other types of national modernization and planning," in J. Fishman (ed.), *Advances in Language Planning*. The Hague: Mouton, pp. 79–102.

Fujisaki, H. 1984. "Wadopurosessa wa nihongo ni ihen o motarasu ka (Will the word processor bring about a disaster for Japanese?)," *Kokubungaku (Kaishaku to Kyōiku no Kenkyū* 29 (6): 111–115.

Fukui Chamber of Commerce 2001. *2001nen 9gatsu no Chōsa: Dokusho Chōsa (Survey of Reading, September 2001)*. Online at http://www.fcci.or.jp/chousa/totteoki/dokusyo/index.htm, accessed 25 February 2004.

Fukuoka, Y. 2000. *Lives of Young Koreans in Japan*, tr. T. Gill. Melbourne: Trans Pacific Press.

Fukuoka, Y. 1996. "Beyond assimilation and dissimilation: diverse resolutions to identity crises among younger generation Koreans in Japan," Saitama University Review 31 (2). Online at http://www.han.org/a/fukuoka96b.html, accessed 1 March 2004.

Garvin, P. 1974. "Some comments on language planning," in J. Fishman (ed.), *Advances in Language Planning*. The Hague: Mouton, pp. 69–78.

Global Internet Statistics by Language 2003. *Online Language Populations Sept. 2003*. Online at http://www.glreach.com/globstats/index.php3, accessed 29 February 2004.

Gomi, M. 1987. "Senzen no Nihongo Kyōiku to Nihongo Kyōiku Shinkōkai (Prewar Japanese language education and the Nihongo Kyōiku Shinkōkai)," *Nihongo Gakkō Ronshū* 14: 155–171.

Goodman, R. 1990. *Japan's "International Youth": The Emergence of a New Class of Schoolchildren*. New York: Oxford University Press.

Gottlieb, N. 2001. "Language and disability in Japan," *Disability & Society* 16 (7): 981–995.

Gottlieb, N. 2000. *Word-Processing Technology in Japan: Kanji and the Keyboard*. Richmond: Curzon Press.

Gottlieb, N. 1995. *Kanji Politics: Language Policy and Japanese Script*. London: Kegan Paul International.

Gottlieb, N. 1994a. "Language and imperialism: Japan's wartime language policies in Asia and the Pacific," *New Zealand Journal of East Asian Studies* 2 (2): 3–21.

Gottlieb, N. 1994b. "Language and politics: the reversal of postwar script policy in Japan," *Journal of Asian Studies* 53 (4): 3–21.

Graddol, D. 2000. *The Future of English?* London: The British Council.

Hanazaki, K. 1996. "Ainu Moshir and Yaponesia: Ainu and Okinawan identities in contemporary Japan," in D. Denoon, M. Hudson, G. McCormack and T. Morris-Suzuki (eds.), *Multicultural Japan: Paleolithic to Postmodern*. Cambridge University Press, pp. 117–131.

Hannas, W. 1997. *Asia's Orthographic Dilemma*. Honolulu: University of Hawaii Press.

Hansen, A. 2001. *The Institutionalization of Language in Nineteenth Century Japan: When Language became a Manifestation of National Identity, a Commodity and a Full-time Profession.* Unpublished PhD dissertation, University of Copenhagen.

Hattori, S. (ed.) 1964. *Ainugo Hōgen Jiten (A Dictionary of Ainu Dialects).* Tokyo: Iwanami Shoten.

Hattori, S. 1960. *Gengogaku no Hōhō (Methods in Linguistics).* Tokyo: Iwanami Shoten.

Henshall, K. 1999. *Dimensions of Japanese Society: Gender, Margins and Mainstream.* New York: St. Martin's Press.

Hicks, G. 1997. *Japan's Hidden Apartheid: The Korean Minority and The Japanese.* Aldershot: Ashgate.

Hirose, T. and Hatta, T. 1988. "Reading disabilities in modern Japanese children," *Journal of Research in Reading* 11 (2): 152–160.

Holden, T. and Tsuruki, T. 2003. "*Deai-kei*: Japan's new culture of encounter," in N. Gottlieb and M. McLelland (eds.), *Japanese Cybercultures.* London: Routledge, pp. 34–49.

Honna, N. 1995. "English in Japanese society: language within language," in J. Maher and K. Yashiro (eds.), *Multilingual Japan.* Clevedon: Multilingual Matters, pp. 45–62.

Ide, S. 1991. "How and why do women speak more politely in Japanese?", in S. Ide and N. McGloin (eds.), *Aspects of Japanese Women's Language,* Tokyo: Kurosio, pp. 63–79.

Ide, S. 1982. "Japanese sociolinguistics: politeness and women's language," *Lingua* 57: 357–385.

Imidas 2002. "Kokusai Kōryū: Nihon no ichi (International Cultural Exchange: Japan's Position)," *Imidas.* Tokyo: Shueisha, p. 1085.

Inoguchi, T. 1999. "Eigo shippai kokka o dō tatenaosu?" *Chūō Kōron* (August). Translated as "Japan's failing grade in English," *Japan Echo* 26 (5). Summary available online at http://www.japanecho.co.jp/sum/1999/b2605.html, accessed 4 March 2004.

Izumi, K. *et al.* 2003. *An Appeal to the Ministry of Education against the Discriminatory Treatment of Ethnic Schools in Japan.* Online at http://www.jca.apc.org/~komagome/english.html, accessed 23 February 2004.

Jackson, P. and Thrift, N. 1995. "Geographies of consumption," in Miller, D. (ed.), *Acknowledging Consumption: A Review of New Studies.* London: Routledge, pp. 204–237.

Japan Foundation 2000. *Present condition of overseas Japanese-language education.* Online at http://www.jpf.go.jp/e/urawa/e_world/e_gaiyou.pdf, accessed 6 March 2004.

Japan Foundation Nihongo Kokusai Sentaa 2000. *Kaigai no Nihongo Kyōiku no Genjō (The Current State of Japanese Language Education Overseas).* Tokyo: Kokusai Kōryū Kikin Nihongo Kokusai Sentaa.

Japan Information Network 2003. *Manga Goes International: Popular Weekly Magazine Debuts in America.* Online at http://http://www.jinjapan.org/trends01/article/030107fas_index.html, accessed 7 March 2004.

Japan Magazine Publishers Association 2003. *Danseimuke, Omo ni Yangu Taishōshi (Magazines for Men, Mainly for Younger Readers).* Online at http://www.j-magazine.or.jp/FIPP/FIPPJ/F/busuuB.htm, accessed 26 February 2004.

Japan MarkeTracker: Internet and Multimedia Report 1998. *18 Million Japanese Language Web Pages* (1 December). Online. Formerly available at HTTP: http://www.internetjapan.com, accessed 15 February 2002.

Japan Statistical Association (eds.) 1992. *Japan Statistical Yearbook 1992.* Tokyo: Statistics Bureau, Management and Coordination Office.

Japan Statistical Association (eds.) 1995. *Japan Statistical Yearbook 1995.* Tokyo: Statistics Bureau, Management and Coordination Office.

Japan Times Online 2002. "Japan reaps benefits from World Cup: survey," *Japan Times* 3 July 2002. Online at http://www.japantimes.co.jp/cgi-bin/getarticle.pl5?nn20020703a5.htm, accessed 22 February 2004.

Jet Programme 2003. *2003–2004 Participant Totals by Country.* Online at http://www.jetprogramme.org/e/outline/data/Page1.html, accessed 22 February 2004.

Jorden, E. 1991. "Overview," in S. Ide and N. McGloin (eds.) *Aspects of Japanese Women's Language.* Tokyo: Kurosio, pp. 1–4.

Joseph, J. 1987. *Eloquence and Power: the Rise of Language Standards and Standard Languages.* London: Frances Pinter.

J-SLA (School Library Association of Japan) 2004. *Dai49kai Dokusho Chōsa no Kekka ga Matomarimashita (Results of the 49th Reading Survey).* Online at http://www.j-sla.or.jp/oshirase/kekka1.html, accessed 25 February 2004.

Kabashima, T. 1988. "Waapuro wa nihongo o kaeru ka (Will the word processor change Japanese?)," *Nihongogaku* 7: 22–29.

Kanisawa, S. 1999. "New directions in foreign student policy," *Look Japan* 45: 519. Online at http://www.lookjapan.com/LBcoverstory/99JunCS.htm, accessed 6 March 2004.

Katō, H. 2000. *Nihongo no Kaikoku* (The Globalization of Japanese). Tokyo: TBS Brittanica.

Katsuno, H. and Yano, C. 2002. "Face to face: on-line subjectivity in contemporary Japan," *Asian Studies Review* 26 (2): 205–231.

Kawaijuku Educational Information Network 2003. "Kokugoryoku teika to sono eikyō: bunkachō 'kokugo ni kansuru seron chōsa' kekka o chūshin ni (A decline in Japanese language ability and its effects: the Agency of Cultural Affairs survey on language)," *Kokugoryoku Kō* special issue 1. Online at http://www.keinet.ne.jp/keinet/doc/keinet/jyohoshi/gl/toku0309/prt1_1.html and http://www.keinet.ne.jp/keinet/doc/keinet/jyohoshi/gl/toku0309/prt1_2.html, accessed 26 February 2004.

Kawamoto, Y. 1995. *Sabetsu to hyōgen: kakuitsu kara sai e (Discrimination and Language: From Uniformity to Difference).* Tokyo: San'ichi Shobo.

Keizai Kikakuchō (ed.) 1990. *Heisei Ninenhan Kokumin Seikatsu Hakusho (White Paper on Living Conditions 1990).* Tokyo: Ōkurashō Insatsukyoku.

Kida, Furuse *et al.* 1987. *Wapuro Kōgengaku (Modernology of the Word Processor).* Tokyo: Nihon Sofuto Banku Shuppan Jigyōbu.

Kindaichi, H. 1978. *The Japanese Language.* Tokyo: Tuttle.

Kinsella, S. 2000. *Adult Manga: Culture & Power in Contemporary Japanese Society.* Surrey: Curzon Press.

Kinsella, S. 1998. "Japanese subculture in the 1990s: *otaku* and the amateur *manga* movement," *Journal of Japanese Studies* 24 (2): 289–316.

Kitao, K., Kitao, S. Nozawa, K. and Yamamoto, M. 1994. *Teaching English in Japan*. Online at http://www.ling.lancs.ac.uk/staff/visitors/kenji/kitao/tejk.htm, accessed 24 February 2004.

Kitao, S. and Kitao, K. 1997. *Changes in English Language Education in Japan*. Online at http://ilc2.doshisha.ac.jp/users/kkitao/library/article/wca.htm, accessed 6 March 2004

Kitta, H. 1989. *Nippon no Rōmazi-undō 1789–1988 (The Romanization Movement in Japan 1789–1988)*. Tokyo: Nippon Rōmazi-sha.

Kiyota, Y. 2002. "Difficult times for bookstores," *Japanese Book News* 39: 7.

Kiyota, Y. 2003. "The ten big stories in 2002", *Japanese Book News* 41: 7.

Kodama, F. 1991. *Analyzing Japanese High Technologies: The Techno-Paradigm Shift*. London and New York: Pinter Publishers.

Koh, C. 2000. "Japan considers own TOEFL test," *The Straits Times* 20 December.

Koike, I. and Tanaka, H. 1995. "English in foreign language education policy in Japan: toward the twenty-first century," *World Englishes* 14 (1): 13–25.

Kokugo Shingikai 2000. *Kokusai Shakai ni okeru Nihongo no Arikata (The Ideal State of Japanese in International Society)*, online at http://www.mext.go.jp/b_menu/shingi/12/kokugo/toushin/001217.htm, accessed 4 March 2004.

Kokugo Shingikai 1999. *Dai22ki Kokugo Shingikai Dai3 Iinkai (Dai2kai) Giji Yōshi) (Outline of the second meeting of the third committee of the twenty-second session of the National Language Council) (Minutes of the 15 April 1999 meeting)*. Online at http://www.mext.go.jp/b_menu/shingi/12/kokugo/gijiroku/001/990401.htm, accessed 8 March 2004.

Kokugo Shingikai 1995. "Atarashii jidai ni ōjita kokugo shisaku ni tsuite (Toward a language policy for a new era)," in Kokuritsu Kokugo Kenkyūjo (ed.) 1996. *Kokugo Nenkan 1995 (Japanese Language Yearbook 1995)*, Tokyo: Shūei Shuppan, pp. 427–451.

Kokugo Shingikai 2000. *Gendai Shakai ni okeru Kei-i Hyōgen: Kokugo Shingikai Tōshin (Report of the National Language Council: Honorifics in Today's Society)*. Online at http://www.bunka.go.jp/kokugo/frame.asp?tm=20040306100053, accessed 6 March 2004.

Komori, Y. 2002. "Japanese language booms and nationalism," *Japanese Book News* 40: 1–2.

Kornicki, P. 1998. *The Book in Japan: A Cultural History from the Beginnings to the Nineteenth Century*. Leiden: Brill.

Koshida, K. 1993. "From a 'perishing people' to self-determination," *AMPO* 24 (3): 2–6.

Kotoba to Onna o kangaeru Kai (eds.) 1985. *Kokugo Jiten no miru Josei Sabetsu (Discrimination against Women in Japanese Dictionaries)*, Tokyo: San'ichi Shobo.

Large, T. 2001. "Sacred river doubly dammed by pork-barrel Japan," *Reuters News Service*. Online at http://www.planetark.org/dailynewsstory.cfm?newsid=9410, accessed 6 March 2004.

Lo Bianco, J. 1999. *Globalisation: Frame Word for Education and Training, Human Capital and Human Development/Rights*. Melbourne: Language Australia.

Loveday, L. 1996. *Language Contact in Japan: A Socio-linguistic History*. New York: Clarendon Press.

Loveday, L. 1981. "Pitch, politeness and sexual role: an exploratory investigation into the pitch correlates of English and Japanese politeness formulae," *Language and Speech* 24 (1): 71–89.

Lunde, K. 1993. *Understanding Japanese Information Processing*. Sebastopol, California: O'Reilly and Associates.

McConnell, D. 2000. *Importing Diversity: Inside Japan's JET Program*. Berkeley: University of California Press.

McLaughlin, J. 2000. "Foreign Worker Groups Protest Gov. Ishihara's Racist Remarks," *The New Observer*, May.

McLelland, M. 2001. "Out on the global stage: authenticity, interpretation and Orientalism in Japanese coming out narratives," *Electronic Journal of Contemporary Japanese Studies* 1. Online at http://www.japanesestudies.org.uk/articles/McLelland.html, accessed 7 March 2004.

McLelland, M. 2000. *Male Homosexuality in Modern Japan: Cultural Myths and Social Realities*. Richmond: Curzon.

McVeigh, B. 2003. "Individualization, individuality, interiority, and the Internet: Japanese university students and e-mail," in N. Gottlieb and M. McLelland (eds.), *Japanese Cybercultures*. London: Routledge, pp. 19–33.

Maher, J. 2002. "Language policy for multicultural Japan: establishing the new paradigm," in S. Baker (ed.), *Language Policy: Lessons from Global Models*. Monterey: Monterey Institute of International Relations, 164–180. Online at http://www.miis.edu/docs/langpolicy/ch11.pdf, accessed 17 February 2004.

Maher, J. 1995a. "On being there: Korean in Japan," in J. Maher and K. Yashiro (eds.) *Multilingual Japan*. Cleveland: Multilingual Matters, pp. 87–101.

Maher, J. 1995b. "The *Kakyo*: Chinese in Japan," in J. Maher and K. Yashiro (eds.) *Multilingual Japan*. Cleveland: Multilingual Matters, pp. 125–138.

Maher, J. and Macdonald, G. (eds.) 1995. *Diversity in Japanese Culture and Language*. London: Kegan Paul International.

Maher, J. and Yashiro, K. (eds.) 1995. *Multilingual Japan*. Clevedon: Multilingual Matters.

Mainichi Daily News (2004) "Everybody's talking about 'gal talk'," 25 January 2004. Online at http://mdn.mainichi.co.jp/news/archive/200401/25/20040125p2a00m0dm002001c.html, accessed 17 March 2004.

Mainichi Shimbun 2004. "Immigration Bureau introduces 'xenophobic home page'." 21 February 2004. Online at http://mdn.mainichi.co.jp/news/20040221p2a00m0dm017000c.html, accessed 22 February 2004.

Mainichi Shimbun 2003. "Universities open doors to foreign students, high school dropouts," 5 August. Online at http://www12.mainichi.co.jp/news/mdn/search-news/897791/foreign20schools-0–7.html, accessed 20 February 2004.

Mainichi Shimbun 2002a. "Nihongoryoku teika: 'katsujibanare gen'in'" to shiteki 8 wari" (80% say decline in reading is cause of fall in language ability), 26 August 2002.

Mainichi Shimbun 2002b. "Gov't to promote Japanese language studies at schools," 3 August 2002. Online at http://www12.mainichi.co.jp/news/mdn/search-news/898135/Japanese20language-20–36.html, accessed 25 February 2004.

Makita, K. 1968. "The rarity of reading disability in Japanese children," *American Journal of Orthopsychiatry* 38: 599–613.

Mason, J., Anderson, R., Omura, A., Uchida, N. and Imai, M. 1989. "Learning to read in Japan," *Journal of Curriculum Studies* 21 (5): 389–407.

Matsumori, A. 1995. "Ryūkyūan: Past, Present and Future," in J. Maher and K. Yashiro (eds.) *Multilingual Japan*. Cleveland: Multilingual Matters, pp. 19–44.

Mehl, M. 2003. *Private Academies of Chinese Learning in Meiji Japan: The Decline and Transformation of the Kangaku Juku*. Copenhagen: Nordic Institute of Asian Studies.

MEXT 2004. *Shō, chū gakkō ni okeru LD (Gakushū Shōgai), ADHD (Chūi Kekkan/ Tadōsei Shōgai), Kōkinō Jiheishō no Jidō Seito e no Kyōiku Shien Taisei no Seibi no tame no Gaidorain (Shian) (Proposed Guidelines for the Provision of an Educational Support System for Young Students with Learning Difficulties, ADHD and Autism in Elementary and Middle Schools)*. Online at http://www.mext.go.jp/b_menu/houdou/16/01/04013002.htm#1, accessed 26 February 2004.

MEXT 2003a. *Regarding the Establishment of an Action Plan to Cultivate "Japanese with English Abilities."* Online at http://www.mext.go.jp/english/topics/03072801.htm, accessed 6 March 2004.

MEXT 2003b. *Action Plan to Cultivate "Japanese with English Abilities."* Online at http://www.mext.go.jp/b_menu/houdou/15/03/03033101/001.pdf, accessed 22 February 2004.

MEXT 2003c. *The Course of Study for Foreign Languages*. Online at http://www.mext.go.jp/english/shotou/030301.htm, accessed 22 February 2004.

MEXT 2002a. *Tsūjō no Gakkyū ni Zaiseki suru Tokubetsu na Kyōikuteki Shien o Hitsuyō to suru Jidō Seito ni kansuru Zenkoku Jittai Chōsa: Chōsa Kekka (Results of a National Survey of Children Who Require Special Educational Support to be Enrolled in Ordinary Classrooms)*. Online at http://www.mext.go.jp/b_menu/public/2002/021004c.htm, accessed 26 February 2004.

MEXT 2002b. *Developing a Strategic Plan to Cultivate "Japanese with English Abilities."* Online at http://www.mext.go.jp/english/news/2002/07/020901.htm, accessed 22 February 2004.

MEXT 2001a. *'JET Puroguramu Hyōka Chōsa' Ankeeto Kekka Gaiyō (Summary of Results of a Survey Evaluating the JET Program)*. Online at http://www.mext.go.jp/b_menu/houdou/13/11/011121/02.htm, accessed 22 February 2004.

MEXT 2001b. *"Nihongo Shidō ga Hitsuyō na Gaikokujin Jidō Seito no Ukeire Jōkyō nado ni kansuru Chōsa" no Kekka (Results of a Survey on the Reception of Foreign Children who require Instruction in Japanese Language)*. Online at http://www.mext.go.jp/b_menu/houdou/13/02/010221.htm, accessed 29 February 2004.

MEXT 1999. *Heisei10 nendo: Kōtō Gakkō ni okeru Kokusai Kōryū nado no Jōkyō (International Cultural Exchange Activities in High Schools in 1999)*. Cited in The Japan Forum, *Gaikokugo, Eigo Kyōiku (Foreign and English Language Education)*. Online at http://www.tjf.or.jp/deai/contents/teacher/mini_en/html/gaikokugo_j.html, accessed 22 February 2004.

MEXT 1991. *'Wagakuni no Bunkyō Shisaku' Heisei 3nendo: Dai2 Bunkyō Shisaku no Dōkō to Tenkai: Dai1shō Kyōiku Kaikaku (Japan's Cultural Policies 1991: No. 2 Trends and Development in Cultural Policy: Chapter One, Education Reform)*. Tokyo: Okurasho Insatsukyoku.

Miller, R. 1982. *Japan's Modern Myth: The Language and Beyond.* New York: Weatherhill.

Miller, R. 1971. *Japanese and the Other Altaic Languages.* University of Chicago Press.

Ministry of Education 1998a. *Gakushū Shidō Yōryō (Course of Study Guidelines).* Online at http://www.mext.go.jp/b_menu/shuppan/sonota/990301.htm, accessed 27 February 2004.

Ministry of Education 1998b. *Synopsis of the Curriculum Council's Midterm Report.* Online at http://www.monbu.go.jp/series-en/00000011/, accessed 12 June 1999.

Ministry of Education 1997. *Monbusho's budget for the Fiscal Year 1997.* Online at http:www.mext.go.jp/english/yosan/970401.htm, accessed 6 March 2004.

Ministry of Education 1951. *Gakusei Shidō Yōryō: Gaikokugoka Eigo-hen (Course of Study: Foreign Languages (English)).* Online at http://nierdb.nier.go.jp/db/cofs/s22ejl/index.htm, accessed 24 February 2004.

Ministry of Education 1947. *Gakusei Shidō Yōryō Eigo-hen (Course of Study: English).* Online at http://nierdb.nier.go.jp/db/cofs/s22ejl/index.htm, accessed 24 February 2004.

Ministry of Foreign Affairs of Japan (MOFAJ) 2000. *The Number of JET Participants from 1987 to 2000.* Online at http://www.mofa.go.jp/j_info/visit/jet/participants.html, accessed 6 March 2004.

Ministry of Foreign Affairs of Japan (MOFAJ) 1999. *International Convention on the Elimination of All Forms of Racial Discrimination: First and Second Report.* Online at http:www.mofa.go.jp/policy/global/human/race_rep1/intro.html, accessed 12 March 2001.

Ministry of Justice 2003. *Heisei 14nenmatsu Genzai ni okeru Gaikokujintōrokusha Tōkei ni tsuite (Statistics on Foreign Residents of Japan as of the end of 2002).* Online at http://www.moj.go.jp/PRESS/030530-1/030530-1.html, accessed 20 February 2004.

Ministry of Posts and Telecommunications 2001. *Communications in Japan 2000.* Online at http://www.soumu.go.jp/joho_tsusin/eng/Resources/WhitePaper/WP2001/2001-index.html, accessed 7 March 2004.

Ministry of Posts and Telecommunications 2000. *Tsūshin Hakusho (White Paper on Communications) 1999.* Online at http://www.soumu.go.jp/joho_tsusin/policyreports/japanese/papers/99wp/99wp-1-index.html, accessed 7 March 2004.

Ministry of Public Management, Home Affairs, Posts and Telecommunications Japan 2003. *Information and Communications in Japan: Building a New "Japan-Inspired" IT Society*, White Paper 2003. Online at http://www.johotsusintokei.soumu.go.jp/whitepaper/eng/WP2003/2003-index.html, accessed 7 March 2004.

Mitchell, R. 1976. *Thought Control in Prewar Japan.* Ithaca and London: Cornell University Press.

160   References

Moriyoshi, N., Trelfa, D. n.d. *Components of National Education Standards in Japan.* Online at http://www.ed.gov/pubs/Research5/Japan/standards_j.html, accessed 24 February 2004.

Morris-Suzuki, T. 1998. *Re-Inventing Japan: Time, Space, Nation.* Armonk: M. E. Sharpe.

Morris-Suzuki, T. 2000. "Packaging prejudice for the global marketplace: chauvinism incited by Tokyo Governor Ishihara," *Sekai* 678. Online at http://www.iwanami.co.jp/jpworld/text/packaging01.html, accessed 1 March 2004.

Muto, I. 1997. "The Birth of the Women's Liberation Movement in the 1970s," in J. Moore (ed.), *The Other Japan: Conflict, Compromise and Resistance Since 1945.* Armonk, New York: M. E. Sharpe, pp. 147–175.

Nagano, T. 1994. *Zainichi Chūgokujin: Rekishi to Aidentitei (Resident Chinese in Japan: History and Identity).* Tokyo: Akashi Shoten.

Nagasaki Industrial Promotion Foundation 2002. *Shuppan Gyōkai no Genjō to Tembō: Daiwa Ginkō Sōgō Kenkyūjo Shirabe (Present Situation and Outlook for the Publishing Industry: An Investigation by the Daiwa Bank Research Section).* Online at http://www.joho-nagasaki.or.jp/book/johod/txt213d.html, accessed 25 February 2004.

Nagata, Y. 1991. "Linguistic apartheid – some thoughts on Kan'yaku Nihongo (special Japanese)," in Japanese Studies Association of Australia (eds.), *Japan and the World: Social, Political and Economic Change. Seventh Biennial Conference of the Japanese Studies Association of Australia*, Canberra: Australia-Japan Research Centre, Australian National University. Vol. 3, pp. 231–236.

Namase, K. 1994. *Shōgaisha to Sabetsu Hyōgen (People with Disabilities and Discriminatory Language).* Tokyo: Akashi Shoten.

National Language Research Institute 1988. *Jidō Seito no Jōyō Kanji no Shūtoku (The Acquisition of the Jōyō Kanji by School Children).* Tokyo: Shoseki.

Neary, I. 1989. *Political Protest and Social Control in Pre-war Japan: The Origins of Buraku Liberation.* Manchester University Press.

Neustupný, J. 1987. *Communicating with the Japanese.* Tokyo: The Japan Times.

NHK 1999. "NHK's foreign language programs bridge the gap between Japan and the rest of the world," *NHK Broadcasting Services Roundup* 7. Online at http://www.nhk.or.jp/bunken/bcri-ruo/h07-d3.html, accessed 20 February 2004.

NHK Broadcasting Culture Research Unit 1995. Survey questions report obtained from J-Poll, Roper Center for Public Opinion Research. Online at http://www.ropercenter.uconn.edu/jpoll/JPOLL.html, accessed 22 February 2004.

Nihon PEN Kurabu (ed.) 1995. *Sabetsu Hyōgen o kangaeru (On Discriminatory Language).* Tokyo: Kobunsha.

Nikkei 2003a. *Comparison between Japan and Overseas Media.* Online at http://www.nikkei.co.jp/ad/info/jpmarket/comparison.html, accessed 12 February 2004.

Nikkei 2003b. *Newspapers in Japan.* Online at www.nikkei.co.jp/ad/info/jpmarket/paperinjp.html, accessed 12 February 2004.

Nishio, M. 1943. "Nihongo Sōryokusen Taisei no Juritsu (Establishing Japanese on a total-war footing)," *Nihongo* 3 (1).

Nomura, M. 1986. "Wapuro wa kokugo mondai o kaiketsu suru ka (Will the word processor solve our language problems?)," *Gengo* 15 (7): 66–71.

Noyama 1998. *Bunkachō kara (From the Agency for Cultural Affairs)*. Online at http://www.kikokusha_center.or.jp/network/tongsheng/12/12gyosei.htm, accessed 8 March 2003.

Ogino, T. 1994. "Waapuro to gengo seikatsu (Word processors and our linguistic life)," *Gendai no Esupuri* 319: 102–114.

Ogino, T. 1987. "Wapuro no fukyū wa nani o motarasu ka (What will the spread of the word processor bring about?)," *Kagaku Asahi* April: 31–35.

Oguri (no initial given) 2003. "Yūisei ni Igi" (A challenge to dominance), Kōtō Gakkō KankokuChōsengo Kyōiku Nettowaaku bulletin board. Online at http://www.iie.ac.kr/~jakehs/message/yuuisei.html, accessed 24 February 2004.

Okada, T. 2003. "Changing the Japanese name for the Society of Japanese Linguistics: from Kokugo Gakkai to Nihongo Gakkai." Paper presented at the International Symposium on Globalization, Localization and Japanese Studies in the Asia-Pacific Region, University of Sydney, November 2003.

Okamoto, S. 1994. "'Gendered' speech styles and social identity among young Japanese women," in M. Bucholtz, A. Liang, L. Sutton and C. Hines (eds.), *Proceedings of the Third Berkeley Women and Language Conference*. Berkeley: Berkeley Women and Language Group, pp. 569–581.

Okano, K. and Tsuchiya, M. 1999. *Education in Contemporary Japan: Inequality and Diversity*. Cambridge University Press.

Osedo, H. 2001. "Japan worry at brash posting," *Courier Mail* 28 April.

Pang, C. 2000. *Negotiating Identity in Contemporary Japan: The Case of Kikokushijo*. London: Kegan Paul International.

Passin, H. 1982. *Society and Education in Japan*, Tokyo: Kodansha International.

People's Daily 2000. "Ishihara's Anti-China Ravings Castigated by Overseas Chinese in Japan." Online at http://fpeng.peopledaily.com.cn/200004/14/eng20000414_38953.html, accessed 23 February 2004.

Pharr, S. 1990. *Losing Face: Status Politics in Japan*. Berkeley: University of California Press.

Phillipson, R. 2002. "Global English and local language policies," in A. Kirkpatrick (ed.), *Englishes in Asia: Communication, Identity, Power and Education*. Melbourne: Language Australia, pp. 7–28.

Prime Minister's Commission on Japan's Goals in the Twenty-First Century 2000. *The Frontier Within: Individual Empowerment and Better Governance in the New Millennium*. Online at http://www.kantei.go.jp/jp/21century/report/overview.html, accessed 20 February 2004.

Rabson, S. 1996. *Assimilation Policy in Okinawa: Promotion, Resistance and "Reconstruction,"* Japan Policy Research Institute (JPRI) Occasional Paper 8. Online at http://www.jpri.org/publications/occasionalpapers/op8.html, accessed 18 February 2004.

Refsing, K. (ed.) 1996. *Early European Writings on the Ainu Language*. Richmond: Curzon.

Refsing, K. 1986. *The Ainu Language: The Morphology and Syntax of the Shizunai Dialect*. Aarhus: Aarhus University Press.

Reynolds, K. 1991. "Female speakers of Japanese in transition," in S. Ide and N. McGloin (eds.), *Aspects of Japanese Women's Language*. Tokyo: Kurosio, pp. 129–146.

Roscoe, B. 1986. "No place for the Ainu," *Far Eastern Economic Review* 13 November: 66–67.

Rubinger, R. 1982. *Private Academies of Tokugawa Japan*. Princeton University Press.

Rudofsky, B. 1974. *The Kimono Mind*. Tokyo: Tuttle.

Ryang, S. 1997. *North Koreans in Japan: Language, Ideology and Identity*. Boulder, Colorado: Westview Press.

Sabin, B. 2002. "Kawasaki's Koreatown," *The East* 38 (1). Online at http://www.theeast.co.jp/places.htm, accessed 20 February 2004.

Sakamoto, T. 1981. "Beginning reading in Japan," in L. Ollila (ed.), *Beginning Reading Instruction in Different Countries*. Newark: International Reading Association, pp. 16–25.

Sala, G. 1975. "Protest and the Ainu of Hokkaido," *The Japan Interpreter* 10 (1): 44–65.

Sasaki-Uemura, W. 2002. "Competing publics: citizen groups, mass media and the state in the 1960s," *Positions: East Asia Cultures Critique* 10 (1): 79–110.

Savage Landor, A. 1893. *Alone with the Hairy Ainu, or, 3,800 Miles on a Pack Saddle in Yezo and a Cruise to the Kurile Islands*. London: J. Murray.

Schodt, F. 1996. *Dreamland Japan: Writings on Modern Manga*. Berkeley: Stonebridge Press.

Schodt, F. and Tezuka, O. 1986. *Manga! Manga! The World of Japanese Comics*. Tokyo: Kodansha International (paperback edition).

Seeley, C. 1991. *A History of Writing in Japan*. Leiden: Brill.

Sheridan, M. 1993. "Reading disabilities: are there fewer in Japan?" *Reading Horizons* 33 (3): 245–257.

Shibamoto, J. 1985. *Japanese Women's Language*. London: Academic Press.

Shibatani, M. 1990. *The Languages of Japan*. Cambridge University Press.

Shinohara, T. 1944. "Nihongo kyōiku no kisoteki na mondai (Fundamental issues in teaching Japanese as a foreign language)," *Nihongo* 3 (10): 17–27.

Shu n.d. *Kokusaika Jidai no Nihongo (Japanese in the Age of Internationalization)*. Online. Formerly available at http://www.oak.dti.ne.jp/~phoenix/jp03.html, accessed 8 November 2003.

Siddle, R. 2002. "An epoch-making event? the 1997 Ainu Cultural Promotion Act and its impact," *Japan Forum* 14 (3): 405–423.

Siddle, R. 1997. "Ainu: Japan's indigenous people," in M. Weiner (ed.) *Japan's Minorities: The Illusion of Homogeneity*. London: Routledge, pp. 17–49.

Siddle, R. 1996. *Race, Resistance and the Ainu of Japan*. London: Routledge.

Silverstone, R., Hirsch, E. *et al.* 1992. "Information and communication technologies and the moral economy of the household," in R. Silverstone and E. Hirsch (eds.), *Consuming Technologies: Media and Information in Domestic Spaces*. London: Routledge, pp. 15–31.

Sōzō, T. 2001. "Vocabulary of the Korea boom," *Japanese Book News* 36: 3–4.

Spaeth, A. 2003. "Minds at Risk," *Time Asia* 162 (9) 8 September 2003. Online at http://www.time.com/time/asia/magazine/printout/0,13675,501030908–480333,00.html, accessed 12 February 2004.

Statistics Bureau, Ministry of Public Management, Home Affairs, Posts and Telecommunications 2002. *Todōfuken, Danjo-betsu Jinkō oyobi Jinkō Seibi Sōjinkō, Nihonjin Jinkō (Population of Japan by Area and with Population Ratios: Total Population, Number of Japanese, with Male-Female Ratios)*. Online at http://www.stat.go.jp/data/jinsui/2002np/zuhyou/05k3f-4.xls, accessed 19 February 2004.

Stevenson, H., Stigler, J., Lucker, G. and Lee, S. 1982. "Reading disabilities: the case of Chinese, Japanese, and English," *Child Development* 53: 1164–1181.

Sugimoto, Y. 2003. *An Introduction to Japanese Society*. Cambridge University Press.

Sugimoto, Y. and Mouer, R. (eds.) 1989. *Constructs for Understanding Japan*. London: Kegan Paul International.

Sukigara, Rika 1995. *Language and Discrimination: a Critical Examination of 'Sabetsu-go' in the Media*. Unpublished Master of Arts thesis, International Christian University, Tokyo.

Suzuki, T. 1999. *Nihonjin wa naze Eigo ga dekinai ka (Why can't the Japanese speak English?)*. Tokyo: Iwanami Shoten.

Suzuki, T. 1991. "What's happening to the Japanese language?: a side-effect of Japan's self-colonizing mentality," in Japanese Studies Association of Australia (eds.), *Japan and the World Vol. 3: Social, Political and Economic Change: Japanese Language and Studies in Australia. Proceedings of the Seventh Biennial Conference*. The Australian National University, Canberra: Australia-Japan Research Centre, pp. 99–103.

Suzuki, T. 1987. "Language barriers between Japan and the countries of Asia," in *Reflections on Japanese Language and Culture*. Tokyo: Keio University Institute of Cultural and Linguistic Studies, pp. 107–118.

Suzuki, T. 1975. *Tozasareta Gengo: Nihongo no Sekai (The Shut-in Language: The World of Japanese)*. Tokyo: Shinchōsha.

Taira, K. 1996. "The Ainu in Japan," *International Education e-j* 1 (1). Online at http://pandora.nla.gov.au/parchive/1999/Z1999-Sep-22/www2. canberra.edu.au/education/crie/1996–1997/ieej1/Ainu_ ieej1.html, accessed 4 March 2004.

Taira, K. 1997. "Troubled national identity: the Ryukyuans/Okinawans," in M. Weiner (ed.) *Japan's Minorities: The Illusion of Homogeneity*. London: Routledge, pp. 140–177.

Takagi, M. 1999. *Sabetsu Yōgo no Kiso Chishiki'99 (Basic Information on Discriminatory Language'99)*. Tokyo: Doyō Bijitsusha.

Tamura, T. 2000. *The Ainu Language*. Tokyo: Sanseido. ICHEL Linguistic Studies V.2.

Tanaka, H. 1991. *Zainichi Gaikokujin (Foreigners Resident in Japan)*. Tokyo: Iwanami Shoten.

Tanaka, R. 1991. *Wapuro ga Shakai o Kaeru (The Word Processor Will Change Society)*. Tokyo: Chūō Kōron.

Tanaka, S. 1993. *Japan's Orient: Rendering Pasts into History*. Berkeley: University of California Press.

Taylor, I. and Taylor, M. 1995. *Writing and Literacy in Chinese, Korean and Japanese*, Amsterdam: John Benjamins.

The Japan Forum 1998. *Kankoku Chōsengo to Chūgokugo Kyōiku no Torikumikō (Schools involved in Korean and Chinese language Education)*. Online at http://www.tjf.or.jp/Korean/pdf/jk_j2.pdf, accessed 23 February 2004.

The Japan Forum 2003. *Kōtō Gakkō ni okeru KankoguChōsengo Jugyō no Kaisetsu Jōkyō (The Teaching of Korean in High Schools)*. Online at http://www.tjf.or.jp/korean/pdf/f60_joukyou.pdf, accessed 21 February 2004.

TOEFL 2003. *TOEFL Test and Score Data Summary 02–03 Edition*. Online at ftp://ftp.ets.org/pub/toefl/10496_02_03.pdf, accessed 22 February 2004.

Totsuka, M. 1993. "The golf war on Mt. Kotan," *AMPO* 24 (3): 12–14.

Transnational Radical Party and Esperanto International Federation n.d. *Ecosoc/annex on International Auxiliary Language*. Online at http://www.radicalparty.org/esperanto/ins_un.htm, accessed 8 March 2004.

Tsurumi, P. 1967. *Taiwan under Kodama Gentarō and Gotō Shimpei*. Cambridge: Harvard University East Asian Research Center Papers on Japan.

Tsurumi, Y. 1942. "Daisenshō to Nihongo no sekaiteki Shinshutsu (Victory and the worldwide advance of the Japanese language)," *Kokugo Undō* 6 (8): 2–11.

Tsūsan Daijin Kanbō Chōsa Tōkeibu (eds.) 1986. *Wagakuni Sangyō no Genjō (The Current State of Industry in Japan)*. Tokyo: Tsūsan Shiryō Chōsakai.

Tsūsan Daijin Kanbō Chōsa Tōkeibu (eds.) 1987. *Shōwa 61nen Kikai Tōkei Nempō (Machine Statistics Yearbook, 1986)*. Tokyo: Ōkurashō Insatsukyoku.

Turner, M. 2003. "The World's Most Widely Spoken Languages." Online at http://www2.ignatius.edu/faculty/turner/languages.htm, accessed 4 March 2004.

Twine, N. 1991a. *Language and the Modern State: The Reform of Written Japanese*. London: Routledge.

Twine, N. 1991b. "Language and the constitution," *Japan Forum* 3 (1): 125–137.

Ueda, K. 1894. "Kokugo to Kokka to" (Our language and our nation), in *Meiji Bunka Zenshū* 44, Tokyo: Chikuma Shobō, pp. 108–113.

UNESCO 1999. *Resolution 12 of UNESCO's 30th General Conference, 1999*. Online at http://www.unesco.org/education/imld_2002/resolution_en.shtml, accessed 8 March 2004.

Unger, J. 1996. *Literacy and Script Reform in Occupation Japan: Reading Between the Lines*. New York: Oxford University Press.

Unger, J. 1987. *The Fifth Generation Fallacy: Why Japan is Betting its Future on Artificial Intelligence*. New York and Oxford: Oxford University Press.

United Nations Development Programme 2003. *Human Development Indicators 2003*. Online at http://www.undp.org/hdr2003/indicator/indic_2_1_1.html, accessed 7 March 2004.

United Nations 2002. *Problems of Indigenous Peoples Living in Cities Should Be Addressed, Permanent Forum Told*, UN Press Release HR4600. Online at http://www.un.org/rights/indigenous/hr4600.doc.htm, accessed 18 February 2004.

Upham, F. 1987. *Law and Social Change in Postwar Japan*. Cambridge: Harvard University Press.

Valentine, J. 1997. "Pots and pans: identification of queer Japanese in terms of discrimination," in A. Livia and K. Hall (eds.) *Queerly Phrased: Language, Gender and Sexuality*. New York and Oxford: Oxford University Press, pp. 95–114.

Vasishth, A. 1997. "The model minority: the Chinese community in Japan," in M. Weiner (ed.) *Japan's Minorities: The Illusion of Homogeneity*. London: Routledge, pp. 108–139.

Walker, B. 1999. "The early modern Japanese state and Ainu vaccinations: redefining the body politic 1799–1868," *Past and Present* 163: 121–160.

Weber, G. 1997. "The world's 10 most influential languages," *Language Today* 2.

Weiner, M. 1997. "The representation of absence and the absence of representation: Korean victims of the atomic bomb," in M. Weiner (ed.) *Japan's Minorities: The Illusion of Homogeneity*. London: Routledge, pp. 79–107.

Weiner, M. 1997. *Japan's Minorities: The Illusion of Homogeneity*. London: Routledge.

Wilkinson, E. 1991. *Japan versus the West: Image and Reality*. London: Penguin Books.

Yamada, H. 1994. "Ōsugiru kanji/kango ni dō kotaeru ka (What to do about our oversupply of kanji and Sino-Japanese words?)" *Gakujutsu Jōhō Sentaa Kiyō* 6: 1–56.

Yamada, H. 1984. "Wapuro to nihongo no genjō to shōrai (The present situation and future prospects of Japanese and the word processor)," *Nihongogaku* 3 (7): 4–17.

Yamanaka, Ō. 1995. "'Sabetsu' to Media no Jiko Kisei ('Discrimination' and media self-regulation)," *Buraku Bukkuretto 14*. Osaka: Buraku Mondai Kenkyūjo, pp. 69–72.

Yōgo to Sabetsu o kangaeru Shinpojiumu Jikkō Iinkai (eds.) 1989. *Sabetsu Yōgo(Discriminatory Language) 3*[rd] *ed*. Tokyo: Sekibunsha.

Yokoyama, M. 1984. "Hatokiin seketeshiu: kikai onchi wapuro o kiru (Getting rid of machine-phobic word processing)," *Sakushin* 26: 63–79.

Yumoto, K. 1963. *Ainu no Kajin* (Ainu Writers). Tokyo: Yoyosha.

List of useful websites and journals

Websites

Agency for Cultural Affairs, www.bunka.go.jp

Bibliography of Japanese sociolinguistics in English http://www.age.ne.jp/x/oswcjlrc/jlrc/sl-lib-e.htm

Foundation for Research and Promotion of Ainu Culture http://www.frpac.or.jp/english/e_index2.html

Japan Foundation, http://www.jpf.go.jp/

Jet Program, www.jetprogramme.org

Ministry of Education, Culture, Sports, Science and Technology www.mext.go.jp

National Institute for Japanese Language, www.kokken.go.jp

Journals

Asian Englishes: An International Journal of the Sociolinguistics of English in Asia

Communication (a journal of the Communication Association of the Pacific)

Gengo Kenkyū (Journal of the Linguistic Society of Japan)

Gengo to Bunka (Language and Culture)

Human Communication Studies (a journal of the Communication Association of Japan)

JALT Journal (Japan Association for Language Teaching)

Japan Journal of Multilingualism and Multiculturalism

Japanese Journal of Intercultural Communication

Japanese Journal of Language in Society

Journal of Asian Pacific Communication

Journal of Language, Culture and Communication

Nihongogaku

Nihongo Kyōiku (Journal of Japanese Language Teaching)

Speech Communication Education (a journal of the Communication Association of Japan)

TESOL Journal

TESOL Quarterly

World Englishes

Index

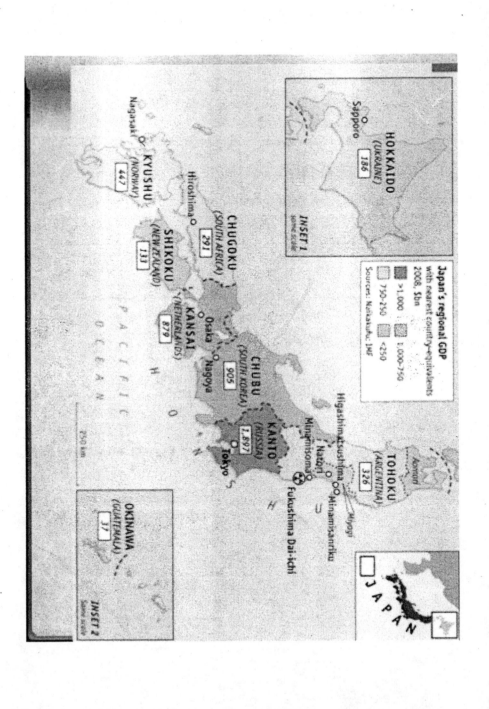

Japan's regional GDP
with nearest country-equivalents
2008, $bn

>1,000   1,000-750
750-250   <250

Sources: Nakasato; IMF

INSET 1
Same scale

HOKKAIDO
(UKRAINE)
135

Sapporo ○

Nagasaki ○
KYUSHU
(NORWAY)
447

Hiroshima ○

CHUGOKU
(SOUTH AFRICA)
291

SHIKOKU
(NEW ZEALAND)
133

KANSAI
(NETHERLANDS)
879

Osaka ○
Nagoya ○

CHUBU
(SOUTH KOREA)
905

KANTO
(RUSSIA)
1,897

Tokyo ○

Higashimatsushima
Natori
Minamisoma

Fukushima Dai-ichi

Minamisanriku

Aomori

TOHOKU
(ARGENTINA)
326

Miyagi

PACIFIC

OCEAN

250 km

OKINAWA
(GUATEMALA)
37

INSET 2
Same scale

J A P A N